THE COMPLETE

POETICAL WORKS

OF

AUSTIN DOBSON

AUSTIN DOBSON

From a photograph by H. Walter Barnett

THE COMPLETE

POETICAL WORKS

OF

AUSTIN DOBSON

Majores majora sonent
MARTIAL

HUMPHREY MILFORD
OXFORD UNIVERSITY PRESS

London   Edinburgh   Glasgow   Copenhagen
New York   Toronto   Melbourne   Cape Town
Bombay   Calcutta   Madras   Shanghai

1923

O.S.A.

Henry Austin Dobson, LL.D.

Born, Plymouth . . . 18 Jan. 1840
Died, Ealing. . . . 2 Sept. 1921

PRINTED IN ENGLAND
AT THE OXFORD UNIVERSITY PRESS
BY FREDERICK HALL

PREFACE

As it has been possible, through the generosity of the
Oxford University Press, to present to the Public, now for
the first time, the complete collected poems of Austin Dobson,
it may be useful to refer briefly to the various volumes that
have preceded the present edition.

Austin Dobson's first volume of verse was published by
Messrs. Henry S. King & Co. in October, 1873, and was
entitled *Vignettes in Rhyme and Vers de Société*.   It contained
poems which had appeared in various magazines, chiefly *St.
Paul's*, then under the editorship of Anthony Trollope, to
whom the volume was dedicated.   A second edition appeared
in 1874, and a third in 1875.

In May, 1877, it was followed by *Proverbs in Porcelain
and other Verses*, a fresh ingathering issued by the same
publishers.   A second edition appeared in 1878, the residue
of which was destroyed by a fire.

In 1880, *Vignettes in Rhyme and Other Verses*, a selection
for the most part of the two earlier volumes, was published
in New York by Messrs. Henry Holt & Co., with a dedication
to Oliver Wendell Holmes and an introduction by Edmund
Clarence Stedman.   A reprint appeared in 1885.

In 1883, by which date the two English volumes above
mentioned were no longer obtainable, the American Selection
of 1880, newly arranged, was reprinted in London by Messrs.
Kegan Paul, Trench & Co. (successors to Messrs. Henry
S. King & Co.) as *Old World Idylls* ; the fifteenth and final
edition appearing in 1906.

Preface

In 1885, a companion volume, entitled *At the Sign of the Lyre*, mainly composed of later poems, was issued in London and New York, although the American edition differed somewhat as to its contents from the English edition. The eleventh and final edition of the English volume appeared in 1904.

It should here be recorded that the sixth edition of *At the Sign of the Lyre* (1889) and the ninth edition of *Old World Idylls* (1889) were also issued under the title *Poems on Several Occasions*. The sixth and seventh editions of *At the Sign of the Lyre* were supplied at the end with extra half-titles and titles bearing this name. *Poems on Several Occasions* was also produced in 1889 in America by Messrs. Dodd, Mead & Co., and reprinted in 1894.

The early nineties saw the publication of three illustrated volumes of Selections. These were *The Ballad of Beau Brocade* (1892), which ran into three editions, and *The Story of Rosina* (1895), both illustrated by Hugh Thomson ; and *Proverbs in Porcelain* (1893), illustrated by Bernard Partridge. These volumes were published by Messrs. Kegan Paul, Trench, Trübner & Co., and the first and third were reprinted in pocket form in 1903 and 1905 respectively.

In 1892, Messrs. Heinemann & Balestier published a volume of *Selected Poems* in *The English Library Series*, for Continental readers only.

In 1895 a new edition, revised and enlarged, of *Poems on Several Occasions* appeared simultaneously in England and America, although there were two additional limited editions printed in America, of which no copies appeared in England. This edition comprised a portrait by William Strang, and seven etchings by Adolphe Lalauze. The English edition was issued by Messrs. Kegan Paul, Trench, Trübner, & Co., and the American edition by Messrs. Dodd, Mead & Co.

In 1897, the first edition of *Collected Poems* was published

Preface

by Messrs. Kegan Paul, Trench, Trübner & Co. This volume
was added to considerably from time to time, with the result
that the latest issue (the third impression of the ninth
edition, appearing in 1920) contains some 88 poems more
than the first edition of 1897.

In 1899–1901, Messrs. Dodd, Mead & Co., of New York,
published in America an eleven-volume edition of the
Author's writings, comprising both prose and poetry. This
edition included two volumes of poetry, practically a reprint of
the *Poems on Several Occasions* of 1895, as well as a volume
of *Miscellanies,* containing a number of poems, the majority
of which had already appeared in a privately printed volume
issued in England in 1901, under the title of *Carmina Votiva*.

In 1905, Messrs. Kegan Paul, Trench, Trübner & Co.
issued a selected edition, containing some 50 of the Author's
most popular poems. This was reprinted in 1909 and is
now published by the Oxford University Press. A certain
number of poems are also to be found in the following
volumes : *De Libris, Prose and Verse,* published by Messrs.
Macmillan & Co. in 1908, second edition 1909, and now
reissued by the Oxford University Press; *A Bookman's
Budget* (1917) and *Later Essays* (1920) both published by
the Oxford University Press.

The present complete edition, issuing from the Oxford
University Press, contains all the poems included in the
last-issued edition of *Collected Poems,* referred to above,
and in addition some 54 War Rondeaus and other Miscellaneous Poems, most of which have already appeared in print.

The various sections into which *Collected Poems* was
divided have been preserved in the present volume. Most
of the new poems will be found in the last section, entitled
Rondeaus of the Great War and other Poems. As, however,
a certain number of these 'other' poems originally appeared
in the privately printed *Carmina Votiva,* these have, for the

Preface

sake of uniformity, been added to the section bearing that
name. To that section have also been transferred a few
poems, originally appearing in *Carmina Votiva*, which were
included in the ninth edition of *Collected Poems*, chiefly in
the section entitled *Additions and Translations*. As this
transference has greatly reduced the size of that section,
it has been combined with the previous section, and is now
named *Later Additions and Translations*. The section
Carmina Votiva now contains practically all the poems
appearing in the volume of that name, and they generally
follow the order in which they there appeared.

To each poem is appended the date of its first appearance
in print. Where this date is not coincident with the date of
its composition, the latter is also shown in brackets. To
such of the poems in the last section as have not appeared
before in print, the necessary explanation is added.

Three indexes are appended. The first is an index to
first lines; the second an index to titles; and the third
a bibliographical index, showing the poems arranged chronologically, according to their first appearance in print, whether
in a magazine, a published volume, or in a privately printed
form. In a few cases, however, it is regretted that it has
not been possible to trace the poems to their earliest
appearance in print. I desire to record the assistance I have
derived, in preparing this index, from Mr. F. E. Murray's
valuable 'Bibliography of Austin Dobson', published at
Derby in 1900.

The Author's notes which appeared in the last edition of
Collected Poems have been included in the present volume,
as far as possible in their entirety. Where, however, they
merely contained the information now comprised in the
bibliographical index, they have been omitted. Modifica-
tions or omissions have also had to be made here and there,
especially in the case of those notes which contained poems

Preface

which have now been transferred to the body of the present volume.

The frontispiece is from the portrait taken by Messrs. Walter Barnett & Co. Ltd., of Knightsbridge, and I desire to acknowledge their courtesy in allowing me to reproduce it. It is generally considered by the Poet's family to be his best portrait, and was taken in 1910, when he was seventy.

Every effort has been made to make the present volume as complete as possible, and I gratefully acknowledge my indebtedness to Mr. Edmund Gosse, for the help and advice he has so readily given me in its compilation. All the Author's known poems have been examined, and most of the early poems, which he is known to have refrained from reprinting in the various editions of *Collected Poems*, have again been excluded. The present volume nevertheless contains all the poems which, it is believed, the Author would wish to have been preserved.

It remains to call attention to the quotation from Martial —*Majores majora sonent*—which appears on the title-page of this volume, as on the title-page of the various editions of *Collected Poems*. I cannot do better than quote my father's words in his preface to the first edition of 1897.

'The motto on my title-page is sincere. Let me here complete it—

mihi parva locuto
Sufficit in vestras saepe redire manus.'

ALBAN DOBSON.

EALING, 1923.

To you I sing, whom towns immure,
And bonds of toil hold fast and sure;—
*   To you across whose aching sight*
*   Come woodlands bathed in April light,*
And dreams of pastime premature.

And you, O Sad, who still endure
Some wound that only Time can cure,—
*   To you, in watches of the night,—*
*   To you I sing!*

But most to you with eyelids pure,
Scarce witting yet of love or lure;—
*   To you, with bird-like glances bright,*
*   Half-paused to speak, half-poised in flight;*
O English Girl, divine, demure,
*   To* YOU *I sing!*

1876.

Ie ne puis tenir registre de ma vie par mes
actions ; fortune les met trop bas : ie le tiens
par mes fantasies.

—MONTAIGNE.

Too low my lot for lofty deed :
I pipe but fancies on a reed.

CONTENTS

Contents

Contents

Contents

(xvi)

Contents

Contents

(xviii)

Contents

Contents

Contents

Contents

Contents

OLD-WORLD IDYLLS

A DEAD LETTER

'*À cœur blessé—l'ombre et le silence.*'—H. DE BALZAC.

I

I DREW it from its china tomb;—
    It came out feebly scented
With some thin ghost of past perfume
    That dust and days had lent it.

An old, old letter,—folded still!
    To read with due composure,
I sought the sun-lit window-sill,
    Above the grey enclosure,

That glimmering in the sultry haze,
    Faint-flowered, dimly shaded,
Slumbered like Goldsmith's Madam Blaize,
    Bedizened and brocaded.

A queer old place! You'd surely say
    Some tea-board garden-maker
Had planned it in Dutch William's day
    To please some florist Quaker,

So trim it was. The yew-trees still,
    With pious care perverted,
Grew in the same grim shapes; and still
    The lipless dolphin spurted;

Still in his wonted state abode
  The broken-nosed Apollo;
And still the cypress-arbour showed
  The same umbrageous hollow.

Only,—as fresh young Beauty gleams
  From coffee-coloured laces,—
So peeped from its old-fashioned dreams
  The fresher modern traces;

For idle mallet, hoop, and ball
  Upon the lawn were lying;
A magazine, a tumbled shawl,
  Round which the swifts were flying;

And, tossed beside the Guelder rose,
  A heap of rainbow knitting,
Where, blinking in her pleased repose,
  A Persian cat was sitting.

'A place to love in,—live,—for aye,
  If we too, like Tithonus,
Could find some god to stretch the grey,
  Scant life the Fates have thrown us;

'But now by steam we run our race,
  With buttoned heart and pocket;
Our Love's a gilded, surplus grace,—
  Just like an empty locket!

' "The time is out of joint." Who will
  May strive to make it better;
For me, this warm old window-sill,
  And this old dusty letter.'

A Dead Letter

' Dear *John* (the letter ran), it can't, can't be,
　For Father 's gone to *Chorley Fair* with *Sam*,
And Mother 's storing Apples,—*Prue* and Me
　Up to our Elbows making Damson Jam :
But we shall meet before a Week is gone,—
" 'Tis a long Lane that has no turning," *John !*

' Only till Sunday next, and then you'll wait
　Behind the White-Thorn, by the broken Stile—
We can go round and catch them at the Gate,
　All to Ourselves, for nearly one long Mile ;
Dear *Prue* won't look, and Father he'll go on,
And *Sam's* two Eyes are all for *Cissy, John !*

' *John*, she 's so smart,—with every Ribbon new,
　Flame-coloured Sack, and Crimson Padesoy :
As proud as proud ; and has the Vapours too,
　Just like My Lady ;—calls poor *Sam* a Boy,
And vows no Sweetheart 's worth the Thinking-on
Till he 's past Thirty . . . I know better, *John !*

' My Dear, I don't think that I thought of much
　Before we knew each other, I and you ;
And now, why, *John*, your least, least Finger-touch,
　Gives me enough to think a Summer through.
See, for I send you Something ! There, 'tis gone !
Look in this corner,—mind you find it, *John !* '

　This was the matter of the note,—
　　A long-forgot deposit,
　Dropped in an Indian dragon's throat,
　　Deep in a fragrant closet,

Old-World Idylls

Piled with a dapper Dresden world,—
    Beaux, beauties, prayers, and poses,—
Bonzes with squat legs undercurled,
    And great jars filled with roses.

Ah, heart that wrote! Ah, lips that kissed!
    You had no thought or presage
Into what keeping you dismissed
    Your simple old-world message!

A reverent one. Though we to-day
    Distrust beliefs and powers,
The artless, ageless things you say
    Are fresh as May's own flowers,

Starring some pure primaeval spring,
    Ere Gold had grown despotic,—
Ere Life was yet a selfish thing,
    Or Love a mere exotic!

I need not search too much to find
    Whose lot it was to send it,
That feel upon me yet the kind
    Soft hand of her who penned it;

And see, through two score years of smoke,
    In by-gone, quaint apparel,
Shine from yon time-black Norway oak
    The face of Patience Caryl,—

The pale, smooth forehead, silver-tressed;
    The grey gown, primly flowered;
The spotless, stately coif whose crest
    Like Hector's horse-plume towered;

And still the sweet half-solemn look
    Where some past thought was clinging,
As when one shuts a serious book
    To hear the thrushes singing.

A Dead Letter

I kneel to you! Of those you were,
　Whose kind old hearts grow mellow,—
Whose fair old faces grow more fair
　As Point and Flanders yellow;

Whom some old store of garnered grief,
　Their placid temples shading,
Crowns like a wreath of autumn leaf
　With tender tints of fading.

Peace to your soul! You died unwed—
　Despite this loving letter.
And what of John? The less that's said
　Of John, I think, the better.

1868.

A GENTLEMAN OF THE OLD SCHOOL

He lived in that past Georgian day,
When men were less inclined to say
That 'Time is Gold,' and overlay
　　　With toil their pleasure;
He held some land, and dwelt thereon,—
Where, I forget,—the house is gone;
His Christian name, I think, was John,—
　　　His surname, Leisure.

Reynolds has painted him,—a face
Filled with a fine, old-fashioned grace,
Fresh-coloured, frank, with ne'er a trace
　　　Of trouble shaded;
The eyes are blue, the hair is drest
In plainest way,—one hand is prest
Deep in a flapped canary vest,
　　　With buds brocaded.

(7)

He wears a brown old Brunswick coat,
With silver buttons,—round his throat,
A soft cravat;—in all you note
      An elder fashion,—
A strangeness, which, to us who shine
In shapely hats,—whose coats combine
All harmonies of hue and line,—
      Inspires compassion.

He lived so long ago, you see!
Men were untravelled then, but we,
Like Ariel, post o'er land and sea
      With careless parting;
He found it quite enough for him
To smoke his pipe in 'garden trim,'
And watch, about the fish-tank's brim,
      The swallows darting.

He liked the well-wheel's creaking tongue,—
He liked the thrush that fed her young,—
He liked the drone of flies among
      His netted peaches;
He liked to watch the sunlight fall
Athwart his ivied orchard wall;
Or pause to catch the cuckoo's call
      Beyond the beeches.

His were the times of Paint and Patch,
And yet no Ranelagh could match
The sober doves that round his thatch
      Spread tails and sidled;
He liked their ruffling, puffed content,—
For him their drowsy wheelings meant
More than a Mall of Beaux that bent,
      Or Belles that bridled.

A Gentleman of the Old School

Not that, in truth, when life began,
He shunned the flutter of the fan;
He too had maybe 'pinked his man'
      In Beauty's quarrel;
But now his 'fervent youth' had flown
Where lost things go; and he was grown
As staid and slow-paced as his own
      Old hunter, Sorrel.

Yet still he loved the chase, and held
That no composer's score excelled
The merry horn, when Sweetlip swelled
      Its jovial riot;
But most his measured words of praise
Caressed the angler's easy ways,—
His idly meditative days,—
      His rustic diet.

Not that his 'meditating' rose
Beyond a sunny summer doze;
He never troubled his repose
      With fruitless prying;
But held, as law for high and low,
What God withholds no man can know,
And smiled away inquiry so,
      Without replying.

We read—alas, how much we read!
The jumbled strifes of creed and creed
With endless controversies feed
      Our groaning tables;
His books—and they sufficed him—were
Cotton's 'Montaigne,' 'The Grave' of Blair,
A 'Walton'—much the worse for wear—
      And 'Æsop's Fables.'

One more,—'The Bible.' Not that he
Had searched its page as deep as we ;
No sophistries could make him see
      Its slender credit ;
It may be that he could not count
The sires and sons to Jesse's fount,—
He liked the 'Sermon on the Mount,'—
      And more, he read it.

Once he had loved, but failed to wed,
A red-cheeked lass who long was dead ;
His ways were far too slow, he said,
      To quite forget her ;
And still when time had turned him gray
The earliest hawthorn buds in May
Would find his lingering feet astray,
      Where first he met her.

In Coelo Quies' heads the stone
On Leisure's grave,—now little known,
A tangle of wild-rose has grown
      So thick across it ;
The 'Benefactions' still declare
He left the clerk an elbow-chair,
And '12 Pence Yearly to Prepare
      A Christmas Posset.'

Lie softly, Leisure ! Doubtless you
With too serene a conscience drew
Your easy breath, and slumbered through
      The gravest issue ;
But we, to whom our age allows
Scarce space to wipe our weary brows,
Look down upon your narrow house,
      Old friend, and miss you !

1870.

A GENTLEWOMAN OF THE OLD SCHOOL

SHE lived in Georgian era too.
Most women then, if bards be true,
Succumbed to Routs and Cards, or grew
      Devout and acid.
But hers was neither fate.   She came
Of good west-country folk, whose fame
Has faded now.   For us her name
      Is 'Madam Placid'.

Patience or Prudence,—what you will,
Some prefix faintly fragrant still
As those old musky scents that fill
      Our grandams' pillows ;
And for her youthful portrait take
Some long-waist child of Hudson's make,
Stiffly at ease beside a lake
      With swans and willows.

I keep her later semblance placed
Beside my desk,—'tis lawned and laced,
In shadowy sanguine stipple traced
      By Bartolozzi ;
A placid face, in which surprise
Is seldom seen, but yet there lies
Some vestige of the laughing eyes
      Of arch Piozzi.

For her e'en Time grew debonair.
He, finding cheeks unclaimed of care,
With late-delayed faint roses there,
      And lingering dimples,
Had spared to touch the fair old face,
And only kissed with Vauxhall grace
The soft white hand that stroked her lace,
      Or smoothed her wimples.

So left her beautiful.   Her age
Was comely as her youth was sage,
And yet she once had been the rage ;--
          It hath been hinted,
Indeed, affirmed by one or two,
Some spark at Bath (as sparks will do)
Inscribed a song to 'Lovely Prue,'
          Which Urban printed.

I know she thought ; I know she felt ;
Perchance could sum, I doubt she spelt ;
She knew as little of the Celt
          As of the Saxon ;
I know she played and sang, for yet
We keep the tumble-down spinet
To which she quavered ballads set
          By Arne or Jackson.

Her tastes were not refined as ours ;
She liked plain food and homely flowers,
Refused to paint, kept early hours,
          Went clad demurely ;
Her art was sampler-work design,
Fireworks for her were 'vastly fine,'
Her luxury was elder-wine,--
          She loved that 'purely.'

She was renowned, traditions say,
For June conserves, for curds and whey,
For finest tea (she called it 'tay'),
          And ratafia ;
She knew, for sprains, what bands to choose,
Could tell the sovereign wash to use
For freckles, and was learned in brews
          As erst Medea.

Yet studied little.   She would read,
On Sundays, 'Pearson on the Creed,'
Though, as I think, she could not heed
    His text profoundly ;
Seeing she chose for her retreat
The warm west-looking window-seat,
Where, if you chanced to raise your feet,
    You slumbered soundly.

This, 'twixt ourselves.   The dear old dame,
In truth, was not so much to blame ;
The excellent divine I name
    Is scarcely stirring ;
Her plain-song piety preferred
Pure life to precept.   If she erred,
She knew her faults.   Her softest word
    Was for the erring.

If she had loved, or if she kept
Some ancient memory green, or wept
Over the shoulder-knot that slept
    Within her cuff-box,
I know not.   Only this I know,
At sixty-five she'd still her beau,
A lean French exile, lame and slow,
    With monstrous snuff-box.

Younger than she, well-born and bred.
She'd found him in St. Giles', half dead
Of teaching French for nightly bed
    And daily dinners ;
Starving, in fact, 'twixt want and pride ;
And so, henceforth, you always spied
His rusty 'pigeon-wings' beside
    Her Mechlin pinners.

He worshipped her, you may suppose.
She gained him pupils, gave him clothes,
Delighted in his dry *bons mots*
      And cackling laughter;
And when, at last, the long duet
Of conversation and picquet
Ceased with her death, of sheer regret
      He died soon after.

Dear Madam Placid! Others knew
Your worth as well as he, and threw
Their flowers upon your coffin too,
      I take for granted.
Their loves are lost; but still we see
Your kind and gracious memory
Bloom yearly with the almond tree
      The Frenchman planted.

1871.

THE BALLAD OF 'BEAU BROCADE'

' Hark! I hear the sound of coaches!'—Beggar's Opera.

Seventeen hundred and thirty-nine :—
That was the date of this tale of mine.

First great George was buried and gone;
George the Second was plodding on.

London then, as the 'Guides' aver,
Shared its glories with *Westminster;*

And people of rank, to correct their 'tone',
Went out of town to *Marybone.*

Those were the days of the War with *Spain,*
Porto-Bello would soon be ta'en;

The Ballad of 'Beau Brocade'

WHITEFIELD preached to the colliers grim,
Bishops in lawn sleeves preached at him;

WALPOLE talked of 'a man and his price';
Nobody's virtue was over-nice :—-

Those, in fine, were the brave days when
Coaches were stopped by . . *Highwaymen !*

And of all the knights of the gentle trade
Nobody bolder than 'BEAU BROCADE'.

This they knew on the whole way down;
Best,—maybe,—at the '*Oak and Crown*'.

(For timorous cits on their pilgrimage
Would 'club' for a 'Guard' to ride the stage :

And the Guard that rode on more than one
Was the Host of this hostel's sister's son.)

Open we here on a March day fine,
Under the oak with the hanging sign.

There was Barber DICK with his basin by;
Cobbler JOE with the patch on his eye;

Portly product of Beef and Beer,
JOHN the host, he was standing near.

Straining and creaking, with wheels awry,
Lumbering came the '*Plymouth Fly*';—

Lumbering up from *Bagshot Heath*,
Guard in the basket armed to the teeth;

Passengers heavily armed inside;
Not the less surely the coach had been tried !

Tried !—but a couple of miles away,
By a well-dressed man !—in the open day !

Tried successfully, never a doubt,—
Pockets of passengers all turned out !

Cloak-bags rifled, and cushions ripped,—
Even an Ensign's wallet stripped !

Even a Methodist hosier's wife
Offered the choice of her Money or Life !

Highwayman's manners no less polite,
Hoped that their coppers (returned) were right ;—

Sorry to find the company poor,
Hoped next time they'd travel with more ;—

Plucked them all at his ease, in short :—
Such was the '*Plymouth Fly's*' report.

Sympathy ! horror ! and wonderment !
'Catch the Villain !'   (But Nobody went.)

Hosier's wife led into the Bar ;
(That 's where the best strong waters are !)

Followed the tale of the hundred-and-one
Things that Somebody ought to have done.

Ensign (of BRAGG'S) made a terrible clangour :
But for the Ladies had drawn his hanger !

Robber, of course, was 'BEAU BROCADE,'
Out-spoke DOLLY the Chambermaid.

Devonshire DOLLY, plump and red,
Spoke from the gallery overhead ;—

Spoke it out boldly, staring hard :—
'Why didn't you shoot then, GEORGE the Guard ?'

Spoke it out bolder, seeing him mute :
'GEORGE the Guard, why didn't you shoot ?'

Portly JOHN grew pale and red,
(JOHN was afraid of her, people said ;)

Gasped that 'DOLLY was surely cracked,'
(JOHN was afraid of her—that 's a fact !)

The Ballad of 'Beau Brocade'

GEORGE the Guard grew red and pale,
Slowly finished his quart of ale :—

'Shoot?   Why—Rabbit him !—didn't he shoot?'
Muttered—'The Baggage was far too 'cute!'

'Shoot?   Why he'd flashed the pan in his eye!'
Muttered—'She'd pay for it by and by!'
Further than this made no reply.

Nor could a further reply be made,
For GEORGE *was in league with* 'BEAU BROCADE'!

And JOHN the Host, in his wakefullest state,
Was not—on the whole—immaculate.

But nobody's virtue was over-nice
When WALPOLE talked of 'a man and his price';

And wherever Purity found abode,
'Twas certainly *not* on a posting road.

II

'Forty' followed to 'Thirty-nine.'
Glorious days of the *Hanover* line !

Princes were born, and drums were banged ;
Now and then batches of Highwaymen hanged.

'Glorious news !'—from the *Spanish Main ;*
PORTO-BELLO at last was ta'en.

'Glorious news !'—for the liquor trade ;
Nobody dreamed of 'BEAU BROCADE.'

People were thinking of *Spanish Crowns ;*
Money was coming from seaport towns !

Nobody dreamed of 'BEAU BROCADE,'
(Only DOLLY the Chambermaid !)

Blessings on VERNON !   Fill up the cans ;
Money was coming in ' *Flys* ' and ' *Vans.* '

Possibly JOHN the Host had heard ;
Also, certainly, GEORGE the Guard.

And DOLLY had possibly tidings, too,
That made her rise from her bed anew,

Plump as ever, but stern of eye,
With a fixed intention to warn the ' *Fly.* '

Lingering only at JOHN his door,
Just to make sure of a jerky snore ;

Saddling the grey mare, *Dumpling Star ;*
Fetching the pistol out of the bar ;

(The old horse-pistol that, they say,
Came from the battle of *Malplaquet ;*)

Loading with powder that maids would use,
Even in ' Forty,' to clear the flues ;

And a couple of silver buttons, the Squire
Gave her, away in *Devonshire.*

These she wadded—for want of better—
With the B—SH—P of L—ND—N's ' Pastoral Letter ' ;

Looked to the flint, and hung the whole,
Ready to use, at her pocket-hole.

Thus equipped and accoutred, DOLLY
Clattered away to ' *Exciseman's Folly* ' ;—

Such was the name of a ruined abode,
Just on the edge of the *London* road.

Thence she thought she might safely try,
As soon as she saw it, to warn the ' *Fly.* '

But, as chance fell out, her rein she drew,
As the BEAU came cantering into the view.

The Ballad of 'Beau Brocade'

By the light of the moon she could see him drest
In his famous gold-sprigged tambour vest;

And under his silver-grey surtout,
The laced, historical coat of blue,

That he wore when he went to *London-Spaw*,
And robbed Sir MUNGO MUCKLETHRAW.

Out-spoke DOLLY the Chambermaid,
(Trembling a little, but not afraid,)
'Stand and Deliver, O "BEAU BROCADE"!'

But the BEAU rode nearer, and would not speak,
For he saw by the moonlight a rosy cheek;

And a spavined mare with a rusty hide;
And a girl with her hand at her pocket-side.

So never a word he spoke as yet,
For he thought 'twas a freak of MEG or BET;—
A freak of the '*Rose*' or the '*Rummer*' set.

Out-spoke DOLLY the Chambermaid,
(Tremulous now, and sore afraid,)
'Stand and Deliver, O "BEAU BROCADE"!'—

Firing then, out of sheer alarm,
Hit the BEAU in the bridle-arm.

Button the first went none knows where,
But it carried away his *solitaire*;

Button the second a circuit made,
Glanced in under the shoulder-blade;—
Down from the saddle fell 'BEAU BROCADE''

Down from the saddle and never stirred!—
DOLLY grew white as a *Windsor* curd.

Slipped not less from the mare, and bound
Strips of her kirtle about his wound.

Then, lest his Worship should rise and flee,
Fettered his ankles—tenderly.

Jumped on his chestnut, BET the fleet
(Called after BET of *Portugal Street*);

Came like the wind to the old Inn-door;—
Roused fat JOHN from a three-fold snore;—

Vowed she'd 'peach if he misbehaved . . .
Briefly, the '*Plymouth Fly*' was saved!

Staines and *Windsor* were all on fire:—
DOLLY was wed to a *Yorkshire* squire;
Went to Town at the K—G's desire!

But whether His M—J—STY saw her or not,
HOGARTH jotted her down on the spot;

And something of DOLLY one still may trace
In the fresh contours of his '*Milkmaid's*' face.

GEORGE the Guard fled over the sea:
JOHN had a fit—of perplexity;

Turned King's evidence, sad to state;—
But JOHN was never immaculate.

As for the BEAU, he was duly tried,
When his wound was healed, at *Whitsuntide;*

Served—for a day—as the last of 'sights,'
To the world of *St. James's-Street* and '*White's,*'

Went on his way to TYBURN TREE,
With a pomp befitting his high degree.

Every privilege rank confers:—
Bouquet of pinks at *St. Sepulchre's;*

Flagon of ale at *Holborn Bar;*
Friends (in mourning) to follow his Car—
('t' is omitted where HEROES are!)

The Ballad of 'Beau Brocade'

Every one knows the speech he made ;
Swore that he 'rather admired the Jade ! '—

Waved to the crowd with his gold-laced hat :
Talked to the Chaplain after that ;

Turned to the Topsman undismayed . . .
This was the finish of 'BEAU BROCADE'!

And this is the Ballad that seemed to hide
In the leaves of a dusty 'LONDONER'S GUIDE' ;

' Humbly Inscrib'd (with curls and tails)
By the Author to FREDERICK, *Prince of* WALES :—

' Published by FRANCIS *and* OLIVER PINE ;
Ludgate-Hill, at the Blackmoor Sign,
Seventeen-Hundred-and-Thirty-Nine.'

1876.

UNE MARQUISE

A RHYMED MONOLOGUE IN THE LOUVRE

' Belle Marquise, vos beaux yeux me font mourir d'amour.'—MOLIÈRE.

I

As you sit there at your ease,
                    O Marquise !
And the men flock round your knees
                    Thick as bees,
Mute at every word you utter,
Servants to your least frill-flutter,
                    ' Belle Marquise !'—
As you sit there growing prouder,
    And your ringed hands glance and go,
And your fan's *frou-frou* sounds louder,
    And your *' beaux yeux'* flash and glow ;—

Ah, you used them on the Painter,
   As you know,
For the Sieur Larose spoke fainter,
   Bowing low,
Thanked Madame and Heaven for Mercy
That each sitter was not Circe,
 Or at least he told you so ;—
Growing proud, I say, and prouder
 To the crowd that come and go,
Dainty Deity of Powder,
 Fickle Queen of Fop and Beau,
As you sit where lustres strike you,
   Sure to please,
Do we love you most, or like you,
   ' *Belle Marquise !* '

II

You are fair ; O yes, we know it
   Well, Marquise :
For he swore it, your last poet,
   On his knees ;
And he called all heaven to witness
Of his ballad and its fitness,
   ' *Belle Marquise !* '—
You were everything in *ère*
(With exception of *sévère*),—
You were *cruelle* and *rebelle*,
With the rest of rhymes as well ;
You were ' *Reine*,' and ' *Mère d'Amour*,'
 You were ' *Vénus à Cythère* ' ;
' *Sappho mise en Pompadour*,'
 And ' *Minerve en Parabère* ' ;
You had every grace of heaven
 In your most angelic face,
With the nameless finer leaven
 Lent of blood and courtly race ;

Une Marquise

And he added, too, in duty,
Ninon's wit and Boufflers' beauty;
And La Vallière's *yeux veloutés*
        Followed these,
And you liked it, when he said it
        (On his knees),
And you kept it, and you read it,
        ' Belle Marquise !'

III

Yet with us your toilet graces
        Fail to please,
And the last of your last faces,
        And your *mise ;*
For we hold you just as real,
        ' Belle Marquise !'

As your *Bergers* and *Bergères*,
Iles d'Amour and *Batelières ;*
As your *parcs*, and your Versailles,
Gardens, grottoes, and *rocailles ;*
As your Naiads and your trees ;—
   Just as near the old ideal
        Calm and ease,
As the Venus there, by Coustou,
   That a fan would make quite flighty,
Is to her the gods were used to,—
   Is to grand Greek Aphroditè,
        Sprung from seas.
You are just a porcelain trifle,
        ' Belle Marquise !'
Just a thing of puffs and patches,
Made for madrigals and catches,
Not for heart-wounds, but for scratches,
        O Marquise !
Just a pinky porcelain trifle,
        ' Belle Marquise !'

Wrought in rarest *rose-Dubarry*,
Quick at verbal point and parry,
Clever, doubtless ;—but to marry,
      No, Marquise !

IV

For your Cupid, you have clipped him,
Rouged and patched him, nipped and snipped him
And with *chapeau-bras* equipped him,
      ' *Belle Marquise !* '
Just to arm you through your wife-time,
And the languors of your life-time,
      ' *Belle Marquise !* '
Say, to trim your toilet tapers,
Or,—to twist your hair in papers,
Or,—to wean you from the vapours ;—
      As for these,
You are worth the love they give you,
Till a fairer face outlive you,
  Or a younger grace shall please ;
Till the coming of the crows' feet,
And the backward turn of beaux' feet,
      ' *Belle Marquise !* '—
Till your frothed-out life's commotion
Settles down to Ennui's ocean,
Or a dainty sham devotion,
      ' *Belle Marquise !* '

V

No : we neither like nor love you,
      ' *Belle Marquise !* '
Lesser lights we place above you,—
  Milder merits better please.

Une Marquise

We have passed from *Philosophe*-dom
    Into plainer modern days,—
Grown contented in our oafdom,
    Giving grace not all the praise ;
And, *en partant, Arsinoé*,—
    Without malice whatsoever,—
We shall counsel to our Chloë
    To be rather good than clever ;
For we find it hard to smother
    Just one little thought, Marquise !
Wittier perhaps than any other,—
You were neither Wife nor Mother,
                ' *Belle Marquise !* '

1868.

THE STORY OF ROSINA

AN INCIDENT IN THE LIFE OF FRANÇOIS BOUCHER

' *On ne badine pas avec l'amour.* '

THE scene, a wood.   A shepherd tip-toe creeping,
    Carries a basket, whence a billet peeps,
To lay beside a silk-clad Oread sleeping
    Under an urn ; yet not so sound she sleeps
But that she plainly sees his graceful act ;
' He thinks she thinks he thinks she sleeps,' in fact.

One hardly needs the ' *Peint par François Boucher.* '
    All the sham life comes back again,—one sees
Alcôves, Ruelles, the *Lever* and the *Coucher*,
    Patches and Ruffles, *Roués* and *Marquises ;*
The little great, the infinite small thing
That ruled the hour when Louis Quinze was king.

For these were yet the days of halcyon weather,—
  A 'Martin's summer,' when the nation swam,
Aimless and easy as a wayward feather,
  Down the full tide of jest and epigram ;—
A careless time, when France's bluest blood
Beat to the tune of 'After us the Flood.'

Plain Roland still was placidly 'inspecting,'
  Not now Camille had stirred the Café Foy ;
Marat was young, and Guillotin dissecting,
  Corday unborn, and Lamballe in Savoie ;
No *faubourg* yet had heard the Tocsin ring :—
This was the summer—when Grasshoppers sing.

And far afield were sun-baked savage creatures,
  Female and male, that tilled the earth, and wrung
Want from the soil ;—lean things with livid features,
  Shape of bent man, and voice that never sung :
These were the Ants, for yet to Jacques Bonhomme
Tumbrils were not, nor any sound of drum.

But Boucher was a Grasshopper, and painted,—
  Rose-water Raphael,—*en couleur de rose,*
The crowned Caprice, whose sceptre, nowise sainted,
  Swayed the light realm of ballets and *bons mots ;*—
Ruled the dim boudoir's *demi-jour*, or drove
Pink-ribboned flocks through some pink-flowered grove.

A laughing Dame, who sailed a laughing cargo
  Of flippant loves along the *Fleuve du Tendre ;*
Whose greatest grace was *jupes à la Camargo*,
  Whose gentlest merit *gentiment se rendre ;*
Queen of the rouge-cheeked Hours, whose footsteps fell
To Rameau's notes, in dances by Gardel ;—

The Story of Rosina

Her Boucher served, till Nature's self betraying,
    As Wordsworth sings, the heart that loved her not,
Made of his work a land of languid Maying,
    Filled with false gods and muses misbegot ;—
A Versailles Eden of cosmetic youth,
Wherein most things went naked, save the Truth.

Once, only once,—perhaps the last night's revels
    Palled in the after-taste,—our Boucher sighed
For that first beauty, falsely named the Devil's,
    Young-lipped, unlessoned, joyous, and clear-eyed ;
Flung down his palette like a weary man,
And sauntered slowly through the Rue Sainte-Anne.

Wherefore, we know not ; but, at times, far nearer
    Things common come, and lineaments half-seen
Grow in a moment magically clearer ;—
    Perhaps, as he walked, the grass he called 'too green'
Rose and rebuked him, or the earth 'ill-lighted'
Silently smote him with the charms he slighted.

But, as he walked, he tired of god and goddess,
    Nymphs that deny, and shepherds that appeal ;
Stale seemed the trick of kerchief and of bodice,
    Folds that confess, and flutters that reveal ;
Then as he grew more sad and disenchanted,
Forthwith he spied the very thing he wanted.

So, in the Louvre, the passer-by might spy some
    Arch-looking head, with half-evasive air,
Start from behind the fruitage of Van Huysum,
    Grape-bunch and melon, nectarine and pear :—
Here 'twas no Venus of Batavian city,
But a French girl, young, *piquante*, bright, and pretty.

(27)

Graceful she was, as some slim marsh-flower shaken
    Among the sallows, in the breezy Spring ;
Blithe as the first blithe song of birds that waken,
    Fresh as a fresh young pear-tree blossoming ;
Black was her hair as any blackbird's feather ;
Just for her mouth, two rose-buds grew together.

Sloes were her eyes ; but her soft cheeks were peaches,
    Hued like an Autumn pippin, where the red
Seems to have burned right through the skin, and reaches
    E'en to the core ; and if you spoke, it spread
Up till the blush had vanquished all the brown,
And, like two birds, the sudden lids dropped down.

As Boucher smiled, the bright black eyes ceased dancing ;
    As Boucher spoke, the dainty red eclipse
Filled all the face from cheek to brow, enhancing
    Half a shy smile that dawned around the lips.
Then a shrill mother rose upon the view ;
' *Cerises, M'sieu ? Rosine, dépéchez-vous !* '

Deep in the fruit her hands Rosina buries,
    Soon in the scale the ruby bunches lay.
The Painter, watching the suspended cherries,
    Never had seen such little fingers play ;—
As for the arm, no Hebe's could be rounder ;
Low in his heart a whisper said ' I've found her.'

' Woo first the mother, if you'd win the daughter ! '
    Boucher was charmed, and turned to *Madame Mère*,
Almost with tears of suppliance besought her
    Leave to immortalize a face so fair ;
Praised and cajoled so craftily that straightway
Voici Rosina,—standing at his gateway.

The Story of Rosina

Shy at the first, in time Rosina's laughter
   Rang through the studio as the girlish face
Peeped from some painter's travesty, or after
   Showed like an Omphale in lion's case ;
Gay as a thrush, that from the morning dew
Pipes to the light its clear ' *Réveillez-vous.*'

Just a mere child with sudden ebullitions,
   Flashes of fun, and little bursts of song,
Petulant pains, and fleeting pale contritions,
   Mute little moods of misery and wrong ;
Only a child, of Nature's rarest making,
Wistful and sweet,—and with a heart for breaking !

Day after day the little loving creature
   Came and returned ; and still the Painter felt,
Day after day, the old theatric Nature
   Fade from his sight, and like a shadow melt
Paniers and Powder, Pastoral and Scene,
Killed by the simple beauty of Rosine.

As for the girl, she turned to her new being,—
   Came, as a bird that hears its fellow call ;
Blessed, as the blind that blesses God for seeing ;
   Grew, as the flower on which the sun-rays fall ;
Loved if you will ; she never named it so :
Love comes unseen,—we only see it go.

There is a figure among Boucher's sketches,
   Slim,—a child-face, the eyes as black as beads,
Head set askance, and hand that shyly stretches
   Flowers to the passer, with a look that pleads.
This was no other than Rosina surely ;—
None Boucher knew could else have looked so purely.

But forth her Story, for I will not tarry:
　Whether he loved the little 'nut-brown maid,'
If, of a truth, he counted this to carry
　Straight to the end, or just the whim obeyed,
Nothing we know, but only that before
More had been done, a finger tapped the door.

Opened Rosina to the unknown comer.
　'Twas a young girl—'*une pauvre fille,*' she said,
'They had been growing poorer all the summer;
　Father was lame, and mother lately dead;
Bread was so dear, and,—oh! but want was bitter,
Would Monsieur pay to have her for a sitter?

Men called her pretty.' Boucher looked a minute:
　Yes, she was pretty; and her face beside
Shamed her poor clothing by a something in it,—
　Grace, and a presence hard to be denied;
This was no common offer, it was certain;—
'*Allez*, Rosina! sit behind the curtain.'

Meanwhile the Painter, with a mixed emotion,
　Drew and re-drew his ill-disguised Marquise,
Passed in due time from praises to devotion;
　Last, when his sitter left him on his knees,
Rose in a maze of passion and surprise,—
Rose, and beheld Rosina's saddened eyes.

Thrice-happy France, whose facile sons inherit
　Still in the old traditionary way,
Power to enjoy—with yet a rarer merit,
　Power to forget! Our Boucher rose, I say,
With hand still prest to heart, with pulses throbbing,
And blankly stared at poor Rosina sobbing.

The Story of Rosina

'This was no model, *M'sieu*, but a lady.'
  Boucher was silent, for he knew it true.
'*Est-ce que vous l'aimez ?*' Never answer made he !
  Ah, for the old love fighting with the new !
'*Est-ce que vous l'aimez ?*' sobbed Rosina's sorrow.
'*Bon !*' murmured Boucher ; 'she will come to-morrow.'

How like a Hunter thou, O Time, dost harry
  Us, thine oppressed, and pleasured with the chase,
Sparest to strike thy sorely-running quarry,
  Following not less with unrelenting face.
Time, if Love hunt, and Sorrow hunt, with thee,
Woe to the Fawn ! There is no way to flee.

Woe to Rosina ! By To-morrow stricken,
  Swift from her life the sun of gold declined.
Nothing remained but those grey shades that thicken,
  Cloud and the cold,—the loneliness—the wind.
Only a little by the door she lingers,—
Waits, with wrung lip and interwoven fingers.

No, not a sign. Already with the Painter
  Grace and the nymphs began recovered reign ;
Truth was no more, and Nature, waxing fainter,
  Paled to the old sick Artifice again.
Seeing Rosina going out to die,
How should he know what Fame had passed him by ?

Going to die ! For who shall waste in sadness,
  Shorn of the sun, the very warmth and light,
Miss the green welcome of the sweet earth's gladness
  Lose the round life that only Love makes bright :
There is no succour if these things are taken.
None but Death loves the lips by Love forsaken.

So, in a little, when those Two had parted,—
    Tired of himself, and weary as before,
Boucher remembering, sick and sorry-hearted,
    Stayed for a moment by Rosina's door.
'Ah, the poor child!' the neighbours cry of her,
'*Morte, M'sieu, morte! On dit,—des peines de cœur!*'

Just for a second, say, the tidings shocked him;
    Say, in his eye a sudden tear-drop shone,—
Just for a second, a dull feeling mocked him
    With a vague sense of something priceless gone,
Then,—for at best 'twas but the empty type,
The husk of man with which the days were ripe,—

Then, he forgot her. But, for you that slew her,
    You, her own sister, that with airy ease,
Just for a moment's fancy could undo her,
    Pass on your way. A little while, Marquise,
Be the sky silent, be the sea serene;
A pleasant passage—*à Sainte Guillotine!*

As for Rosina,—for the quiet sleeper,
    Whether stone hides her, or the happy grass,
If the sun quickens, if the dews beweep her,
    Laid in the Madeleine or Montparnasse,
Nothing we know,—but that her heart is cold,
Poor beating heart! And so the Story's told.

1869.

PROVERBS IN PORCELAIN

'Rien en relief.'

ENVOI

No Moral.   Nothing more than may
　　Enliven hours that seem too long;
Or shred on some beclouded day
　　The light of laughter and of song.

No Moral,—no.   Yet oft they make
　　More than they mean, who would but please;
And something for the Moral's sake
　　May lurk in Fables frail as these.

1905.

PROLOGUE

ASSUME *that we are friends. Assume*
A common taste for old costume,—
    Old pictures,—books. Then dream us sitting—
Us two—in some soft-lighted room.

Outside, the wind ;—the 'ways are mire.'
We, with our faces toward the fire,
    Finished the feast not full but fitting,
Watch the light-leaping flames aspire.

Silent at first, in time we glow ;
Discuss ' eclectics', high and low ;
    Inspect engravings, 'twixt us passing
The fancies of DETROY, MOREAU ;

'Reveils' and 'Couchers', 'Balls' and 'Fêtes' ;
Anon we glide to ' crocks' and plates,
    Grow eloquent on glaze and classing,
And half-pathetic over ' states.'

Then I produce my Prize, in truth ;—
Six groups in SÈVRES, fresh as Youth,
    And rare as Love. You pause, you wonder,
(Pretend to doubt the marks, forsooth !)

And so we fall to why and how
The fragile figures smile and bow ;
    Divine, at length, the fable under . . .
Thus grew the 'Scenes' that follow now.

1877.
C 2   (35)

Proverbs in Porcelain

THE BALLAD À-LA-MODE

' Tout vient à point à qui sait attendre.'

SCENE.—*A Boudoir Louis-Quinze, painted with Cupids shooting at Butterflies.*

THE COUNTESS.   THE BARON (*her cousin and suitor*).

THE COUNTESS (*looking up from her work*).
BARON, you doze.

THE BARON (*closing his book*).

        I, Madame?   No,
I wait your order—Stay or Go.

THE COUNTESS.

Which means, I think, that Go or Stay
Affects you nothing, either way.

THE BARON.

Excuse me,—by your favour graced,
My inclinations are effaced.

THE COUNTESS.

Or much the same.   How keen you grow!
You must be reading MARIVAUX.

THE BARON.

Nay,—'twas a song of SAINTE-AULAIRE.

THE COUNTESS.

Then read me one.   We've time to spare :
If I can catch the clock-face there,
'Tis barely eight.

THE BARON.

        What shall it be,—
A tale of woe, or perfidy?

The Ballad à-la-Mode

THE COUNTESS.

Not woes, I beg.   I doubt your woes:
But perfidy, of course, one knows.

THE BARON (*reads*).

' " *Ah, Phillis! cruel Phillis!*
   (*I heard a Shepherd say,*)
You hold me with your Eyes, and yet
   You bid me—Go my Way!"

' " *Ah, Colin! foolish Colin!*
   (*The Maiden answered so,*)
If that be All, the Ill is small,
   I close them—You may go!"

' *But when her Eyes she opened,*
   (*Although the Sun it shone,*)
She found the Shepherd had not stirred—
   " *Because the Light was gone!*"

' *Ah, Cupid! wanton Cupid!*
   'Twas ever thus your Way:
When Maids would bid you ply your Wings,
   You find Excuse to stay! '

THE COUNTESS.

Famous!   He earned whate'er he got:—
But there's some sequel, is there not?

THE BARON (*turning the page*).

I think not.—No.   Unless 'tis this:
My fate is far more hard than his;—
In fact, *your* Eyes—

THE COUNTESS.

                Now, that's a breach!
Your bond is—not to make a speech.

(37)

And we must start—so call JUSTINE.
I know exactly what you mean !—
Give me your arm—

THE BARON.

If, in return,
Countess, I could your hand but earn !

THE COUNTESS.

I thought as much.   This comes, you see,
Of sentiment, and Arcady,
Where vows are hung on every tree. . . .

THE BARON (*offering his arm, with a low bow*).

And no one dreams—of PERFIDY.

1875.

THE METAMORPHOSIS

' On s'enrichit quand on dort.'

SCENE.—*A high stone Seat in an Alley of clipped Lime-trees.*

THE ABBÉ TIRILI.   MONSIEUR L'ÉTOILE

THE ABBÉ (*writing*).

' THIS shepherdess Dorine adored—'
What rhyme is next ?   *Implored ?—ignored ?*
Poured ?—soared ?—afford ?   That facile Dunce,
L'ÉTOILE, would cap the line at once.
'Twill come in time.   Meanwhile, suppose
We take a meditative doze.

(*Sleeps.   By and by his paper falls.*)

M. L'ÉTOILE (*approaching from the back*).

Some one before me.   What ! 'tis you,
Monsieur the Scholar ?   Sleeping too !

(*Picks up the fluttering paper.*)

(38)

The Metamorphosis

More '*Tales*', of course.   One can't refuse
To chase so fugitive a Muse !
Verses are public, too, that fly
'*Cum privilegio*'—*Zephyri !*
                    (*Reads.*)
'CLITANDER AND DORINE.'   Insane !
He fancies he 's a LA FONTAINE !
'*In early Days, the gods, we find,*
Paid private Visits to Mankind ;—
At least, authentic Records say so
In Publius Ovidius Naso.'
(Three names for one.   This passes all.
'Tis '*furiously*' classical !)
'*No doubt their Purpose oft would be*
Some 'Nodus dignus Vindice' ;
'*On dit,*' *not less, these earthward Tours*
Were mostly Matters of Amours.
And Woe to him whose luckless Flame
Impeded that Olympic Game ;
Ere he could say an 'Ave' *o'er,*
They changed him—like a Louis-d'or.'
('*Aves,*' and current coinage ?   O !—
O shade of NICOLAS BOILEAU !)
'*Bird, Beast, or River he became :*
With Women it was much the same.
In Ovid Case to Case succeeds ;
But Names the Reader never reads.'
(That is, Monsieur the Abbé feels
His quantities are out at heels !)
'*Suffice it that, for this our Tale,*
There dwelt in a Thessalian Vale,
Of Tales like this the frequent Scene,
A Shepherdess, by name Dorine.
Trim Waist, ripe Lips, bright Eyes, had she ;—
In short,—the whole Artillery.
Her Beauty made some local Stir ;—

Men marked it. So did Jupiter.
This Shepherdess Dorine adored. . . .'
Implored, ignored, and *soared,* and *poured—*
(He's scrawled them here!)   We'll sum in brief
His fable on his second leaf.

(Writes.)

There, they shall know who 'twas that wrote:—
' L'Étoile's *is but a mock-bird's note.'*   [*Exit.*

The Abbé (waking).

Implored's the word, I think.   But where,—
Where is my paper?   Ah ! 'tis there !
Eh ! what ?

(Reads.)

The Metamorphosis

(not in Ovid).

The Shepherdess Dorine adored
  The Shepherd-Boy Clitander ;
But Jove himself, Olympus' Lord,
The Shepherdess Dorine adored.
Our Abbé's Aid the Pair Implored ;—
  And changed to Goose and Gander ;
The Shepherdess Dorine adored
  The Shepherd-Boy Clitander !'

L'Étoile,—by all the Muses !

Peste !

He 's off, post-haste, to tell the rest.
No matter.   Laugh, Sir Dunce, to-day ;
Next time 'twill be *my* turn to play.

1877.

(40)

THE SONG OUT OF SEASON

' Point de culte sans mystère.'

SCENE.—*A Corridor in a Château, with Busts and Venice chandeliers.*

MONSIEUR L'ÉTOILE.   TWO VOICES.

M. L'ÉTOILE (*carrying a Rose*).

THIS is the place.   MUTINE said here.
' Through the Mancini room, and near
The fifth Venetian chandelier. . . .'
The fifth?—She knew there were but four ;—
Still, here's the *busto* of the Moor.

(*Humming.*)

Tra-la, tra-la !   If BIJOU wake,
He'll bark, no doubt, and spoil my shake !
I'll tap, I think.   One can't mistake ;
    This surely is the door.

(*Sings softly.*)
' *When Jove, the Skies' Director,*
    First saw you sleep of yore,
He cried aloud for Nectar,
    " *The Nectar quickly pour,—*
    The Nectar, Hebe, pour !" '

(No sound.   I'll tap once more.)

(*Sings again.*)
' *Then came the Sire Apollo,*
    He passed you where you lay ;
" *Come, Dian, rise and follow*
    The dappled Hart to slay,—
    The rapid Hart to slay." '
            (*A rustling within.*)

(Coquette !   She heard before.)

Proverbs in Porcelain

(*Sings again.*)

'And urchin Cupid after
   Beside the Pillow curled,
He whispered you with Laughter,
   "Awake and witch the World,—
    O Venus, witch the World!"'

(Now comes the last. 'Tis scarcely worse,
I think, than Monsieur l'ABBÉ's verse.)

'So waken, waken, waken,
   O You, whom we adore;
Where gods can be mistaken,
   Mere Mortals must be more,—
    Poor Mortals must be more!'

(That merits an *encore*.)

'So waken, waken, waken!
   O YOU, whom we adore!'

(*An energetic* VOICE.)

'Tis thou, ANTOINE? Ah, Addle-pate!
Ah, Thief of Valet, always late!
Have I not told thee half-past eight
A thousand times!

(*Great agitation.*)

      But wait,—but wait,—

M. L'ÉTOILE (*stupefied*).

Just Skies! What hideous roar!—
What lungs! The infamous Soubrette!
This is a turn I sha'n't forget:—
To make me sing my *chansonnette*
Before old JOURDAIN's door!

(*Retiring slowly.*)

And yet, and yet,—it can't be she.
They prompted her. Who can it be?

The Song out of Season

(*A second* Voice.)

It was the Abbé Ti—ri—li!

(*In a mocking falsetto.*)

' *Where gods can be mistaken,*
Mere Poets must be more,—
Bad Poets *must be more.*'

1874.

THE CAP THAT FITS

' *Qui sème épines n'aille déchaux.*'

Scene.—*A Salon with blue and white Panels.   Outside,*
Persons pass and re-pass upon a Terrace.

Hortense.   Armande.   Monsieur Loyal.

Hortense (*behind her fan*).

Not young, I think.

Armande (*raising her eye-glass*).

                    And faded, too !—
Quite faded !   Monsieur, what say you ?

M. Loyal.

Nay,—I defer to you.   In truth,
To me she seems all grace and youth.

Hortense.

Graceful ?   You think it ?   What, with hands
That hang like this (*with a gesture*).

Armande.

                    And how she stands !

M. Loyal.

Nay,—I am wrong again.   I thought
Her air delightfully untaught !

(43)

Proverbs in Porcelain

HORTENSE.

But you amuse me—

M. LOYAL.

          Still her dress,—
Her dress at least, you *must* confess—

ARMANDE.

Is odious simply !   JACOTOT
Did not supply that lace, I know ;
And where, I ask, has mortal seen
A hat unfeathered !

HORTENSE.

          Edged with green !

M. LOYAL.

The words remind me.   Let me say
A Fable that I heard to-day.
Have I permission ?

BOTH (*with enthusiasm*).

          Monsieur, pray !

M. LOYAL.

Myrtilla (lest a Scandal rise
The Lady's Name I thus disguise),
Dying of Ennui, once decided—
Much on Resource herself she prided—
To choose a Hat.   Forthwith she flies
On that momentous Enterprise.
Whether to Petit or Legros,
I know not: only this I know ;—
Head-dresses then, of any Fashion,
Bore Names of Quality or Passion.
Myrtilla tried them, almost all :
' Prudence,' she felt, was somewhat small ;
' Retirement ' seemed the Eyes to hide ;
' Content,' at once, she cast aside.

(44)

The Cap that Fits

' Simplicity,'—'twas out of Place ;
' Devotion,' for an older Face ;
Briefly, Selection smaller grew,
' Vexatious ! odious !'—none would do !
Then, on a Sudden, she espied
One that she thought she had not tried :
Becoming, rather,—' edged with green,'—
Roses in yellow, Thorns between.
' Quick ! Bring me that !' 'Tis brought. ' Complete,
Superb, Enchanting, Tasteful, Neat,'
In all the Tones. 'And this you call——?'
' "ILL NATURE," Madame. It fits all.'

HORTENSE.

A thousand thanks ! So naïvely turned !

ARMANDE.

So useful too . . . to those concerned !
'Tis yours ?

M. LOYAL.

Ah no,—some cynic Wit's ;
And called (I think)—
(*Placing his hat upon his breast*),
' The Cap that Fits.'

1876.

THE SECRETS OF THE HEART

' *Le cœur mène où il va.*'

SCENE.—*A Chalet covered with Honeysuckle.*

NINETTE.   NINON.

NINETTE.

THIS way—

NINON.

No, this way—

(45)

NINETTE.

This way, then.
(*They enter the Chalet.*)
You are as changing, Child,—as Men.

NINON.

But are they? Is it true, I mean?
Who said it?

NINETTE.

Sister SÉRAPHINE.
She was so pious and so good,
With such sad eyes beneath her hood,
And such poor little feet,—all bare!
Her name was EUGÉNIE LA FÈRE.
She used to tell us,—moonlight nights,—
When I was at the Carmelites.

NINON.

Ah, then it must be right. And yet,
Suppose for once—suppose, NINETTE—

NINETTE.

But what?

NINON.

Suppose it were not so?
Suppose there *were* true men, you know!

NINETTE.

And then?

NINON.

Why, if that *could* occur,
What kind of man should you prefer?

NINETTE.

What looks, you mean?

NINON.

Looks, voice and all.

(46)

The Secrets of the Heart

NINETTE.

Well, as to that, he must be tall,
Or say, not 'tall,'—of middle size;
And next, he must have laughing eyes,
And a hook-nose,— with, underneath,
O! what a row of sparkling teeth!

NINON (*touching her cheek suspiciously*).

Has he a scar on this side?

NINETTE.

                         Hush!

Some one is coming. No; a thrush:
I see it swinging there.

NINON.

              Go on.

NINETTE.

Then he must fence, (ah, look, 'tis gone!)
And dance like Monseigneur, and sing
'Love was a Shepherd':—everything
That men do. Tell me yours, NINON.

NINON.

Shall I? Then mine has black, black hair . . .
I mean he *should* have; then an air
Half sad, half noble; features thin;
A little *royale* on the chin;
And such a pale, high brow. And then,
He is a prince of gentlemen ;—
He, too, can ride and fence and write
Sonnets and madrigals, yet fight
No worse for that—

NINETTE.

                I know your man.

NINON.

And I know yours. But you'll not tell,—
Swear it !

NINETTE.

I swear upon this fan,—
My Grandmother's !

NINON.

And I, I swear
On this old turquoise *reliquaire*,—
My great—*great* Grandmother's !—

(*After a pause.*)

NINETTE !

I feel *so* sad.

NINETTE.

I too. But why ?

NINON.

Alas, I know not !

NINETTE (*with a sigh*).

Nor do I.

1876.

'GOOD-NIGHT, BABETTE !'

' Si vieillesse pouvait !—'

SCENE.—*A small neat Room. In a high Voltaire Chair
sits a white-haired old Gentleman.*

MONSIEUR VIEUXBOIS.   BABETTE.

M. VIEUXBOIS (*turning querulously*).

DAY of my life ! Where *can* she get ?
BABETTE ! I say ! BABETTE !—BABETTE !

BABETTE (*entering hurriedly*).

Coming, M'sieu' ! If M'sieu' speaks
So loud he won't be well for weeks !

(48)

'Good-Night, Babette!'

M. VIEUXBOIS.

Where have you been?

BABETTE.

Why, M'sieu' knows:—
April! . . . Ville d'Avray! . . . Ma'am'selle ROSE!

M. VIEUXBOIS.

Ah! I am old,—and I forget.
Was the place growing green, BABETTE?

BABETTE.

But of a greenness!—yes, M'sieu'!
And then the sky so blue!—so blue!
And when I dropped my *immortelle*,
How the birds sang!
(Lifting her apron to her eyes.)
This poor Ma'am'selle!

M. VIEUXBOIS.

You're a good girl, BABETTE, but she,—
She was an Angel, verily.
Sometimes I think I see her yet
Stand smiling by the cabinet;
And once, I know, she peeped and laughed
Betwixt the curtains . . .
Where's the draught?

(She gives him a cup.)

Now I shall sleep, I think, BABETTE;—
Sing me your Norman *chansonnette*.

BABETTE *(sings)*.

' *Once at the Angelus*
(Ere I was dead),
Angels all glorious
Came to my Bed;
Angels in blue and white
Crowned on the Head.'

(49)

Proverbs in Porcelain

M. VIEUXBOIS (*drowsily*).

'She was an Angel'. . . 'Once she laughed'. . .
What, was I dreaming?

Where's the draught?

BABETTE (*showing the empty cup*).

The draught, M'sieu'?

M. VIEUXBOIS.

How I forget!
I am so old!   But sing, BABETTE!

BABETTE (*sings*).

*'One was the Friend I left
Stark in the Snow;
One was the Wife that died
Long,— long ago;
One was the Love I lost . . .
How could she know?'*

M. VIEUXBOIS (*murmuring*).

Ah, PAUL! . . . old PAUL! . . . EULALIE too!
And ROSE . . . And O! 'the sky so blue!'

BABETTE (*sings*).

*'One had my Mother's eyes,
Wistful and mild;
One had my Father's face;
One was a Child:
All of them bent to me,—
Bent down and smiled!'*

(He is asleep!)

M. VIEUXBOIS (*almost inaudibly*).

'How I forget!'
'I am so old!' . . . 'Good-night, BABETTE!'
1876.

(50)

EPILOGUE

HEIGHO! *how chill the evenings get!*
Good-night, NINON! *— good-night,* NINETTE!
   Your little Play is played and finished;—
Go back, then, to your Cabinet!

LOYAL, L'ÉTOILE! *no more to-day!*
Alas! they heed not what we say:
   They smile with ardour undiminished;
But we,—we are not always gay!

1877.

VIGNETTES IN RHYME

'leviore plectro.'

Go, little book, on this thy first emprize:
If that thou 'scape the critic Ogre-land,
And come to where young Beauty, with bright eyes,
Listless at noon, shall take thee in her hand,
Tell her that nought in thy poor Master stirs
Of art, or grace, or song,—that is not Hers.

1873.

THE DRAMA OF THE DOCTOR'S WINDOW

IN THREE ACTS, WITH A PROLOGUE

' A tedious brief scene of young Pyramus,
And his love Thisbe ; very tragical mirth.'
—MIDSUMMER-NIGHT'S DREAM

PROLOGUE

'WELL, I must wait !' The Doctor's room
  Where I used this expression,
Wore the severe official gloom
  Attached to that profession ;
Rendered severer by a bald
  And skinless Gladiator,
Whose raw robustness first appalled
  The entering spectator.

No one would call ' The Lancet ' gay,—
  Few could avoid confessing
That Jones, ' On Muscular Decay,'
  Is—as a rule—depressing :
So, leaving both, to change the scene,
  I turned toward the shutter,
And peered out vacantly between
  A water-butt and gutter.

Below, the Doctor's garden lay,
  If thus imagination
May dignify a square of clay
  Unused to vegetation,
Filled with a dismal-looking swing—
  That brought to mind a gallows—
An empty kennel, mouldering,
  And two dyspeptic aloes.

(55)

Vignettes in Rhyme

No sparrow chirped, no daisy sprung,
    About the place deserted ;
Only across the swing-board hung
    A battered doll, inverted,
Which sadly seemed to disconcert
    The vagrant cat that scanned it,
Sniffed doubtfully around the skirt,
    But failed to understand it.

A dreary spot ! And yet, I own,
    Half hoping that, perchance, it
Might, in some unknown way, atone
    For Jones and for ' The Lancet,'
I watched ; and by especial grace,
    Within this stage contracted,
Saw presently before my face
    A classic story acted.

Ah, World of ours, are you so grey
    And weary, World, of spinning,
That you repeat the tales to-day
    You told at the beginning ?
For lo ! the same old myths that made
    The early ' stage successes,'
Still ' hold the boards,' and still are played,
    ' With new effects and dresses.'

Small, lonely ' three-pair-backs ' behold,
    To-day, Alcestis dying ;
To-day, in farthest Polar cold,
    Ulysses' bones are lying ;
Still in one's morning ' Times ' one reads
    How fell an Indian Hector ;
Still clubs discuss Achilles' steeds,
    Briseis' next protector ;—

Still Menelaus brings, we see,
  His oft-remanded case on ;
Still somewhere sad Hypsipyle
  Bewails a faithless Jason ;
And here, the Doctor's sill beside,
  Do I not now discover
A Thisbe, whom the walls divide
  From Pyramus, her lover ?

ACT THE FIRST.

Act I. began.   Some noise had scared
  The cat, that like an arrow
Shot up the wall and disappeared ;
  And then, across the narrow,
Unweeded path, a small dark thing,
  Hid by a garden-bonnet,
Passed wearily towards the swing,
  Paused, turned, and climbed upon it.

A child of five, with eyes that were
  At least a decade older,
A mournful mouth, and tangled hair
  Flung careless round her shoulder,
Dressed in a stiff ill-fitting frock,
  Whose black, uncomely rigour
Sardonically seemed to mock
  The plaintive, slender figure.

What was it?   Something in the dress
  That told the girl unmothered ;
Or was it that the merciless
  Black garb of mourning smothered
Life and all light :—but rocking so,
  In the dull garden-corner,
The lonely swinger seemed to grow
  More piteous and forlorner.

(57)

Vignettes in Rhyme

Then, as I looked, across the wall
  Of 'next-door's' garden, that is—
To speak correctly—through its tall
  Surmounting fence of lattice,
Peeped a boy's face, with curling hair,
  Ripe lips, half drawn asunder,
And round, bright eyes, that wore a stare
  Of frankest childish wonder.

Rounder they grew by slow degrees,
  Until the swinger, swerving,
Made, all at once, alive to these
  Intentest orbs observing,
Gave just one brief, half-uttered cry,
  And,—as with gathered kirtle,
Nymphs fly from Pan's head suddenly
  Thrust through the budding myrtle,—

Fled in dismay.   A moment's space,
  The eyes looked almost tragic ;
Then, when they caught my watching face,
  Vanished as if by magic ;
And, like some sombre thing beguiled
  To strange, unwonted laughter,
The gloomy garden, having smiled,
  Became the gloomier after.

ACT THE SECOND.

Yes : they were gone, the stage was bare,—
  Blank as before ; and therefore,
Sinking within the patient's chair,
  Half vexed, I knew not wherefore,
I dozed ; till, startled by some call,
  A glance sufficed to show me,
The boy again above the wall,
  The girl erect below me.

(58)

The boy, it seemed, to add a force
  To words found unavailing,
Had pushed a striped and spotted horse
  Half through the blistered paling,
Where now it stuck, stiff-legged and straight,
  While he, in exultation,
Chattered some half-articulate
  Excited explanation.

Meanwhile, the girl, with upturned face,
  Stood motionless, and listened ;
The ill-cut frock had gained a grace,
  The pale hair almost glistened ;
The figure looked alert and bright,
  Buoyant as though some power
Had lifted it, as rain at night
  Uplifts a drooping flower.

The eyes had lost their listless way,—
  The old life, tired and faded,
Had slipped down with the doll that lay
  Before her feet, degraded ;
She only, yearning upward, found
  In those bright eyes above her
The ghost of some enchanted ground
  Where even Nurse would love her.

Ah, tyrant Time ! you hold the book,
  We, sick and sad, begin it ;
You close it fast, if we but look
  Pleased for a meagre minute ;
You closed it now, for, out of sight
  Some warning finger beckoned ;
Exeunt both to left and right ;—
  Thus ended Act the Second.

ACT THE THIRD.

Or so it proved.   For while I still
  Believed them gone for ever,
Half raised above the window sill,
  I saw the lattice quiver ;
And lo, once more appeared the head,
  Flushed, while the round mouth pouted ;
' Give Tom a kiss,' the red lips said,
  In style the most undoubted.

The girl came back without a thought ;
  Dear Muse of Mayfair, pardon,
If more restraint had not been taught
  In this neglected garden ;
For these your code was all too stiff,
  So, seeing none dissented,
Their unfeigned faces met as if
  Manners were not invented.

Then on the scene,—by happy fate,
  When lip from lip had parted,
And, therefore, just two seconds late,—
  A sharp-faced nurse-maid darted ;
Swooped on the boy, as swoops a kite
  Upon a rover chicken,
And bore him sourly off, despite
  His well-directed kicking.

The girl stood silent, with a look
  Too subtle to unravel,
Then, with a sudden gesture took
  The torn doll from the gravel ;

Hid the whole face, with one caress,
　　Under the garden-bonnet,
And, passing in, I saw her press
　　Kiss after kiss upon it.

———

Exeunt omnes.　End of play.
　　It made the dull room brighter,
The Gladiator almost gay,
　　And e'en 'The Lancet' lighter.

1870.

AN AUTUMN IDYLL

'*Sweet Themmes! runne softly, till I end my song.*'—SPENSER.

LAWRENCE.　　FRANK.　　JACK.

LAWRENCE.

HERE, where the beech-nuts drop among the grasses,
　　Push the boat in, and throw the rope ashore.
Jack, hand me out the claret and the glasses;
　　Here let us sit.　We landed here before.

FRANK.

Jack's undecided.　Say, *formose puer*,
　　Bent in a dream above the 'water wan,'
Shall we row higher, for the reeds are fewer,
　　There by the pollards, where you see the swan?

JACK.

Hist! That's a pike.　Look—nose against the river
　　Gaunt as a wolf,—the sly old privateer!
Enter a gudgeon.　Snap,—a gulp, a shiver;—
　　Exit the gudgeon.　Let us anchor here.

(61)

Vignettes in Rhyme

FRANK (*in the grass*).

Jove, what a day ! Black Care upon the crupper
    Nods at his post, and slumbers in the sun;
Half of Theocritus, with a touch of Tupper,
    Churns in my head. The frenzy has begun!

LAWRENCE.

Sing to us then. Damœtas in a choker,
    Much out of tune, will edify the rooks.

FRANK.

Sing you again. So musical a croaker
    Surely will draw the fish upon the hooks.

JACK.

Sing while you may. The beard of manhood still is
    Faint on your cheeks, but I, alas ! am old.
Doubtless you yet believe in Amaryllis ;—
    Sing me of Her, whose name may not be told.

FRANK.

Listen, O Thames ! His budding beard is riper,
    Say—by a week. Well, Lawrence, shall we sing ?

LAWRENCE.

Yes, if you will. But ere I play the piper,
    Let him declare the prize he has to bring.

JACK.

Hear then, my Shepherds. Lo, to him accounted
    First in the song, a Pipe I will impart ;—
This, my Belovèd, marvellously mounted,
    Amber and foam,—a miracle of art.

LAWRENCE.

Lordly the gift. O Muse of many numbers,
    Grant me a soft alliterative song !

An Autumn Idyll

FRANK.

Me too, O Muse! And when the Umpire slumbers,
Sting him with gnats a summer evening long.

LAWRENCE.

Not in a cot, begarlanded of spiders,
Not where the brook traditionally 'purls,'—
No, in the Row, supreme among the riders,
Seek I the gem,—the paragon of girls.

FRANK.

Not in the waste of column and of coping,
Not in the sham and stucco of a square,—
No, on a June-lawn, to the water sloping,
Stands she I honour, beautifully fair.

LAWRENCE.

Dark-haired is mine, with splendid tresses plaited
Back from the brows, imperially curled;
Calm as a grand, far-looking Caryatid,
Holding the roof that covers in a world.

FRANK.

Dark-haired is mine, with breezy ripples swinging
Loose as a vine-branch blowing in the morn;
Eyes like the morning, mouth for ever singing,
Blithe as a bird new risen from the corn.

LAWRENCE.

Best is the song with the music interwoven:
Mine's a musician,—musical at heart,—
Throbs to the gathered grieving of Beethoven,
Sways to the light coquetting of Mozart.

FRANK.

Best? You should hear mine trilling out a ballad,
Queen at a picnic, leader of the glees,
Not too divine to toss you up a salad,
Great in Sir Roger danced among the trees.

Vignettes in Rhyme

LAWRENCE.

Ah, when the thick night flares with dropping torches,
    Ah, when the crush-room empties of the swarm,
Pleasant the hand that, in the gusty porches,
    Light as a snow-flake, settles on your arm.

FRANK.

Better the twilight and the cheery chatting,—
    Better the dim, forgotten garden-seat,
Where one may lie, and watch the fingers tatting,
    Lounging with Bran or Bevis at her feet.

LAWRENCE.

All worship mine.   Her purity doth hedge her
    Round with so delicate divinity, that men
Stained to the soul with money-bag and ledger,
    Bend to the goddess, manifest again.

FRANK.

None worship mine.   But some, I fancy, love her,—
    Cynics to boot.   I know the children run,
Seeing her come, for naught that I discover,
    Save that she brings the summer and the sun.

LAWRENCE.

Mine is a Lady, beautiful and queenly,
    Crowned with a sweet, continual control,
Grandly forbearing, lifting life serenely
    E'en to her own nobility of soul.

FRANK.

Mine is a Woman, kindly beyond measure,
    Fearless in praising, faltering in blame :
Simply devoted to other people's pleasure,—
    Jack's sister Florence,—now you know her name.

An Autumn Idyll

LAWRENCE.

'Jack's sister Florence!' Never, Francis, never.
　Jack, do you hear? Why, it was she I meant.
She like the country! Ah, she's far too clever—

FRANK.

There you are wrong. I know her down in Kent.

LAWRENCE.

You'll get a sunstroke, standing with your head bare.
　Sorry to differ. Jack,—the word's with you.

FRANK.

How is it, Umpire? Though the motto's threadbare,
　'*Coelum, non animum*'—is, I take it, true.

JACK.

'*Souvent femme varie,*' as a rule, is truer;
　Flattered, I'm sure,—but both of you romance.
Happy to further suit of either wooer,
　Merely observing—you haven't got a chance.

LAWRENCE

Yes. But the Pipe —

FRANK.

　　　The Pipe is what we care for, —

JACK.

Well, in this case, I scarcely need explain,
Judgement of mine were indiscreet, and therefore, —
　Peace to you both. The Pipe I shall retain.

1869.

A GARDEN IDYLL

A LADY.   A POET.

THE LADY.

SIR POET, ere you crossed the lawn
  (If it was wrong to watch you, pardon),
Behind this weeping birch withdrawn,
  I watched you saunter round the garden.
I saw you bend beside the phlox,
  Pluck, as you passed, a sprig of myrtle,
Review my well-ranged hollyhocks,
  Smile at the fountain's slender spurtle ;

You paused beneath the cherry-tree,
  Where my marauder thrush was singing,
Peered at the bee-hives curiously,
  And narrowly escaped a stinging ;
And then—you see I watched—you passed
  Down the espalier walk that reaches
Out to the western wall, and last
  Dropped on the seat before the peaches.

What was your thought ? You waited long.
  Sublime or graceful,—grave,—satiric ?
A Morris Greek-and-Gothic song ?
  A tender Tennysonian lyric ?
Tell me.   That garden-seat shall be,
  So long as speech renown disperses,
Illustrious as the spot where he—
  The gifted Blank—composed his verses.

THE POET.

Madam,—whose uncensorious eye
  Grows gracious over certain pages,
Wherein the Jester's maxims lie,
  It may be, thicker than the Sage's—

(66)

A Garden Idyll

I hear but to obey, and could
    Mere wish of mine the pleasure do you,
Some verse as whimsical as Hood,—
    As gay as Praed,—should answer to you.

But, though the common voice proclaims
    Our only serious vocation
Confined to giving nothings names
    And dreams a 'local habitation,'
Believe me there are tuneless days,
    When neither marble, brass, nor vellum,
Would profit much by any lays
    That haunt the poet's cerebellum.

More empty things, I fear, than rhymes,
    More idle things than songs, absorb it;
The 'finely-frenzied' eye, at times,
    Reposes mildly in its orbit;
And—painful truth—at times, to him,
    Whose jog-trot thought is nowise restive,
'A primrose by a river's brim'
    Is absolutely unsuggestive.

The fickle Muse! As ladies will,
    She sometimes wearies of her wooer;
A goddess, yet a woman still,
    She flies the more that we pursue her.;
In short, with worst as well as best,
    Five months in six, your hapless poet
Is just as prosy as the rest,
    But cannot comfortably show it.

You thought, no doubt, the garden scent
    Brings back some brief-winged bright sensation
Of love that came and love that went,—
    Some fragrance of a lost flirtation,

Vignettes in Rhyme

Born when the cuckoo changes song,
 Dead ere the apple's red is on it,
That should have been an epic long,
 Yet scarcely served to fill a sonnet.

Or else you thought,—the murmuring noon
 He turns it to a lyric sweeter,
With birds that gossip in the tune,
 And windy bough-swing in the metre ;
Or else the zigzag fruit-tree arms
 Recall some dream of harp-prest bosoms,
Round singing mouths, and chanted charms,
 And mediaeval orchard blossoms,—

Quite *à la mode*.   Alas for prose !—
 My vagrant fancies only rambled
Back to the red-walled Rectory close,
 Where first my graceless boyhood gamboled,
Climbed on the dial, teased the fish,
 And chased the kitten round the beeches,
Till widening instincts made me wish
 For certain slowly-ripening peaches.

Three peaches.   Not the Graces three
 Had more equality of beauty :
I would not look, yet went to see ;
 I wrestled with Desire and Duty ;
I felt the pangs of those who feel
 The Laws of Property beset them ;
The conflict made my reason reel,
 And, half-abstractedly, I ate them ;—

Or Two of them.   Forthwith Despair—
 More keen that one of these was rotten—
Moved me to seek some forest lair
 Where I might hide and dwell forgotten,

A Garden Idyll

Attired in skins, by berries stained,
  Absolved from brushes and ablution;—
But, ere my sylvan haunt was gained,
  Fate gave me up to execution.

I saw it all but now.   The grin
  That gnarled old Gardener Sandy's features;
My father, scholar-like and thin,
  Unroused, the tenderest of creatures;
I saw—ah me—I saw again
  My dear and deprecating mother;
And then, remembering the cane,
  Regretted—that *I'd left the Other.*

1870.

TU QUOQUE

AN IDYLL IN THE CONSERVATORY.

'— *romprons-nous,*
Ou ne romprons-nous pas?'—LE DÉPIT AMOUREUX.

NELLIE.

IF I were you, when ladies at the play, sir,
  Beckon and nod, a melodrama through,
I would not turn abstractedly away, sir,
  If I were you!

FRANK.

If I were you, when persons I affected,
  Wait for three hours to take me down to Kew,
I would, at least, pretend I recollected,
  If I were you!

NELLIE.

If I were you, when ladies are so lavish,
  Sir, as to keep me every waltz but two,
I would not dance with *odious* Miss M'Tavish,
  If I were you!

Vignettes in Rhyme

FRANK.

If I were you, who vow you cannot suffer
    Whiff of the best,—the mildest 'honey-dew,'
I would not dance with smoke-consuming Puffer,
    If I were you!

NELLIE.

If I were you, I would not, sir, be bitter,
    Even to write the 'Cynical Review';—

FRANK.

No, I should doubtless find flirtation fitter,
    If I were you!

NELLIE.

Really! You would? Why, Frank, you're quite delightful,—
    Hot as Othello, and as black of hue;
Borrow my fan. I would not look so *frightful*,
    If I were you!

FRANK.

'It is the cause.' I mean your chaperon is
    Bringing some well-curled juvenile. Adieu!
I shall retire. I'd spare that poor Adonis,
    If I were you!

NELLIE.

Go, if you will. At once! And by express, sir!
    Where shall it be? To China—or Peru?
Go. I should leave inquirers my address, sir,
    If I were you!

FRANK.

No,—I remain. To stay and fight a duel
    Seems, on the whole, the proper thing to do;—
Ah, you are strong,—I would not then be cruel,
    If I were you!

Tu Quoque

NELLIE.

One does not like one's feelings to be doubted,—

FRANK.

One does not like one's friends to misconstrue,—

NELLIE.

If I confess that I a wee-bit pouted?—

FRANK.

I should admit that I was *piqué*, too.

NELLIE.

Ask me to dance! I'd say no more about it,
    If I were you!

[Waltz—*Exeunt.*

1872.

A DIALOGUE FROM PLATO

'*Le temps le mieux employé est celui qu'on perd.*'—CLAUDE TILLIER.

I'D 'read' three hours. Both notes and text
    Were fast a mist becoming;
In bounced a vagrant bee, perplexed,
    And filled the room with humming,

Then out. The casement's leafage sways,
    And, parted light, discloses
Miss Di., with hat and book,—a maze
    Of muslin mixed with roses.

'You're reading Greek?' 'I am—and you?'
    'O, mine's a mere romancer!'
'So Plato is.' 'Then read him—do;
    And I'll read mine in answer.'

(71)

Vignettes in Rhyme

I read. 'My Plato (Plato, too,—
  That wisdom thus should harden!)
Declares "blue eyes look doubly blue
  Beneath a Dolly Varden."'

She smiled. 'My book in turn avers
  (No author's name is stated)
That sometimes those Philosophers
  Are sadly mis-translated.'

'But hear,—the next's in stronger style:
  The Cynic School asserted
That two red lips which part and smile
  May not be controverted!'

She smiled once more—'My book, I find,
  Observes some modern doctors
Would make the Cynics out a kind
  Of album-verse concoctors.'

Then I—'Why not? "Ephesian law,
  No less than time's tradition,
Enjoined fair speech on all who saw
  DIANA'S apparition."'

She blushed—this time. 'If Plato's page
  No wiser precept teaches,
Then I'd renounce that doubtful sage,
  And walk to Burnham-beeches.'

'Agreed', I said. 'For Socrates
  (I find he too is talking)
Thinks Learning can't remain at ease
  While Beauty goes a-walking.'

She read no more. I leapt the sill:
  The sequel's scarce essential—
Nay, more than this, I hold it still
  Profoundly confidential.

1872.

THE ROMAUNT OF THE ROSE

Poor Rose! I lift you from the street—
    Far better I should own you,
Than you should lie for random feet,
    Where careless hands have thrown you!

Poor pinky petals, crushed and torn!
    Did heartless Mayfair use you,
Then cast you forth to lie forlorn,
    For chariot wheels to bruise you?

I saw you last in Edith's hair.
    Rose, you would scarce discover
That I she passed upon the stair
    Was Edith's favoured lover,

A month—'a little month'—ago—
    O theme for moral writer!—
'Twixt you and me, my Rose, you know,
    She might have been politer;

But let that pass. She gave you then—
    Behind the oleander—
To one, perhaps, of all the men,
    Who best could understand her,—

Cyril that, duly flattered, took,
    As only Cyril's able,
With just the same Arcadian look
    He used, last night, for Mabel;

Then, having waltzed till every star
    Had paled away in morning,
Lit up his cynical cigar,
    And tossed you downward, scorning.

Kismet, my Rose! Revenge is sweet,—
　　She made my heart-strings quiver;
And yet—you sha'n't lie in the street,
　　I'll drop you in the River.

1872.

LOVE IN WINTER

BETWEEN the berried holly-bush
The Blackbird whistled to the Thrush:
'Which way did bright-eyed Bella go?
Look, Speckle-breast, across the snow,—
Are those her dainty tracks I see,
That wind beside the shrubbery?'

The Throstle pecked the berries still.
'No need for looking, Yellow-bill;
Young Frank was there an hour ago,
Half frozen, waiting in the snow;
His callow beard was white with rime,—
'Tchuck,—'tis a merry pairing-time!'

'What would you?' twittered in the Wren;
'These are the reckless ways of men.
I watched them bill and coo as though
They thought the sign of Spring was snow;
If men but timed their loves as we,
'Twould save this inconsistency.'

'Nay, Gossip,' chirped the Robin, 'nay;
I like their unreflective way.
Besides, I heard enough to show
Their love is proof against the snow :—
"Why wait," he said, "why wait for May,
When love can warm a winter's day?"'

1871.

POT-POURRI

' Si jeunesse savait ! —'

I plunge my hand among the leaves :
(An alien touch but dust perceives,
  Nought else supposes ;)
For me those fragrant ruins raise
Clear memory of the vanished days
  When they were roses.

' If youth but knew !' Ah, ' if,' in truth ?—
I can recall with what gay youth,
  To what light chorus,
Unsobered yet by time or change,
We roamed the many-gabled Grange,
  All life before us ;

Braved the old clock-tower's dust and damp,
To catch the dim Arthurian camp
  In misty distance ;
Peered at the still-room's sacred stores,
Or rapped at walls for sliding doors
  Of feigned existence.

What need had we for thoughts or cares !
The hot sun parched the old parterres
  And ' flowerful closes' ;
We roused the rooks with rounds and glees,
Played hide-and-seek behind the trees,—
  Then plucked these roses.

Louise was one—light, glib Louise,
So freshly freed from school decrees

You scarce could stop her;
And Bell, the Beauty, unsurprised
At fallen locks that scandalized
    Our dear 'Miss Proper';—

Shy Ruth, all heart and tenderness,
Who wept—like Chaucer's Prioress,
    When Dash was smitten;
Who blushed before the mildest men,
Yet waxed a very Corday when
    You teased her kitten.

I loved them all.   Bell first and best;
Louise the next—for days of jest
    Or madcap masking;
And Ruth, I thought,—why, failing these,
When my High-Mightiness should please,
    She'd come for asking.

.   .   .   .   .   .

Louise was grave when last we met;
Bell's beauty, like a sun, has set;
    And Ruth, Heaven bless her,
Ruth that I wooed,— and wooed in vain,—
Has gone where neither grief nor pain
    Can now distress her.

1873.

DOROTHY

A REVERIE SUGGESTED BY THE NAME UPON A PANE.

SHE then must once have looked, as I
Look now, across the level rye,—
Past Church and Manor-house, and seen,
As now I see, the village green,
The bridge, and Walton's river—she
Whose old-world name was 'Dorothy.'

Dorothy

The swallows must have twittered, too,
Above her head ; the roses blew
Below, no doubt,—and, sure, the South
Crept up the wall and kissed her mouth,—
That wistful mouth, which comes to me
Linked with her name of Dorothy.

What was she like ? I picture her
Unmeet for uncouth worshipper ;—
Soft,—pensive,—far too subtly graced
To suit the blunt bucolic taste,
Whose crude perception could but see
' Ma'am Fine-airs ' in ' Miss Dorothy.'

How not ? She loved, maybe, perfume,
Soft textures, lace, a half-lit room ;—
Perchance too candidly preferred
' Clarissa ' to a gossip's word ;—
And, for the rest, would seem to be
Or proud, or dull—this Dorothy.

Poor child !—with heart the down-lined nest
Of warmest instincts unconfest,
Soft, callow things that vaguely felt
The breeze caress, the sunlight melt,
But yet, by some obscure decree,
Unwinged from birth ;—poor Dorothy !

Not less I dream her mute desire
To acred churl and booby squire,
Now pale, with timorous eyes that filled
At ' twice-told tales ' of foxes killed ;—
Now trembling when slow tongues grew free
'Twixt sport, and Port—and Dorothy !

'Twas then she'd seek this nook, and find
Its evening landscape balmy-kind;
And here, where still her gentle name
Lives on the old green glass, would frame
Fond dreams of unfound harmony
'Twixt heart and heart.   Poor Dorothy!

L'ENVOI.

These last I spoke.   Then Florence said,
Below me,—'Dreams?   Delusions, Fred!'
Next, with a pause,—she bent the while
Over a rose, with roguish smile—
'But how disgusted, Sir, you'll be
To hear *I* scrawled that "Dorothy."'

1873.

AVICE

'On serait tenté de lui dire, Bonjour, Mademoiselle la Bergeronnette.'
—VICTOR HUGO.

THOUGH the voice of modern schools
        Has demurred,
By the dreamy Asian creed
        'Tis averred,
That the souls of men, released
From their bodies when deceased,
Sometimes enter in a beast,—
        Or a bird.

I have watched you long, Avice,—
        Watched you so,
I have found your secret out;
        And I know
That the restless ribboned things,
Where your slope of shoulder springs,
Are but undeveloped wings
        That will grow.

(78)

Avice

When you enter in a room,
   It is stirred
With the wayward, flashing flight
   Of a bird;
And you speak—and bring with you
Leaf and sun-ray, bud and blue,
And the wind-breath and the dew,
   At a word.

When you called to me my name,
   Then again
When I heard your single cry
   In the lane,
All the sound was as the 'sweet'
Which the birds to birds repeat
In their thank-song to the heat
   After rain.

When you sang the *Schwalbenlied*,
   'Twas absurd,—
But it seemed no human note
   That I heard;
For your strain had all the trills,
All the little shakes and stills,
Of the over-song that rills
   From a bird.

You have just their eager, quick
   '*Airs de tête*,'
All their flush and fever-heat
   When elate;
Every bird-like nod and beck,
And a bird's own curve of neck
When she gives a little peck
   To her mate.

Vignettes in Rhyme

When you left me, only now,
      In that furred,
Puffed, and feathered Polish dress,
      I was spurred
Just to catch you, O my Sweet,
By the bodice trim and neat,—
Just to feel your heart a-beat,
      Like a bird.

Yet, alas ! Love's light you deign
      But to wear
As the dew upon your plumes,
      And you care
Not a whit for rest or hush ;
But the leaves, the lyric gush,
And the wing-power, and the rush
      Of the air.

So I dare not woo you, Sweet,
      For a day,
Lest I lose you in a flash,
      As I may ;
Did I tell you tender things,
You would shake your sudden wings ;—
You would start from him who sings,
      And away.

1868.

THE LOVE-LETTER

' J'ai vu les mœurs de mon tems, et j'ai publié cette lettre.'
      —LA NOUVELLE HÉLOÏSE.

IF this should fail, why then I scarcely know
  What could succeed.   Here's brilliancy (and banter),
Byron *ad lib.*, a chapter of Rousseau ;—
  If this should fail, then *tempora mutantur* ;
Style 's out of date, and love, as a profession,
Acquires no aid from beauty of expression.

(80)

The Love-Letter

'The men who think as I, I fear, are few,'
  (Cynics would say 'twere well if they were fewer);
'I am not what I seem,'—(indeed, 'tis true;
  Though, as a sentiment, it might be newer);
'Mine is a soul whose deeper feelings lie
More deep than words'—(as these exemplify).

'I will not say when first your beauty's sun
  Illumed my life,'—(it needs imagination);
'For me to see you and to love were one,'—
  (This will account for some precipitation);
'Let it suffice that worship more devoted
Ne'er throbbed', *et cetera*.   The rest is quoted.

'If Love can look with all-prophetic eye,'—
  (Ah, if he could, how many would be single!)
'If truly spirit unto spirit cry,'—
  (The ears of some most terribly must tingle!)
'Then I have dreamed you will not turn your face.'
  This next, I think, is more than commonplace.

'Why should we speak, if Love, interpreting,
  Forestall the speech with favour found before?
Why should we plead?—it were an idle thing,
  If Love himself be Love's ambassador!'
Blot, as I live! Shall we erase it? No;—
'Twill show we write *currente calamo*.

'My fate,—my fortune, I commit to you,'—
  (In point of fact, the latter's not extensive);
'Without you I am poor indeed,'—(strike through,
  'Tis true but crude—'twould make her apprehensive);
'My life is yours—I lay it at your feet,'
(Having no choice but Hymen or the Fleet).

'Give me the right to stand within the shrine,
   Where never yet my faltering feet intruded ;
Give me the right to call you wholly mine,'—
   (That is, Consols and Three-per-Cents included) ;
'To guard your rest from every care that cankers,—
To keep your life,'—(and balance at your banker's).

'Compel me not to long for your reply ;
   Suspense makes havoc with the mind—(and muscles) ;
'Winged Hope takes flight,'—(which means that I must fly,
   Default of funds, to Paris or to Brussels) ;
'I cannot wait ! My own, my queen—PRISCILLA !
Write by return.' And *now* for a Manilla !

'Miss Blank,' at 'Blank.' Jemima, let it go ;
   And I, meanwhile, will idle with 'Sir Walter' ;
Stay, let me keep the first rough copy, though—
   'Twill serve again. There's but the name to alter ;
And Love,—that starves,—must knock at every portal,
In formâ pauperis. We are but mortal !

   1872.

THE MISOGYNIST

' Il était un jeune homme d'un bien beau passé.'

WHEN first he sought our haunts, he wore
   His locks in Hamlet-style ;
His brow with thought was 'sicklied o'er,'—
   We rarely saw him smile ;
And, e'en when none was looking on,
His air was always woe-begone.

He kept, I think, his bosom bare
   To imitate Jean Paul ;
His solitary topics were
   Æsthetics, Fate, and Soul ;—
Although at times, but not for long,
He bowed his Intellect to song.

The Misogynist

He served, he said, a Muse of Tears :
   I know his verses breathed
A fine funereal air of biers,
   And objects cypress-wreathed ;—
Indeed, his tried aquaintance fled
An ode he named 'The Sheeted Dead.'

In these light moods, I call to mind,
   He darkly would allude
To some dread sorrow undefined,—
   Some passion unsubdued ;
Then break into a ghastly laugh,
And talk of Keats his epitaph.

He railed at women's faith as Cant ;
   We thought him grandest when
He named them Siren-shapes that 'chant
   On blanching bones of Men' ;—
Alas, not e'en the great go free
From that insidious minstrelsy !

His lot, he oft would gravely urge,
   Lay on a lone Rock where
Around Time-beaten bases surge
   The Billows of Despair.
We dreamed it true.   We never knew
What gentler ears he told it to.

We, bound with him in common care,
   One-minded, celibate,
Resolved to Thought and Diet spare
   Our lives to dedicate ;—
We, truly, in no common sense,
Deserved his closest confidence !

But soon, and yet, though soon, too late,
　　We, sorrowing, sighed to find
A gradual softness enervate
　　That all superior mind,
Until,—in full assembly met,
He dared to speak of Etiquette.

The verse that we severe had known,
　　Assumed a wanton air,—
A fond effeminate monotone
　　Of eyebrows, lips, and hair;
Not ἦθος stirred him now or νοῦς,
He read 'The Angel in the House'!

Nay worse.　He, once sublime to chaff,
　　Grew ludicrously sore
If we but named a photograph
　　We found him simpering o'er;
Or told how in his chambers lurked
A watch-guard intricately worked.

Then worse again.　He tried to dress;
　　He trimmed his tragic mane;
Announced at length (to our distress)
　　He had not 'lived in vain';—
Thenceforth his one prevailing mood
Became a base beatitude.

And O Jean Paul, and Fate, and Soul!
　　We met him last, grown stout,
His throat with wedlock's triple roll,
　　'All wool,' enwound about;
His very hat had changed its brim;—
Our course was clear,—WE BANISHED HIM!

1874.

A VIRTUOSO

Be seated, pray. 'A grave appeal'?
　　The sufferers by the war, of course;
Ah, what a sight for us who feel,—
　　This monstrous *mélodrame* of Force!
We, Sir, we connoisseurs, should know,
　　On whom its heaviest burden falls;
Collections shattered at a blow,
　　Museums turned to hospitals!

'And worse,' you say; 'the wide distress!'
　　Alas, 'tis true distress exists,
Though, let me add, our worthy Press
　　Have no mean skill as colourists;
Speaking of colour, next your seat
　　There hangs a sketch from Vernet's hand;
Some Moscow fancy, incomplete,
　　Yet not indifferently planned;

Note specially the gray old guard,
　　Who tears his tattered coat to wrap
A closer bandage round the scarred
　　And frozen comrade in his lap;—
But, as regards the present war,—
　　Now don't you think our pride of pence
Goes—may I say it?—somewhat far
　　For objects of benevolence?

You hesitate. For my part, I—
　　Though ranking Paris next to Rome,
Aesthetically—still reply
　　That 'Charity begins at Home.'
The words remind me. Did you catch
　　My so-named 'Hunt'? The girl's a gem;
And look how those lean rascals snatch
　　The pile of scraps she brings to them!

(85)

Vignettes in Rhyme

'But your appeal's for home,'—you say,—
   For home, and English poor ! Indeed ! .
I thought Philanthropy to-day
   Was blind to mere domestic need—
However sore—Yet though one grants
   That home should have the foremost claims,
At least these Continental wants
   Assume intelligible names ;

While here with us—Ah ! who could hope
   To verify the varied pleas,
Or from his private means to cope
   With all our shrill necessities !
Impossible ! One might as well
   Attempt comparison of creeds ;
Or fill that huge Malayan shell
   With these half-dozen Indian beads.

Moreover, add that every one
   So well exalts his pet distress,
'Tis—Give to all, or give to none,
   If you'd avoid invidiousness.
Your case, I feel, is sad as A.'s,
   The same applies to B.'s and C.'s ;
By my selection I should raise
   An alphabet of rivalries ;

And life is short,—I see you look
   At yonder dish, a priceless bit ;
You'll find it etched in Jacquemart's book,
   They say that Raphael painted it ;—
And life is short, you understand ;
   So, if I only hold you out
An open though an empty hand,
   Why, you'll forgive me, I've no doubt.

A Virtuoso

Nay, do not rise.   You seem amused ;
   One can but be consistent, Sir !
'Twas on these grounds I just refused
   Some gushing lady-almoner,—
Believe me, on these very grounds.
   Good-bye, then.   Ah, a rarity !
That cost me quite three hundred pounds,—
   That Dürer figure,— 'Charity.'

1871.

LAISSEZ FAIRE

' Prophete rechts, Prophete links,
Das Weltkind in der Mitten.'

          —GOETHE'S *Diné zu Coblenz.*

To left, here's B., half-Communist,
   Who talks a chastened treason,
And C., a something-else in 'ist,'
   Harangues, to right, on Reason.

B., from his 'tribune,' fulminates
   At Throne and Constitution,
Nay—with the walnuts—advocates
   Reform by revolution ;

While C.'s peculiar coterie
   Have now in full rehearsal
Some patent new Philosophy
   To make doubt universal.

And yet—why not ?   If zealots burn,
   Their zeal has not affected
My taste for salmon and Sauterne,
   Or I might have objected :—

Vignettes in Rhyme

Friend B., the argument you choose
   Has been by France refuted;
And C., *mon cher*, your novel views
   Are just Tom Paine, diluted;

There's but one creed,—that's *Laissez faire*,
   Behold its mild apostle!
My dear, declamatory pair,
   Although you shout and jostle,

Not your ephemeral hands, nor mine,
   Time's Gordian knots shall sunder,—
WILL laid three casks of this old wine:
   Who'll drink the last, I wonder?

1872.

TO Q. H. F.

SUGGESTED BY A CHAPTER IN SIR THEODORE
MARTIN'S 'HORACE'

('ANCIENT CLASSICS FOR ENGLISH READERS')

'HORATIUS FLACCUS, B.C. 8,'
There's not a doubt about the date,—
    You're dead and buried:
As you observed, the seasons roll;
And 'cross the Styx full many a soul
    Has Charon ferried,
Since, mourned of men and Muses nine,
They laid you on the Esquiline.

And that was centuries ago!
You'd think we'd learned enough, I know
    To help refine us,

To Q. H. F.

Since last you trod the Sacred Street,
And tacked from mortal fear to meet
   The bore Crispinus ;
Or, by your cold Digentia, set
The web of winter birding-net.

Ours is so far-advanced an age !
Sensation tales, a classic stage,
   Commodious villas !
We boast high art, an Albert Hall,
Australian meats, and men who call
   Their sires gorillas !
We have a thousand things, you see,
Not dreamt in your philosophy.

And yet, how strange ! Our 'world,' to-day,
Tried in the scale, would scarce outweigh
   Your Roman cronies ;
Walk in the Park—you'll seldom fail
To find a Sybaris on the rail
   By Lydia's ponies,
Or hap on Barrus, wigged and stayed,
Ogling some unsuspecting maid.

The great Gargilius, then, behold !
His 'long-bow' hunting tales of old
   Are now but duller ;
Fair Neobule too ! Is not
One Hebrus here—from Aldershot ?
   Aha, you colour !
Be wise. There old Canidia sits ;
No doubt she's tearing you to bits.

And look, dyspeptic, brave, and kind,
Comes dear Maecenas, half behind
   Terentia's skirting ;

Vignettes in Rhyme

Here's Pyrrha, 'golden haired' at will;
Prig Damasippus, preaching still;
    Asterie flirting,—
Radiant, of course.   We'll make her black,—
Ask her when Gyges' ship comes back.

So with the rest.   Who will may trace
Behind the new each elder face
    Defined as clearly;
Science proceeds, and man stands still;
Our 'world' to-day's as good or ill,—
    As cultured (nearly),—
As yours was, Horace!   You alone,
Unmatched, unmet, we have not known.

1873.

TO 'LYDIA LANGUISH'

' Il me faut des émotions.'—BLANCHE AMORY.

You ask me, Lydia, 'whether I,
If you refuse my suit, shall die.'
    (Now pray don't let this hurt you!)
Although the time be out of joint,
I should not think a bodkin's point
    The sole resource of virtue;
Nor shall I, though your mood endure,
Attempt a final Water-cure
    Except against my wishes;
For I respectfully decline
To dignify the Serpentine,
    And make *hors-d'œuvres* for fishes;
But if you ask me whether I
    Composedly can go,
Without a look, without a sigh,
    Why, then I answer—No.

To 'Lydia Languish'

'You are assured,' you sadly say
(If in this most considerate way
   To treat my suit your will is),
That I shall 'quickly find as fair
Some new Neæra's tangled hair—
   Some easier Amaryllis.'
I cannot promise to be cold
If smiles are kind as yours of old
   On lips of later beauties ;
Nor can I, if I would, forget
The homage that is Nature's debt,
   While man has social duties ;
But if you ask shall I prefer
   To you I honour so,
A somewhat visionary Her,
   I answer truly—No.

You fear, you frankly add, 'to find
In me too late the altered mind
   That altering Time estranges.'
To this I make response that we
(As physiologists agree)
   Must have septennial changes ;
This is a thing beyond control,
And it were best upon the whole
   To try and find out whether
We could not, by some means, arrange
This not-to-be-avoided change
   So as to change together :
But, had you asked me to allow
   That you could ever grow
Less amiable than you are now,—
   Emphatically—No.

But—to be serious—if you care
To know how I shall really bear

This much-discussed rejection,
I answer you.   As feeling men
Behave, in best romances, when
   You outrage their affection ;—
With that gesticulatory woe,
By which, as melodramas show,
   Despair is indicated ;
Enforced by all the liquid grief
Which hugest pocket-handkerchief
   Has ever simulated ;
And when, arrived so far, you say
   In tragic accents 'Go,'
Then, Lydia, then . . . I still shall stay,
   And firmly answer—No.

1872.

A GAGE D'AMOUR

(HORACE, III. 8)

*' Martiis coelebs quid agam Kalendis
——— miraris ? '*

CHARLES,—for it seems you wish to know,—
You wonder what could scare me so,
And why, in this long-locked bureau,
      With trembling fingers,—
With tragic air, I now replace
This ancient web of yellow lace,
Among whose faded folds the trace
      Of perfume lingers.

Friend of my youth, severe as true,
I guess the train your thoughts pursue ;
But this my state is nowise due
      'To indigestion ;
I had forgotten it was there,
A scarf that Some-one used to wear.
Hinc illae lacrimae,—so spare
      Your cynic question.

A Gage d'Amour

Some-one who is not girlish now,
And wed long since.   We meet and bow;
I don't suppose our broken vow
        Affects us keenly;
Yet, trifling though my act appears,
Your Sternes would make it ground for tears;—
One can't disturb the dust of years,
        And smile serenely.

'My golden locks' are gray and chill,
For hers,—let them be sacred still;
But yet, I own, a boyish thrill
        Went dancing through me,
Charles, when I held yon yellow lace;
For, from its dusty hiding-place,
Peeped out an arch, ingenuous face
        That beckoned to me.

We shut our heart up, nowadays,
Like some old music-box that plays
Unfashionable airs that raise
        Derisive pity;
Alas,—a nothing starts the spring,
And lo, the sentimental thing
At once commences quavering
        Its lover's ditty.

Laugh, if you like.   The boy in me,—
The boy that was,—revived to see
The fresh young smile that shone when she,
        Of old, was tender.
Once more we trod the Golden Way,—
That mother you saw yesterday,—
And I, whom none can well portray
        As young, or slender.

She twirled the flimsy scarf about
Her pretty head, and stepping out
Slipped arm in mine, with half a pout
       Of childish pleasure.
Where we were bound no mortal knows,
For then you plunged in Ireland's woes,
And brought me blankly back to prose
       And Gladstone's measure.

Well, well, the wisest bend to Fate.
My brown old books around me wait,
My pipe still holds, unconfiscate,
       Its wonted station.
Pass me the wine.   To Those that keep
The bachelor's secluded sleep
Peaceful, inviolate, and deep,
       I pour libation !

1870.

CUPID'S ALLEY

A MORALITY

O, Love's but a dance,
    Where Time plays the fiddle!
See the couples advance,—
O, Love's but a dance!
A whisper, a glance,—
    ' Shall we twirl down the middle ? '
O, Love's but a dance,
    Where Time plays the fiddle!

It runs (so saith my Chronicler)
   Across a smoky City ;—
A Babel filed with buzz and whirr,
   Huge, gloomy, black and gritty ;
Dark-louring looks the hill-side near,
   Dark-yawning looks the valley,—
But here 'tis always fresh and clear,
   For here—is ' Cupid's Alley.'

(94)

Cupid's Alley

And, from an Arbour cool and green
　　With aspect down the middle,
An ancient Fiddler, gray and lean,
　　Scrapes on an ancient fiddle;
Alert he seems, but aged enow
　　To punt the Stygian galley;—
With wisp of forelock on his brow,
　　He plays—in 'Cupid's Alley.'

All day he plays,—a single tune!—
　　But, by the oddest chances,
Gavotte, or Brawl, or Rigadoon,
　　It suits all kinds of dances;
My Lord may walk a *pas de Cour*
　　To Jenny's *pas de Chalet;*—
The folks who ne'er have danced before
　　Can dance—in 'Cupid's Alley.'

And here, for ages yet untold,
　　Long, long before my ditty,
Came high and low, and young and old,
　　From out the crowded City;
And still to-day they come, they go,
　　And just as fancies tally,
They foot it quick, they foot it slow,
　　All day—in 'Cupid's Alley.'

Strange Dance!　'Tis free to Rank and Rags;
　　Here no distinction flatters,
Here Riches shakes its money-bags,
　　And Poverty its tatters;
Church, Army, Navy, Physic, Law;—
　　Maid, Mistress, Master, Valet;
Long locks, gray hairs, bald heads, and a',—
　　They bob—in 'Cupid's Alley.'

(95)

Strange pairs !   To laughing, light Fifteen
   Here capers Prudence thrifty ;
Here Prodigal leads down the green
   A blushing Maid of fifty ;
Some treat it as a serious thing,
   And some but shilly-shally ;
And some have danced without the ring
   (Ah me !)—in ' Cupid's Alley.'

And sometimes one to one will dance,
   And think of one behind her ;
And one by one will stand, perchance,
   Yet look all ways to find her ;
Some seek a partner with a sigh,
   Some win him with a sally ;
And some, they know not how nor why,
   Strange fate !— of ' Cupid's Alley.'

And some will dance an age or so
   Who came for half a minute ;
And some, who like the game, will go
   Before they well begin it ;
And some will vow they 're ' danced to death,'
   Who (somehow) always rally ;
Strange cures are wrought (mine Author saith),
   Strange cures !—in ' Cupid's Alley.'

It may be one will dance to-day,
   And dance no more to-morrow ;
It may be one will steal away
   And nurse a life-long sorrow ;
What then ?   The rest advance, evade,
   Unite, dispart, and dally,
Re-set, coquet, and gallopade,
   Not less—in ' Cupid's Alley.'

For till that City's wheel-work vast
    And shuddering beams shall crumble ;—
And till that Fiddler lean at last
    From off his seat shall tumble ;—
Till then (the Civic records say),
    This quaint, fantastic *ballet*
Of Go and Stay, of Yea and Nay,
    Must last—in ' Cupid's Alley.'

1876.

THE IDYLL OF THE CARP

(The SCENE is in a garden,—where you please,
    So that it lie in France, and have withal
Its gray-stoned pond beneath the arching trees,
    And Triton huge, with moss for coronal.
A PRINCESS,—feeding fish. To her DENISE.)

THE PRINCESS.

THESE, Denise, are my Suitors !

DENISE.

                Where ?

THE PRINCESS.

                    These fish.
I feed them daily here at morn and night
With crumbs of favour,—scraps of graciousness,
Not meant, indeed, to mean the thing they wish,
But serving just to edge an appetite.
            (*Throwing bread.*)
Make haste, *Messieurs!* Make haste, then ! Hurry.
    See,—
See how they swim ! Would you not say, confess,
Some crowd of Courtiers in the audience hall,
When the King comes ?

E

Vignettes in Rhyme

DENISE.

You're jesting!

THE PRINCESS.

Not at all.

Watch but the great one yonder! There's the Duke;—
Those gill-marks mean his Order of St. Luke;
Those old skin-stains his boasted quarterings.
Look what a swirl and roll of tide he brings;
Have you not marked him thus, with crest in air,
Breathing disdain, descend the palace-stair?
You surely have, DENISE.

DENISE.

I think I have.

But there's another, older and more grave,—
The one that wears the round patch on the throat,
And swims with such slow fins. Is he of note?

THE PRINCESS.

Why, that's my good *chambellan*—with his seal.
A kind old man!—he carves me orange-peel
In quaint devices at refection-hours,
Equips my sweet-pouch, brings me morning flowers,
Or chirrups madrigals with old, sweet words,
Such as men loved when people wooed like birds
And spoke the true note first. No suitor he,
Yet loves me too,—though in a graybeard's key.

DENISE.

Look, Madam, look!—a fish without a stain!
O speckless, fleckless fish! Who is it, pray,
That bears him so discreetly?

THE PRINCESS.

FONTENAY.

You know him not? My prince of shining locks!
My pearl!—my Phoenix!—my pomander-box!
He loves not Me, alas! The man's too vain!

The Idyll of the Carp

He loves his doublet better than my suit,—
His graces than my favours.   Still his sash
Sits not amiss, and he can touch the lute
Not wholly out of tune—

DENISE.

                                    Ai ! what a splash !
Who is it comes with such a sudden dash
Plump i' the midst, and leaps the others clear ?

THE PRINCESS.

Ho ! for a trumpet !   Let the bells be rung !
Baron of *Sans-terre*, Lord of *Prés-en-Cieux*,
Vidame of *Vol-au-Vent*—" *et aultres lieux !* "
Bah !   How I hate his Gasconading tongue !
Why, that 's my bragging Bravo-Musketeer—
My carpet cut-throat, valiant by a scar
Got in a brawl that stands for Spanish war :—
His very life 's a splash !

DENISE.

                                    I'd rather wear
E'en such a patched and melancholy air,
As his,—that motley one,—who keeps the wall,
And hugs his own lean thoughts for carnival.

THE PRINCESS.

My frankest wooer !   Thus *his* love he tells
To mournful moving of his cap and bells.
He loves me (so he saith) as Slaves the Free,—
As Cowards War,—as young Maids Constancy.
Item, he loves me as the Hawk the Dove ;
He loves me as the Inquisition Thought ;—

DENISE.

' He loves ?—he loves ? '   Why all this loving 's naught !

THE PRINCESS.

And ' Naught (quoth JACQUOT) makes the sum of Love !'

E 2   (99)

Vignettes in Rhyme

DENISE.

The cynic knave !   How call you this one here ?—
This small shy-looking fish, that hovers near,
And circles, like a cat around a cage,
To snatch the surplus.

THE PRINCESS.

CHÉRUBIN, the page.

'Tis but a child, yet with that roguish smile,
And those sly looks, the child will make hearts ache
Not five years hence, I prophesy.   Meanwhile,
He lives to plague the swans upon the lake,
To steal my comfits, and the monkey's cake.

DENISE.

And these—that swim aside—who may these be ?

THE PRINCESS.

Those—are two gentlemen of Picardy,
Equal in blood,—of equal bravery :—
MOREUIL and MONTCORNET.   They hunt in pair ;
I mete them morsels with an equal care,
Lest they should eat each other,—or eat Me.

DENISE.

And that—and that—and that ?

THE PRINCESS.

I name them not.

Those are the crowd who merely think their lot
The lighter by my land.

DENISE.

And is there none

More prized than most ?   There surely must be one,—
A Carp of carps !

The Idyll of the Carp

Ah me !—he will not come !
He swims at large,—looks shyly on,—is dumb.
Sometimes, indeed, I think he fain would nibble,
But while he stays with doubts and fears to quibble,
Some gilded fop, or mincing courtier-fribble,
Slips smartly in,—and gets the proffered crumb.
He should have all my crumbs—if he'd but ask ;
Nay, an he would, it were no hopeless task
To gain a something more.   But though he 's brave,
He 's far too proud to be a dangling slave ;
And then—he 's modest !   So . . . he will not come !

1875.

THE SUNDIAL

'TIS an old dial, dark with many a stain ;
    In summer crowned with drifting orchard bloom,
Tricked in the autumn with the yellow rain,
    And white in winter like a marble tomb ;

And round about its gray, time-eaten brow
    Lean letters speak—a worn and shattered row :
J am a Shade: a Shadowe too arte thou:
    J marke the Time: saye, Gossip, dost thou soe?

Here would the ringdoves linger, head to head ;
    And here the snail a silver course would run,
Beating old Time ; and here the peacock spread
    His gold-green glory, shutting out the sun.

The tardy shade moved forward to the noon ;
    Betwixt the paths a dainty Beauty stept,
That swung a flower, and, smiling, hummed a tune,—
    Before whose feet a barking spaniel leapt.

Vignettes in Rhyme

O'er her blue dress an endless blossom strayed ;
    About her tendril-curls the sunlight shone ;
And round her train the tiger-lilies swayed,
    Like courtiers bowing till the queen be gone.

She leaned upon the slab a little while,
    Then drew a jewelled pencil from her zone,
Scribbled a something with a frolic smile,
    Folded, inscribed, and niched it in the stone.

The shade slipped on, no swifter than the snail ;
    There came a second lady to the place,
Dove-eyed, dove-robed, and something wan and pale—
    An inner beauty shining from her face.

She, as if listless with a lonely love,
    Straying among the alleys with a book,—
Herrick or Herbert,—watched the circling dove,
    And spied the tiny letter in the nook.

Then, like to one who confirmation found
    Of some dread secret half-accounted true,—
Who knew what hands and hearts the letter bound,
    And argued loving commerce 'twixt the two,

She bent her fair young forehead on the stone ;
    The dark shade gloomed an instant on her head ;
And 'twixt her taper-fingers pearled and shone
    The single tear that tear-worn eyes will shed.

The shade slipped onward to the falling gloom ;
    There came a soldier gallant in her stead,
Swinging a beaver with a swaling plume,
    A ribboned love-lock rippling from his head ;

Blue-eyed, frank-faced, with clear and open brow,
    Scar-seamed a little, as the women love ;
So kindly fronted that you marvel how
    The frequent sword-hilt had so frayed his glove ;

The Sundial

Who switched at Psyche plunging in the sun ;
 Uncrowned three lilies with a backward swinge,
And standing somewhat widely, like to one
 More used to ' Boot and Saddle ' than to cringe

As courtiers do, but gentleman withal,
 Took out the note ; held it as one who feared
The fragile thing he held would slip and fall ;
 Read and re-read, pulling his tawny beard ;

Kissed it, I think, and hid it in his breast ;
 Laughed softly in a flattered happy way,
Arranged the broidered baldrick on his chest,
 And sauntered past, singing a roundelay.

 . . . .

The shade crept forward through the dying glow ;
 There came no more nor dame nor cavalier ;
But for a little time the brass will show
 A small gray spot—the record of a tear.

1865.

AN UNFINISHED SONG

' Cantat Deo qui vivit Deo.'

YES, he was well-nigh gone and near his rest,
 The year could not renew him ; nor the cry
Of building nightingales about the nest ;
 Nor that soft freshness of the May-wind's sigh

That fell before the garden scents, and died
 Between the ampler leafage of the trees :
All these he knew not, lying open-eyed,
 Deep in a dream that was not pain nor ease,

(103)

But death not yet.   Outside a woman talked—
   His wife she was—whose clicking needles sped
To faded phrases of complaint that balked
   My rising words of comfort.   Overhead,

A cage that hung amid the jasmine stars
   Trembled a little, and a blossom dropped.
Then notes came pouring through the wicker bars,
   Climbed half a rapid arc of song, and stopped.

'Is it a thrush?' I asked.   'A thrush,' she said.
   'That was Will's tune.   Will taught him that before
He left the doorway settle for his bed,
   Sick as you see, and couldn't teach him more.

'He'd bring his Bible here o' nights, would Will,
   Following the light, and whiles when it was dark
And days were warm, he'd sit there whistling still,
   Teaching the bird.   He whistled like a lark.'

'Jack! Jack!'   A joyous flutter stirred the cage,
   Shaking the blossoms down.   The bird began;
The woman turned again to want and wage,
   And in the inner chamber sighed the man.

How clear the song was!   Musing as I heard,
   My fancies wandered from the droning wife
To sad comparison of man and bird,—
   The broken song, the uncompleted life,

That seemed a broken song; and of the two,
   My thought a moment deemed the bird more blest,
That, when the sun shone, sang the notes it knew,
   Without desire or knowledge of the rest.

Nay, happier man.   For him futurity
   Still hides a hope that this his earthly praise
Finds heavenly end, for surely will not He,
   Solver of all, above his Flower of Days,

Teach him the song that no one living knows?
   Let the man die, with that half-chant of his,—
What Now discovers not Hereafter shows,
   And God will surely teach him more than this.

Again the Bird.   I turned, and passed along;
   But Time and Death, Eternity and Change,
Talked with me ever, and the climbing song
   Rose in my hearing, beautiful and strange.

1871.

THE CHILD-MUSICIAN

He had played for his lordship's levee,
   He had played for her ladyship's whim,
Till the poor little head was heavy,
   And the poor little brain would swim.

And the face grew peaked and eerie,
   And the large eyes strange and bright,
And they said—too late—'He is weary!
   He shall rest for, at least, To-night!'

But at dawn, when the birds were waking,
   As they watched in the silent room,
With the sound of a strained cord breaking,
   A something snapped in the gloom.

'Twas a string of his violoncello,
   And they heard him stir in his bed :—
'Make room for a tired little fellow,
   Kind God!'— was the last that he said.

1876.

Vignettes in Rhyme

THE CRADLE

How steadfastly she'd worked at it !
　How lovingly had drest
With all her would-be-mother's wit
　That little rosy nest !

How longingly she'd hung on it !—
　It sometimes seemed, she said,
There lay beneath its coverlet
　A little sleeping head.

He came at last, the tiny guest,
　Ere bleak December fled ;
That rosy nest he never prest . . .
　Her coffin was his bed.

1877.

BEFORE SEDAN

' The dead hand clasped a letter.'—SPECIAL CORRESPONDENCE.

HERE in this leafy place
　Quiet he lies,
Cold, with his sightless face
　Turned to the skies.
'Tis but another dead ;
All you can say is said.

Carry his body hence,—
　Kings must have slaves ;
Kings climb to eminence
　Over men's graves :
So this man's eye is dim ;—
Throw the earth over him.

(106)

Before Sedan

What was the white you touched,
    There, at his side?
Paper his hand had clutched
    Tight ere he died ;—
Message or wish, may be ;—
Smooth the folds out and see.

Hardly the worst of us
    Here could have smiled !—
Only the tremulous
    Words of a child ;—
Prattle, that has for stops
Just a few ruddy drops.

Look.   She is sad to miss,
    Morning and night,
His—her dead father's—kiss ;
    Tries to be bright,
Good to mamma, and sweet.
That is all.   ' Marguerite.'

Ah, if beside the dead
    Slumbered the pain !
Ah, if the hearts that bled
    Slept with the slain !
If the grief died ;—But no ;—
Death will not have it so.

1870.

THE FORGOTTEN GRAVE

A SKETCH IN A CEMETERY

OUT from the City's dust and roar,
You wandered through the open door ;
Paused at a plaything pail and spade
Across a tiny hillock laid ;
Then noted on your dexter side
Some moneyed mourner's 'love or pride,'
And so,—beyond a hawthorn-tree,
Showering its rain of rosy bloom
Alike on low and lofty tomb,---
You came upon it—suddenly.

How strange !   The very grasses' growth
Around it seemed forlorn and loath ;
The very ivy seemed to turn
Askance that wreathed the neighbour urn
The slab had sunk ; the head declined,
And left the rails a wreck behind.
No name ; you traced a ' 6,'—a ' 7,'
Part of 'affliction' and of 'Heaven'
And then, in letters sharp and clear,
You read—O Irony austere !—
' *Tho' lost to Sight, to Mem'ry dear.*'

1876.

Vignettes in Rhyme

MY LANDLADY

A SMALL brisk woman, capped with many a bow :
   'Yes,' so she says, 'and younger, too, than some,'
Who bids me, bustling, 'God speed,' when I go,
   And gives me, rustling, 'Welcome,' when I come.

'Ay, sir, 'tis cold,—and freezing hard,—they say ;
   I'd like to give that hulking brute a hit—
Beating his horse in such a shameful way !—
   Step here, sir, till your fire's blazed up a bit.'

A musky haunt of lavender and shells,
   Quaint-figured Chinese monsters, toys, and trays—
A life's collection—where each object tells
   Of fashions gone and half-forgotten ways :—

A glossy screen, where wide-mouth dragons ramp ;
   A vexed inscription in a sampler-frame ;
A shade of beads upon a red-capped lamp ;
   A child's mug graven with a golden name ;

A pictured ship, with full-blown canvas set,
   A card, with sea-weed twisted to a wreath,
Circling a silky curl as black as jet,
   With yellow writing faded underneath.

Looking, I sink within the shrouded chair,
   And note the objects slowly, one by one,
And light at last upon a portrait there,—
   Wide-collared, raven-haired.   'Yes, 'tis my son !'

'Where is he ?'   'Ah, sir, he is dead—my boy !
   Nigh ten long years ago—in 'sixty-three ;
He's always living in my head—my boy !
   He was left drowning in the Southern Sea.

'There were two souls washed overboard, they said,
  And one the waves brought back ; but he was left.
They saw him place the life-buoy o'er his head ;
  The sea was running wildly ;—he was left.

'He was a strong, strong swimmer. Do you know,
  When the wind whistled yesternight, I cried,
And prayed to God,—though 'twas so long ago,—
  He did not struggle much before he died.

''Twas his third voyage. That's the box he brought,–
  Or would have brought—my poor deserted boy !
And these the words the agents sent—they thought
  That money, perhaps, could make my loss a joy.

'Look, sir, I've something here that I prize more :
  This is a fragment of the poor lad's coat,—
That other clutched him as the wave went o'er,
  And this stayed in his hand. That's what they wrote.

'Well, well, 'tis done. My story's shocking you ;—
  Grief is for them that have both time and wealth :
We can't mourn much, who have much work to do ;—
  Your fire is bright. Thank God, I have my health !

1872.

BEFORE THE CURTAIN

'Miss Peacock's called.' And who demurs ?
  Not I who write, for certain ;
If praise be due, one sure prefers
That some such face as fresh as hers
  Should come before the curtain.

And yet, most strange to say, I find
  (E'en bards are sometimes prosy)
Her presence here but brings to mind
That undistinguished crowd behind
  For whom life's not so rosy.

Before the Curtain

The pleased young *premier* led her on,
　　But where are all the others?
Where is that nimble servant John?
And where's the comic Uncle gone?
　　And where that best of Mothers?

Where is 'Sir Lumley Leycester, Bart.'?
　　And where the crafty Cousin?—
That man *may* have a kindly heart,
And yet each night ('tis in the part)
　　Must poison half-a-dozen!

Where is the cool Detective,—he
　　Should surely be applauded?
The Lawyer, who refused the fee?—
The Wedding Guests (in number three)?—
　　Why are they all defrauded?

The men who worked the cataract?
　　The plush-clad carpet lifters?—
Where is the countless host, in fact,
Whose cue is not to speak, but act,—
　　The 'supers' and the shifters?

Think what a crowd whom none recall,
　　Unsung,—unpraised,—unpitied;
Women for whom no bouquets fall,
And men whose names no galleries baw
　　The Great unBenefit-ed!

Ah, Reader, ere you turn the page,
　　I leave you this for Moral:—
Remember those who tread Life's stage
With weary feet and scantest wage,
　　And ne'er a leaf for laurel!

1874.

A NIGHTINGALE IN KENSINGTON GARDENS

THEY paused,—the cripple in the chair,
  More bent with pain than age ;
The mother with her lines of care ;
  The many-buttoned page ;

The noisy, red-cheeked nursery-maid,
  With straggling train of three ;
The Frenchman with his frogs and braid ;—
  All, curious, paused to see,

If possible, the small, dusk bird
  That from the almond bough
Had poured the joyous chant they heard,
  So suddenly, but now.

And one poor POET stopped and thought—
  How many a lonely lay
That bird had sung ere fortune brought
  It near the common way,

Where the crowd hears the note.   And then,—
  What birds must sing the song,
To whom that hour of listening men
  Could ne'er in life belong !

But 'Art for Art !' the Poet said,
  ''Tis still the Nightingale,
That sings where no men's feet will tread,
  And praise and audience fail.'

1874.

MISCELLANEOUS   PIECES

A SONG OF THE FOUR SEASONS

WHEN Spring comes laughing
  By vale and hill,
By wind-flower walking
  And daffodil,—
Sing stars of morning,
  Sing morning skies,
Sing blue of speedwell,—
  And my Love's eyes.

When comes the Summer,
  Full-leaved and strong,
And gay birds gossip
  The orchard long,—
Sing hid, sweet honey
  That no bee sips ;
Sing red, red roses,—
  And my Love's lips.

When Autumn scatters
  The leaves again,
And piled sheaves bury
  The broad-wheeled wain,—
Sing flutes of harvest
  Where men rejoice ;
Sing rounds of reapers,—
  And my Love's voice.

But when comes Winter
With hail and storm,
And red fire roaring
And ingle warm,—
Sing first sad going
Of friends that part;
Then sing glad meeting,—
And my Love's heart.

1877.

THE PARADOX OF TIME

(A VARIATION ON RONSARD)

' *Le temps s'en va, le temps s'en va, ma dame!*
Las! le temps non : mais NOUS *nous en allons!*'

TIME goes, you say?   Ah no!
Alas, Time stays, *we* go;
    Or else, were this not so,
What need to chain the hours,
For Youth were always ours?
    Time goes, you say?—ah no!

Ours is the eyes' deceit
Of men whose flying feet
    Lead through some landscape low;
We pass, and think we see
The earth's fixed surface flee :—
    Alas, Time stays,—we go!

Once in the days of old,
Your locks were curling gold,
    And mine had shamed the crow.
Now, in the self-same stage,
We've reached the silver age;
    Time goes, you say?—ah no!

(116)

The Paradox of Time

Once, when my voice was strong,
I filled the woods with song
   To praise your 'rose' and 'snow';
My bird, that sang, is dead;
Where are your roses fled?
   Alas, Time stays,—we go!

See, in what traversed ways,
What backward Fate delays
   The hopes we used to know;
Where are our old desires?—
Ah, where those vanished fires?
   Time goes, you say?—ah no!

How far, how far, O Sweet,
The past behind our feet
   Lies in the even-glow!
Now, on the forward way,
Let us fold hands, and pray;
   Alas, Time stays,—*we* go!

1875.

TO A GREEK GIRL

WITH breath of thyme and bees that hum,
   Across the years you seem to come,—
Across the years with nymph-like head,
And wind-blown brows unfilleted;
A girlish shape that slips the bud
   In lines of unspoiled symmetry;
A girlish shape that stirs the blood
   With pulse of Spring, Autonoë!

Where'er you pass,—where'er you go,
I hear the pebbly rillet flow;
Where'er you go,—where'er you pass,
There comes a gladness on the grass

You bring blithe airs where'er you tread,—
    Blithe airs that blow from down and sea
You wake in me a Pan not dead,—
Not wholly dead !—Autonoë !

How sweet with you on some green sod
To wreathe the rustic garden-god ;
How sweet beneath the chestnut's shade
With you to weave a basket-braid ;
To watch across the stricken chords
    Your rosy-twinkling fingers flee ;
To woo you in soft woodland words,
    With woodland pipe, Autonoë !

In vain,—in vain !   The years divide :
Where Thamis rolls a murky tide,
I sit and fill my painful reams,
And see you only in my dreams ;—
A vision, like Alcestis, brought
    From under-lands of Memory,—
A dream of Form in days of Thought,—
    A dream,—a dream, Autonoë !

1875.

THE DEATH OF PROCRIS

A VERSION SUGGESTED BY THE SO-NAMED PICTURE OF
PIERO DI COSIMO, IN THE NATIONAL GALLERY

PROCRIS the nymph had wedded Cephalus :
He, till the spring had warmed to slow-winged days
Heavy with June, untired and amorous,
Named her his love ; but now, in unknown ways,
His heart was gone ; and evermore his gaze
Turned from her own, and ever farther ranged
His woodland war ; while she, in dull amaze,
Beholding with the hours her husband changed,
Sighed for his lost caress, by some hard god estranged.

(118)

The Death of Procris

So, on a day, she rose and found him not.
Alone, with wet, sad eye, she watched the shade
Brighten below a soft-rayed sun that shot
Arrows of light through all the deep-leaved glade;
Then, with weak hands, she knotted up the braid
Of her brown hair, and o'er her shoulders cast
Her crimson weed; with faltering fingers made
Her golden girdle's clasp to join, and past
Down to the trackless wood, full pale and overcast.

And all day long her slight spear devious flew,
And harmless swerved her arrows from their aim,
For ever, as the ivory bow she drew,
Before her ran the still unwounded game.
Then, at the last, a hunter's cry there came,
And, lo, a hart that panted with the chase;
Thereat her cheek was lightened as with flame,
And swift she gat her to a leafy place,
Thinking, 'I yet may chance unseen to see his face.'

Leaping he went, this hunter Cephalus,
Bent in his hand his cornel bow he bare,
Supple he was, round-limbed and vigorous,
Fleet as his dogs, a lean Laconian pair.
He, when he spied the brown of Procris' hair
Move in the covert, deeming that apart
Some fawn lay hidden, loosed an arrow there;
Nor cared to turn and seek the speeded dart,
Bounding above the fern, fast following up the hart.

But Procris lay among the white wind-flowers,
Shot in the throat.   From out the little wound
The slow blood drained, as drops in autumn showers
Drip from the leaves upon the sodden ground.

None saw her die but Lelaps, the swift hound,
That watched her dumbly with a wistful fear,
Till, at the dawn, the hornèd woodmen found
And bore her gently on a sylvan bier,
To lie beside the sea,—with many an uncouth tear.

1869.

THE PRAYER OF THE SWINE TO CIRCE

HUDDLING they came, with shag sides caked of mire,—
With hoofs fresh sullied from the troughs o'erturned,—
With wrinkling snouts,—yet eyes in which desire
Of some strange thing unutterably burned,
Unquenchable ; and still where'er She turned
They rose about her, striving each o'er each,
With restless, fierce impórtuning that yearned
Through those brute masks some piteous tale to teach,
Yet lacked the words thereto, denied the power of speech.

For these—Eurylochus alone escaping—
In truth, that small exploring band had been,
Whom wise Odysseus, dim precaution shaping,
Ever at heart, of peril unforeseen,
Had sent inland ;—whom then the islet-Queen,—
The fair disastrous daughter of the Sun,—
Had turned to likeness of the beast unclean,
With evil wand transforming one by one
To shapes of loathly swine, imbruted and undone.

But ' the men's minds remained,' and these for ever
Made hungry suppliance through the fire-red eyes ;
Still searching aye, with impotent endeavour,
To find, if yet, in any look, there lies
A saving hope, or if they might surprise

The Prayer of the Swine to Circe

In that cold face soft pity's spark concealed,
Which she, still scorning, evermore denies;
Nor was there in her any ruth revealed
To whom with such mute speech and dumb words they
appealed.

What hope is ours—what hope!   To find no mercy
After much war, and many travails done?—
Ah, kinder far than thy fell philtres, Circe,
The ravening Cyclops and the Læstrigon!
And O, thrice cursèd be Laertes' son,
By whom, at last, we watch the days decline
With no fair ending of the quest begun,
Condemned in sties to weary and to pine,
And with men's hearts to beat through this foul front of swine!

For us not now,—for us, alas! no more
The old green glamour of the glancing sea;
For us not now the laughter of the oar,—
The strong-ribbed keel wherein our comrades be;
Not now, at even, any more shall we,
By low-browed banks and reedy river places,
Watch the beast hurry and the wild fowl flee;
Or steering shoreward, in the upland spaces
Have sight of curling smoke and fair-skinned foreign faces.

Alas for us!—for whom the columned houses
We left afore-time, cheerless must abide;
Cheerless the hearth where now no guest carouses,—
No minstrel raises song at eventide;
And O, more cheerless than aught else beside,
The wistful hearts with heavy longing full;—
The wife that watched us on the waning tide,—
The sire whose eyes with weariness are dull,—
The mother whose slow tears fall on the carded wool.

Miscellaneous Pieces

If swine we be,—if we indeed be swine,
Daughter of Persé, make us swine indeed,
Well pleased on litter-straw to lie supine,—
Well pleased on mast and acorn-shales to feed,
Stirred by all instincts of the bestial breed;
But O Unmerciful!   O Pitiless!
Leave us not thus with sick men's hearts to bleed!—
To waste long days in yearning, dumb distress,
And memory of things gone, and utter hopelessness!

Leave us at least, if not the things we were,
At least consentient to the thing we be;
Not hapless doomed to loathe the forms we bear,
And senseful roll in senseless savagery;
For surely cursed above all cursed are we,
And surely this the bitterest of ill;—
To feel the old aspirings fair and free,
Become blind motions of a powerless will
Through swine-like frames dispersed to swine-like issues still.

But make us men again, for that thou may'st!
Yea, make us men, Enchantress, and restore
These grovelling shapes, degraded and debased,
To fair embodiments of men once more;
Yea, by all men that ever woman bore;
Yea, e'en by him hereafter born in pain,
Shall draw sustainment from thy bosom's core,
O'er whom thy face yet kindly shall remain,
And find its like therein,—make thou us men again!

Make thou us men again,—if men but groping
That dark Hereafter which th' Olympians keep;
Make thou us men again,—if men but hoping
Behind death's doors security of sleep;—
For yet to laugh is somewhat, and to weep;—

The Prayer of the Swine to Circe

To feel delight of living, and to plough
The salt-blown acres of the shoreless deep ;
Better,—yea better far all these than bow
Foul faces to foul earth, and yearn—as we do now !

So they in speech unsyllabled.   But She,
The fair-tressed Goddess, born to be their bane,
Uplifting straight her wand of ivory,
Compelled them groaning to the sties again ;
Where they in hopeless bitterness were fain
To rend the oaken woodwork as before,
And tear the troughs in impotence of pain,—
Not knowing, they, that even at the door
Divine Odysseus stood,—as Hermes told of yore.

1875.

A CASE OF CAMEOS

AGATE.

(*The Power of Love.*)

First, in an Agate-stone, a Centaur strong,
With square man-breasts and hide of dapple dun,
His brown arms bound behind him with a thong,
On strained croup strove to free himself from one,—
A bolder rider than Bellerophon.
For, on his back, by some strange power of art,
There sat a laughing Boy with bow and dart,
Who drave him where he would, and driving him,
With that barbed toy would make him rear and start.
To this was writ 'World-victor' on the rim.

CHALCEDONY.

(*The Thefts of Mercury.*)

The next in legend bade 'Beware of show !'
'Twas graven this on pale Chalcedony.
Here great Apollo, with unbended bow,

His quiver hard by on a laurel tree,
For some new theft was rating Mercury.
Who stood with downcast eyes, and feigned distress,
As daring not, for utter guiltiness,
To meet that angry voice and aspect joined.
His very heel-wings drooped; but yet, not less,
His backward hand the Sun-God's shafts purloined.

SARDONYX.

(*The Song of Orpheus.*)

THEN, on a Sardonyx, the man of Thrace,
The voice supreme that through Hell's portals stole,
With carved white lyre and glorious song-lit face,
(Too soon, alas! on Hebrus' wave to roll!)
Played to the beasts, from a great elm-tree bole.
And lo! with half-shut eyes the leopard spread
His lissome length; and deer with gentle tread
Came through the trees; and, from a nearer spring,
The prick-eared rabbit paused; while overhead
The stock-dove drifted downward, fluttering.

AMETHYST.

(*The Crowning of Silenus.*)

NEXT came an Amethyst,—the grape in hue.
On a mock throne, by fresh excess disgraced,
With heavy head, and thyrsus held askew,
The Youths, in scorn, had dull Silenus placed,
And o'er him 'King of Topers' they had traced.
Yet but a King of Sleep he seemed at best,
With wine-bag cheeks that bulged upon his breast,
And vat-like paunch distent from his carouse.
Meanwhile, his ass, by no respect represt,
Munched at the wreath upon her Master's brows.

BERYL

(*The Sirens.*)

LASTLY, with 'Pleasure' was a Beryl graven,
Clear-hued, divine. Thereon the Sirens sung.
What time, beneath, by rough rock-bases caven,
And jaw-like rifts where many a green bone clung,
The strong flood-tide, in-rushing, coiled and swung.
Then,—in the offing,—on the lift of the sea,
A tall ship drawing shoreward—helplessly.
For, from the prow, e'en now the rowers leap
Headlong, nor seek from that sweet fate to flee . . .
Ah me, those Women-witches of the Deep!
1876.

LOVE'S QUEST

(FOR A MURAL PAINTING)

WHENAS the watches of the night had grown
    To that deep loneliness where dreams begin,
    I saw how Love, with visage worn and thin,—
With wings close-bound, went through a town alone.
Death-pale he showed, and inly seemed to moan
    With sore desire some dolorous place to win;
    Sharp brambles passed had streaked his dazzling skin,—
His bright feet eke were gashed with many a stone.
And, as he went, I, sad for piteousness,
    Might see how men from door and gate would move
To stay his steps; or womankind would press,
    With wistful eyes, to balconies above,
And bid him enter in. But Love not less,
    Mournful, kept on his way. Ah! hapless Love.
    1873.

THE SICK MAN AND THE BIRDS

ÆGROTUS.

Spring,—art thou come, O Spring!
  I am too sick for words;
How hast thou heart to sing,
  O Spring, with all thy birds?

MERULA.

I sing for joy to see again
The merry leaves along the lane,
  The little bud grown ripe;
And look, my love upon the bough!
Hark, how she calleth to me now,—
      'Pipe! pipe!'

ÆGROTUS.

Ah! weary is the sun:
  Love is an idle thing;
But, Bird, thou restless one,
  What ails thee, wandering?

HIRUNDO.

By shore and sea I come and go
To seek I know not what; and lo!
  On no man's eaves I sit,
But voices bid me rise once more,
To flit again by sea and shore,—
      Flit! Flit!

ÆGROTUS.

This is Earth's bitter cup:—
  Only to seek, not know.
But Thou, that strivest up,
  Why dost thou carol so?

The Sick Man and the Birds

ALAUDA.

A secret Spirit gifteth me
With song, and wing that lifteth me,—
   A Spirit for whose sake,
Striving amain to reach the sky,
Still to the old dark earth I cry,—
         ' Wake ! wake !'

ÆGROTUS.

My hope hath lost its wing.
   Thou, that to Night dost call,
How hast thou heart to sing
   Thy tears made musical ?

PHILOMELA.

Alas for me ! a dry desire
Is all my song,—a waste of fire
   That will not fade nor fail ;
To me, dim shapes of ancient crime
Moan through the windy ways of time,
         ' Wail ! wail !'

ÆGROTUS.

This is the sick man's song,—
   Mournful, in sooth, and fit ;
Unrest that cries ' How long !'—
   And the Night answers it.

1869.

A FLOWER SONG OF ANGIOLA

Down where the garden grows,
   Gay as a banner,
Spake to her mate the Rose
   After this manner :—
'We are the first of flowers,
   Plain-land or hilly,
All reds and whites are ours,
   Are they not, Lily ?'

Then to the flowers I spake,—
   'Watch ye my Lady
Gone to the leafy brake,
   Silent and shady ;
When I am near to her,
   Lily, she knows ;
How I am dear to her,
   Look to it, Rose.'

Straightway the Blue-bell stooped,
   Paler for pride,
Down where the Violet drooped,
   Shy, at her side :—
'Sweetheart, save me and you,
   Where has the summer kist
Flowers of as fair a hue,—
   Turkis or Amethyst ?'

Therewith I laughed aloud,
   Spake on this wise,
'O little flowers so proud,
   Have ye seen eyes
Change through the blue in them,—
   Change till the mere
Loving that grew in them
   Turned to a tear?

(128)

A Flower Song of Angiola

'Flowers, ye are bright of hue,
 Delicate, sweet;
Flowers, and the sight of you
 Lightens men's feet;
Yea, but her worth to me,
 Flowerets, even,
Sweetening the earth to me,
 Sweeteneth heaven.

'This, then, O Flowers, I sing;
 God, when He made ye,
Made yet a fairer thing
 Making my Lady;—
Fashioned her tenderly,
 Giving all weal to her;—
Girdle ye slenderly,
 Go to her, kneel to her,—

'Saying, "He sendeth us,
 He the most dutiful,
Meetly he endeth us,
 Maiden most beautiful!
Let us get rest of you,
 Sweet, in your breast;—
Die, being prest of you,
 Die, being blest."'

1871.

A SONG OF ANGIOLA IN HEAVEN

' Vale, unica !'

FLOWERS,—that have died upon my Sweet,
Lulled by the rhythmic dancing beat
  Of her young bosom under you,—
Now will I show you such a thing
As never, through thick buds of Spring,
  Betwixt the daylight and the dew,
The Bird whose being no man knows—
  The voice that waketh all night through—
    Tells to the Rose.

For lo,—a garden-place I found,
Well filled of leaves, and stilled of sound,
  Well flowered, with red fruit marvellous,
And 'twixt the shining trunks would flit
Tall knights and silken maids, or sit
  With faces bent and amorous ;—
There, in the heart thereof, and crowned
  With woodbine and amaracus,
    My Love I found.

Alone she walked,—ah, well I wis,
My heart leapt up for joy of this !—
  Then when I called to her her name,—
The name, that like a pleasant thing
Men's lips remember, murmuring,
  At once across the sward she came,—
Full fain she seemed, my own dear maid,
  And askèd ever as she came,
    ' Where hast thou stayed ?'

' Where hast thou stayed ?'—she asked as though
The long years were an hour ago ;
  But I spake not, nor answerèd,

A Song of Angiola in Heaven

For, looking in her eyes, I saw,
A light not lit of mortal law ;
   And in her clear cheek's changeless red,
And sweet, unshaken speaking found
   That in this place the Hours were dead,
      And Time was bound.

' This is well done,'—she said,—' in thee,
O Love, that thou art come to me,
   To this green garden glorious ;
Now truly shall our life be sped
In joyance and all goodlihed,
   For here all things are fair to us,
And none with burden is oppressed,
   And none is poor or piteous,—
      For here is Rest.

' No formless Future blurs the sky ;
Men mourn not here, with dull dead eye,
   By shrouded shapes of Yesterday ;
Betwixt the Coming and the Past
The flawless life hangs fixen fast
   In one unwearying To-Day,
That darkens not ; for Sin is shriven,
   Death from the doors is thrust away,
      And here is Heaven.'

At ' Heaven ' she ceased ;—and lifted up
Her fair head like a flower-cup,
   With rounded mouth, and eyes aglow ;
Then set I lips to hers, and felt,—
Ah, me !—the hard pain fade and melt,
   And past things change to painted show ;
The song of quiring birds outbroke ;
   The lit leaves laughed,—sky shook, and lo,
      I swooned,—and woke.

And now, O Flowers,
   —Ye that indeed are dead,—
Now for all waiting hours,
   Well am I comforted ;
For of a surety, now, I see,
   That, without dim distress
   Of tears, or weariness,
My Lady, verily, awaiteth me ;
So that until with Her I be,
   For my dear Lady's sake
   I am right fain to make
Out from my pain a pillow, and to take
  Grief for a golden garment unto me ;
   Knowing that I, at last, shall stand
   In that green garden-land,
And, in the holding of my dear Love's hand,
  Forget the grieving and the misery.

1868.

ANDRÉ LE CHAPELAIN

(Clerk of Love, 1170)

HIS PLAINT TO VENUS OF THE COMING YEARS

     ' *Plus ne suis ce que j'ay esté*
      Et ne le sçaurois jamais estre ;
     Mon beau printemps et mon esté
      Ont fait le saut par la fenestre.'

QUEEN VENUS, round whose feet,
   To tend thy sacred fire,
With service bitter-sweet
   Nor youths nor maidens tire ;—
Goddess, whose bounties be
Large as the un-oared sea ;—

André le Chapelain

Mother, whose eldest born
   First stirred his stammering tongue
In the world's youngest morn,
   When the first daisies sprung :—
Whose last, when Time shall die,
In the same grave shall lie :—

Hear thou one suppliant more !
   Must I, thy Bard, grow old,
Bent, with the temples frore,
   Not jocund be nor bold
To tune for folk in May
Ballad and virelay ?

Shall the youths jeer and jape,
   ' Behold his verse doth dote,—
Leave thou Love's lute to scrape,
   And tune thy wrinkled throat
To songs of " Flesh is Grass," '—
Shall they cry thus and pass ?

And the sweet girls go by ?
   ' Beshrew the gray-beard's tune !—
What ails his minstrelsy
   To sing us snow in June !'
Shall they too laugh, and fleet
Far in the sun-warmed street ?

But Thou whose beauty bright,
   Upon thy wooded hill,
With ineffectual light
   The wan sun seeketh still ;—
Woman, whose tears are dried,
Hardly, for Adon's side,—

Have pity, Erycine !
   Withhold not all thy sweets ;
Must I thy gifts resign
   For Love's mere broken meats ;
And suit for alms prefer
That was thine Almoner ?

Must I, as bondsman, kneel
   That, in full many a cause,
Have scrolled thy just appeal ?
   Have I not writ thy Laws ?
That none from Love shall take
Save but for Love's sweet sake ; —

That none shall aught refuse
To Love of Love's fair dues ; —
That none dear Love shall scoff
Or deem foul shame thereof ; —
That none shall traitor be
To Love's own secrecy ; —

Avert, — avert it, Queen !
   Debarred thy listed sports,
Let me at least be seen
   An usher in thy courts,
Outworn, but still indued
With badge of servitude.

When I no more may go,
   As one who treads on air,
To string-notes soft and slow,
   By maids found sweet and fair—
When I no more may be
Of Love's blithe company ; —

André le Chapelain

When I no more may sit
 Within thine own pleasance,
To weave, in sentence fit,
 Thy golden dalliance ;
When other hands than these
Record thy soft decrees ;—

Leave me at least to sing
 About thine outer wall,
To tell thy pleasuring,
 Thy mirth, thy festival ;
Yea, let my swan-song be
Thy grace, thy sanctity.

[Here ended André's words :
 But One, that writeth, saith—
Betwixt his stricken chords
 He heard the Wheels of Death ;
And knew the fruits Love bare
But Dead-Sea apples were.]

1873

THE DYING OF TANNEGUY DU BOIS

En los nidos de antaño
No hay pájaros hogaño.—Spanish Proverb.

YEA, I am passed away, I think, from this ;
 Nor helps me herb, nor any leechcraft here,
But lift me hither the sweet cross to kiss,
 And witness ye, I go without a fear.
Yea, I am sped, and never more shall see,
 As once I dreamed, the show of shield and crest,
Gone southward to the fighting by the sea ;—
 There is no bird in any last year's nest !

Yea, with me now all dreams are done, I ween,
 Grown faint and unremembered ; voices call
High up, like misty warders dimly seen
 Moving at morn on some Burgundian wall ;

(135)

And all things swim—as when the charger stands
    Quivering between the knees, and East and West
Are filled with flash of scarves and waving hands ;—
    There is no bird in any last year's nest!

Is she a dream I left in Aquitaine ?—
    My wife Giselle,—who never spoke a word,
Although I knew her mouth was drawn with pain,
    Her eyelids hung with tears ; and though I heard
The strong sob shake her throat, and saw the cord
    Her necklace made about it ;—she that prest
To watch me trotting till I reached the ford ;—
    There is no bird in any last year's nest!

Ah! I had hoped, God wot,—had longed that she
    Should watch me from the little-lit tourelle,
Me, coming riding by the windy lea—
    Me, coming back again to her, Giselle ;
Yea, I had hoped once more to hear him call,
    The curly-pate, who, rushen lance in rest,
Stormed at the lilies by the orchard wall ;—
    There is no bird in any last year's nest!

But how, my Masters, ye are wrapt in gloom !
    This Death will come, and whom he loves he cleaves
Sheer through the steel and leather ; hating whom
    He smites in shameful wise behind the greaves.
'Tis a fair time with Dennis and the Saints,
    And weary work to age, and want for rest,
When harness groweth heavy, and one faints,
    With no bird left in any last year's nest!

Give ye good hap, then, all.   For me, I lie
    Broken in Christ's sweet hand, with whom shall rest
To keep me living, now that I must die ;—
    There is no bird in any last year's nest!
1869.

PALOMYDES

Hɪᴍ best in all the dim Arthuriad,
   Of lovers of fair women, him I prize,—
The Pagan Palomydes.   Never glad
   Was he with sweetness of his lady's eyes,
       Nor joy he had.

But, unloved ever, still must love the same,
   And riding ever through a lonely world,
Whene'er on adverse shield or crest he came,
   Against the danger desperately hurled,
       Crying her name.

So I, who strove to You I may not earn,
   Methinks, am come unto so high a place,
That though from hence I can but vainly yearn
   For that averted favour of your face,
       I shall not turn.

No, I am come too high.   Whate'er betide,
   To find the doubtful thing that fights with me,
Towards the mountain tops I still shall ride,
   And cry your name in my extremity,
       As Palomyde,

Until the issue come.   Will it disclose
   No gift of grace, no pity made complete,
After much labour done,—much war with woes?
   Will you deny me still in Heaven, my sweet;—
       Ah, Death—who knows?

1871.

THE MOSQUE OF THE CALIPH

Unto Seyd the vizier spake the Caliph Abdallah :—
' Now hearken and hear, I am weary, by Allah !
I am faint with the mere over-running of leisure ;
I will rouse me and rear up a palace to Pleasure ! '

To Abdallah the Caliph spake Seyd the vizier :
' All faces grow pale if my Lord draweth near ;
And the breath of his mouth not a mortal shall scoff it ;—
They must bend and obey, by the beard of the Prophet ! '

Then the Caliph that heard, with becoming sedateness,
Drew his hand down *his* beard as he thought of his greatness ;
Drained out the last bead of the wine in the chalice :
' I have spoken, O Seyd ; I will build it, my palace !

' As a drop from the wine where the wine-cup hath spilled it,
As a gem from the mine, O my Seyd, I will build it ;
Without price, without flaw, it shall stand for a token
That the word is a law which the Caliph hath spoken ! '

Yet again to the Caliph bent Seyd the vizier :
' Who shall reason or rail if my Lord speaketh clear ?
Who shall strive with his might ?   Let my Lord live for ever !
He shall choose him a site by the side of the river.'

Then the Caliph sent forth unto Kür, unto Yemen,—
To the South, to the North,—for the skilfullest freemen ;
And soon, in a close, where the river breeze fanned it,
The basement uprose, as the Caliph had planned it.

Now the courses were laid and the corner-piece fitted ;
And the butments and set-stones were shapen and knitted,
When lo ! on a sudden the Caliph heard, frowning,
That the river had swelled, and the workmen were drowning.

The Mosque of the Caliph

Then the Caliph was stirred, and he flushed in his ire as
He sent forth his word from Teheran to Shiraz ;
And the workmen came new, and the palace, built faster,
From the bases up-grew unto arch and pilaster.

And the groinings were traced, and the arch-heads were
    chasen,
When lo ! in hot haste there came flying a mason,
For a cupola fallen had whelmed half the workmen ;
And Hamet the chief had been slain by the Turc'-men.

Then the Caliph's beard curled, and he foamed in his rage as
Once more his scouts whirled from the Tell to the Hedjaz ;
'Is my word not my word ?' cried the Caliph Abdallah ;
'I *will* build it up yet . . . *by the aiding of Allah !*'

Though he spoke in his haste like King David before him,
Yet he felt as he spoke that a something stole o'er him ;
And his soul grew as glass, and his anger passed from it
As the vapours that pass from the Pool of Mahomet.

And the doom seemed to hang on the palace no longer,
Like a fountain it sprang when the sources feed stronger ;
Shaft, turret, and spire leaped upward, diminished,
Like the flames of a fire,—till the palace was finished !

Without price, without flaw. And it lay on the azure
Like a diadem dropped from an emperor's treasure ;
And the dome of pearl white and the pinnacles fleckless,
Flashed back to the light, like the gems in a necklace.

So the Caliph looked forth on the turret-tops gilded ;
And he said in his pride, 'Is my palace not builded ?
Who is more great than I that his word can avail if
My will is my will ?'—said Abdallah the Caliph.

But lo ! with the light he repented his scorning,
For an earthquake had shattered the whole ere the morning ;
Of the pearl-coloured dome there was left but a ruin,—
But an arch as a home for the ring-dove to coo in.

Shaft, turret, and spire—all were tumbled and crumbled;
And the soul of the Caliph within him was humbled;
And he bowed in the dust :—' There is none great but Allah !
I will build Him a Mosque,'—said the Caliph Abdallah.

And the Caliph has gone to his fathers for ever,
But the Mosque that he builded shines still by the river;
And the pilgrims up-stream to this day slacken sail if
They catch the first gleam of the ' Mosque of the Caliph.'

1876.

IN THE BELFRY

WRITTEN UNDER RETHEL'S ' DEATH, THE FRIEND '

TOLL ! Is it night, or daylight yet?
Somewhere the birds seem singing still,
Though surely now the sun has set.

Toll ! But who tolls the Bell once more ?
He must have climbed the parapet.
Did I not bar the belfry door ?

Who can it be?—the Bernardine,
That wont to pray with me of yore ?
No,—for the monk was not so lean.

This must be He who, legend saith,
Comes sometimes with a kindlier mien
And tolls a knell.—This shape is Death !

Good-bye, old Bell ! So let it be.
How strangely now I draw my breath !
What is this haze of light I see ? . . .
IN MANUS TUAS, DOMINE !

1876.

ARS VICTRIX

(IMITATED FROM THÉOPHILE GAUTIER)

Yes; when the ways oppose—
  When the hard means rebel,
Fairer the work out-grows,—
  More potent far the spell.

O Poet, then, forbear
  The loosely-sandalled verse,
Choose rather thou to wear
  The buskin—strait and terse;

Leave to the tiro's hand
  The limp and shapeless style,
See that thy form demand
  The labour of the file.

Sculptor, do thou discard
  The yielding clay,—consign
To Paros marble hard
  The beauty of thy line;—

Model thy Satyr's face
  For bronze of Syracuse;
In the veined agate trace
  The profile of thy Muse.

Painter, that still must mix
  But transient tints anew,
Thou in the furnace fix
  The firm enamel's hue;

Let the smooth tile receive
  Thy dove-drawn Erycine;
Thy Sirens blue at eve
  Coiled in a wash of wine.

(141)

Miscellaneous Pieces

All passes. ART alone
   Enduring stays to us ;
The Bust outlasts the throne,—
   The Coin, Tiberius ;

Even the gods must go ;
   Only the lofty Rhyme
Not countless years o'erthrow,—
   Not long array of time.

Paint, chisel, then, or write ;
   But, that the work surpass,
With the hard fashion fight,—
   With the resisting mass.

1876.

AT THE SIGN OF THE LYRE

'Autant ici qu'ailleurs'

' At the Sign of the Lyre,
  Good Folk, we present you
With the pick of our quire—
  And we hope to content you !

Here be Ballad and Song,
  The fruits of our leisure,
Some short and some long,—
  May they all give you pleasure !

But if, when you read,
  They should fail to restore you,
Farewell, and God-speed—
  The world is before you !

1885.

THE LADIES OF ST. JAMES'S

A PROPER NEW BALLAD OF THE COUNTRY AND THE TOWN

' Phyllida amo ante alias.'—VIRG.

THE ladies of St. James's
  Go swinging to the play ;
Their footmen run before them,
  With a 'Stand by ! Clear the way !'
But Phyllida, my Phyllida !
  She takes her buckled shoon,
When we go out a-courting
  Beneath the harvest moon.

The ladies of St. James's
  Wear satin on their backs ;
They sit all night at *Ombre*,
  With candles all of wax :
But Phyllida, my Phyllida !
  She dons her russet gown,
And hastes to gather May dew
  Before the world is down.

The ladies of St. James's !
  They are so fine and fair,
You'd think a box of essences
  Was broken in the air :
But Phyllida, my Phyllida !
  The breath of heath and furze,
When breezes blow at morning,
  Is not so fresh as hers.

(145)

At the Sign of the Lyre

The ladies of St. James's!
    They're painted to the eyes,
Their white it stays for ever,
    Their red it never dies:
But Phyllida, my Phyllida!
    Her colour comes and goes;
It trembles to a lily,—
    It wavers to a rose.

The ladies of St. James's!
    You scarce can understand
The half of all their speeches,
    Their phrases are so grand:
But Phyllida, my Phyllida!
    Her shy and simple words
Are clear as after rain-drops
    The music of the birds.

The ladies of St. James's!
    They have their fits and freaks;
They smile on you—for seconds;
    They frown on you—for weeks:
But Phyllida, my Phyllida!
    Come either storm or shine,
From Shrove-tide unto Shrove-tide,
    Is always true—and mine.

My Phyllida! my Phyllida!
    I care not though they heap
The hearts of all St. James's,
    And give me all to keep;
I care not whose the beauties
    Of all the world may be,
For Phyllida—for Phyllida
    Is all the world to me!

1883.

THE OLD SEDAN CHAIR

'What's not destroy'd by Time's devouring Hand?
Where's Troy, and where's the May-Pole in the Strand?'
—BRAMSTON'S 'ART OF POLITICKS.'

IT stands in the stable-yard, under the eaves,
Propped up by a broom-stick and covered with leaves :
It once was the pride of the gay and the fair,
But now 'tis a ruin,—that old Sedan chair !

It is battered and tattered,—it little avails
That once it was lacquered, and glistened with nails ;
For its leather is cracked into lozenge and square,
Like a canvas by Wilkie,—that old Sedan chair !

See,—here came the bearing-straps ; here were the holes
For the poles of the bearers—when once there were poles ;
It was cushioned with silk, it was wadded with hair,
As the birds have discovered,—that old Sedan chair !

' Where's Troy ? ' says the poet ! Look,—under the seat,
Is a nest with four eggs,—'tis the favoured retreat
Of the Muscovy hen, who has hatched, I dare swear,
Quite an army of chicks in that old Sedan chair !

And yet—Can't you fancy a face in the frame
Of the window,—some high-headed damsel or dame,
Be-patched and be-powdered, just set by the stair,
While they raise up the lid of that old Sedan chair !

Can't you fancy Sir Plume, as beside her he stands,
With his ruffles a-droop on his delicate hands,
With his cinnamon coat, with his laced solitaire,
As he lifts her out light from that old Sedan chair ?

Then it swings away slowly.   Ah, many a league
It has trotted 'twixt sturdy-legged Terence and Teague;
Stout fellows!—but prone, on a question of fare,
To brandish the poles of that old Sedan chair!

It has waited by portals where Garrick has played;
It has waited by Heidegger's 'Grand Masquerade';
For my Lady Codille, for my Lady Bellair,
It has waited—and waited, that old Sedan chair!

Oh, the scandals it knows! Oh, the tales it could tell
Of Drum and Ridotto, of Rake and of Belle,—
Of Cock-fight and Levee, and (scarcely more rare!)
Of Fête-days at Tyburn, that old Sedan chair!

' *Heu! quantum mutata,*' I say as I go.
It deserves better fate than a stable-yard, though!
We must furbish it up, and dispatch it,—'With Care,'—
To a Fine-Art Museum—that old Sedan chair!

    1884.

TO AN INTRUSIVE BUTTERFLY

    ' *Kill not—for Pity's sake—and lest ye slay*
    The meanest thing upon its upward way.'

                —FIVE RULES OF BUDDHA.

I WATCH you through the garden walks,
   I watch you float between
The avenues of dahlia stalks,
   And flicker on the green;
You hover round the garden seat,
   You mount, you waver.   Why,—
Why storm us in our still retreat,
   O saffron Butterfly!

(148)

To an Intrusive Butterfly

Across the room in loops of flight
   I watch you wayward go ;
Dance down a shaft of glancing light,
   Review my books a-row ;
Before the bust you flaunt and flit
   Of 'blind Mæonides'—
Ah, trifler, on his lips there lit
   Not butterflies, but bees !

You pause, you poise, you circle up
   Among my old Japan ;
You find a comrade on a cup,
   A friend upon a fan ;
You wind anon, a breathing-while,
   Around AMANDA'S brow ;—
Dost dream her then, O Volatile !
   E'en such an one as thou ?

Away ! Her thoughts are not as thine.
   A sterner purpose fills
Her steadfast soul with deep design
   Of baby bows and frills ;
What care hath she for worlds without,
   What heed for yellow sun,
Whose endless hopes revolve about
   A planet, *ætat* One !

Away ! Tempt not the best of wives ;
   Let not thy garish wing
Come fluttering our Autumn lives
   With truant dreams of Spring !
Away ! Reseek thy 'Flowery Land' ;
   Be Buddha's law obeyed ;
Lest Betty's undiscerning hand
   Should slay . . . a future PRAED !

1882.

THE CURÉ'S PROGRESS

MONSIEUR the Curé down the street
  Comes with his kind old face,—
With his coat worn bare, and his straggling hair,
  And his green umbrella-case.

You may see him pass by the little '*Grande Place*,'
  And the tiny '*Hôtel-de-Ville*';
He smiles, as he goes, to the *fleuriste* Rose,
  And the *pompier* Théophile.

He turns, as a rule, through the '*Marché*' cool,
  Where the noisy fish-wives call;
And his compliment pays to the '*Belle Thérèse*,'
  As she knits in her dusky stall.

There's a letter to drop at the locksmith's shop,
  And Toto, the locksmith's niece,
Has jubilant hopes, for the Curé gropes
  In his tails for a *pain d'épice*.

There's a little dispute with a merchant of fruit,
  Who is said to be heterodox,
That will ended be with a '*Ma foi, oui!*'
  And a pinch from the Curé's box.

There is also a word that no one heard
  To the furrier's daughter Lou.;
And a pale cheek fed with a flickering red,
  And a '*Bon Dieu garde M'sieu!*'

But a grander way for the *Sous-Préfet*,
  And a bow for Ma'am'selle Anne;
And a mock 'off-hat' to the Notary's cat,
  And a nod to the Sacristan:—

The Curé's Progress

For ever through life the Curé goes
  With a smile on his kind old face—
With his coat worn bare, and his straggling hair,
  And his green umbrella-case.

1878.

THE MASQUE OF THE MONTHS

(FOR A FRESCO)

FIRST com'st thou, churl son of Janus,
  Rough for cold, in drugget clad,
Born with rack and rheum to pain us ;—
First com'st thou, churl son of Janus.
Caverned now is old Sylvanus ;
  Numb and chill are maid and lad.

After thee thy dripping brother,
  Dank his weeds around him cling ;
Fogs his footsteps swathe and smother,—
After thee thy dripping brother.
Hearth-set couples hush each other,
  Listening for the cry of Spring.

Hark ! for March thereto doth follow
  Blithe,—a herald tabarded ;
O'er him flies the shifting swallow,—
Hark ! for March thereto doth follow.
Swift his horn, by holt and hollow,
  Wakes the flowers in winter dead.

Thou then, April, Iris' daughter,
  Born between the storm and sun ;
Coy as nymph ere Pan hath caught her,—
Thou then, April, Iris' daughter.
Now are light, and rustling water ;
  Now are mirth, and nests begun.

(151)

At the Sign of the Lyre

May the jocund cometh after,
 Month of all the Loves (and mine);
Month of mock and cuckoo-laughter,—
May the jocund cometh after.
Beaks are gay on roof and rafter;
 Luckless lovers peak and pine.

June the next, with roses scented,
 Languid from a slumber-spell;
June in shade of leafage tented;—
June the next, with roses scented.
Now her Itys, still lamented,
 Sings the mournful Philomel.

Hot July thereafter rages,
 Dog-star smitten, wild with heat;
Fierce as pard the hunter cages,—
Hot July thereafter rages.
Traffic now no more engages;
 Tongues are still in stall and street.

August next, with cider mellow,
 Laughs from out the poppied corn;
Hook at back, a lusty fellow,—
August next, with cider mellow.
Now in wains the sheafage yellow
 'Twixt the hedges slow is borne.

Laden deep with fruity cluster,
 Then September, ripe and hale;
Bees about his basket fluster,—
Laden deep with fruity cluster.
Skies have now a softer lustre;
 Barns resound to flap of flail.

The Masque of the Months

Thou then, too, of woodlands lover,
　　Dusk October, berry-stained ;
Wailed about of parting plover,—
Thou then, too, of woodlands lover.
Fading now are copse and cover ;
　　Forests now are sere and waned.

Next November, limping, battered,
　　Blinded in a whirl of leaf,
Worn of want and travel-tattered,—
Next November, limping, battered.
Now the goodly ships are shattered,
　　Far at sea, on rock and reef.

Last of all the shrunk December
　　Cowled for age, in ashen gray ;
Fading like a fading ember,—
Last of all the shrunk December.
Him regarding, men remember
　　Life and joy must pass away.

1877.

TWO SERMONS

Between the rail of woven brass,
　　That hides the 'Strangers' Pew,'
I hear the gray-haired Vicar pass
　　From Section One to Two.

And somewhere on my left I see—
　　Whene'er I chance to look—
A soft-eyed girl St. Cecily,
　　Who notes them—in a book.

Ah, worthy Goodman,—sound divine !
　　Shall I your wrath incur,
If I admit these thoughts of mine
　　Will sometimes stray—to her ?

(153)

I know your theme, and I revere;
   I hear your precepts tried;
Must I confess I also hear
   A sermon at my side?

Or how explain this need I feel,—
   This impulse prompting me
Within my secret self to kneel
   To Faith,—to Purity!

1879.

'AU REVOIR'

A Dramatic Vignette

Scene.—*The Fountain in the Garden of the Luxembourg.*
It is surrounded by Promenaders.

Monsieur Jolicœur.   A Lady (*unknown*).

M. Jolicœur.

'Tis she, no doubt. Brunette,—and tall:
A charming figure, above all!
This promises.—Ahem!

The Lady.

            Monsieur?
Ah! it is three. Then Monsieur's name
Is Jolicœur? . . .

M. Jolicœur.

        Madame, the same.

The Lady.

And Monsieur's goodness has to say? . . .
Your note? . . .

(154)

'Au Revoir'

M. JOLICŒUR.

Your note.

THE LADY.

Forgive me.—Nay.

(*Reads*)

'*If Madame* [I omit] *will be*
Beside the Fountain-rail at Three,
Then Madame—possibly—may hear
News of her Spaniel.   JOLICŒUR.'
Monsieur denies his note?

M. JOLICŒUR.

I do.

Now let me read the one from you.
'*If Monsieur Jolicœur will be*
Beside the Fountain-rail at Three,
Then Monsieur—possibly—may meet
An old Acquaintance.   "INDISCREET."'

THE LADY (*scandalized*).

Ah, what a folly!   'Tis not true.
I never met Monsieur.   And you?

M. JOLICŒUR (*with gallantry*).

Have lived in vain till now.   But see:
We are observed.

THE LADY (*looking round*).

I comprehend . . .

(*After a pause.*)

Monsieur, malicious brains combine
For your discomfiture, and mine.
Let us defeat that ill design.
If Monsieur but . . . (*hesitating*).

(155)

At the Sign of the Lyre

M. JOLICŒUR (*bowing*).

> Rely on me.

THE LADY (*still hesitating*).

Monsieur, I know, will understand . . .

M. JOLICŒUR.

Madame, I wait but your command.

THE LADY.

You are too good.   Then condescend
At once to be a new-found Friend !

M. JOLICŒUR (*entering upon the part forthwith*).

How?   I am charmed,—enchanted.   Ah !
What ages since we met . . . at *Spa* ?

THE LADY (*a little disconcerted*).

At *Ems*, I think.   Monsieur, maybe,
Will recollect the Orangery ?

M. JOLICŒUR.

At *Ems*, of course.   But Madame's face
Might make one well forget a place.

THE LADY.

It seems so.   Still, Monsieur recalls
The Kurhaus, and the concert-balls ?

M. JOLICŒUR.

Assuredly.   Though there again
'Tis Madame's image I retain.

THE LADY.

Monsieur is skilled in . . . repartee.
(How do they take it ?—Can you see ?)

'Au Revoir'

M. Jolicœur.

Nay,—Madame furnishes the wit.
(They don't know what to make of it!)

The Lady.

And Monsieur's friend who sometimes came? . . .
That clever . . . I forget the name.

M. Jolicœur.

The Baron? . . . It escapes me, too.
'Twas doubtless he that Madame knew?

The Lady (*archly*).

Precisely.   But, my carriage waits.
Monsieur will see me to the gates?

M. Jolicœur (*offering his arm*).

I shall be charmed.   (Your stratagem
Bids fair, I think, to conquer them.)
                                    (*Aside.*)
(Who is she?   I must find that out.)
—And Madame's husband thrives, no doubt?

The Lady (*off her guard*).

Monsieur de Beau—? . . . He died at *Dôle!*

M. Jolicœur.

Truly.   How sad!
                    (*Aside.*)
                        (Yet, on the whole,
How fortunate!   Beau-*pré?*—Beau-*vau?*
Which can it be?   Ah, there they go!)
—Madame, your enemies retreat
With all the honours of . . . defeat.

The Lady.

Thanks to Monsieur.   Monsieur has shown
A skill Préville could not disown.

At the Sign of the Lyre

M. Jolicœur.

You flatter me.   We need no skill
To act so nearly what we will.
Nay,—what may come to pass, if Fate
And Madame bid me cultivate . . .

The Lady (*anticipating*).

Alas !—no farther than the gate.
Monsieur, besides, is too polite
To profit by a jest so slight.

M. Jolicœur.

Distinctly.   Still, I did but glance
At possibilities . . . of Chance.

The Lady.

Which must not serve Monsieur, I fear,
Beyond the little grating here.

M. Jolicœur (*aside*).

(She's perfect.   One may push too far,
Piano, sano.)
     (*They reach the gates.*)
        Here we are.
Permit me, then . . .
    (*Placing her in the carriage.*)
         And Madame goes ? . . .
Your coachman ? . . . Can I ? . . .

The Lady (*smiling*).

               Thanks ! he knows.
Thanks !   Thanks !

M. Jolicœur (*insidiously*).

          And shall we not renew
Our . . . '*Ems* acquaintanceship' ?

' *Au Revoir* '

THE LADY (*still smiling*).

Adieu !

My thanks instead !

M. JOLICŒUR (*with pathos*).

It is too hard !
(*Laying his hand on the grating.*)
To find one's Paradise is barred ! !

THE LADY.

Nay.—'Virtue is her own Reward !'

[*Exit.*

M. JOLICŒUR (*solus*).

BEAU-*vau ?*—BEAU-*vallon ?*—BEAU-*manoir ?*—
But that's a detail !
(*Waving his hand after the carriage.*)
AU REVOIR !

1878.

THE CARVER AND THE CALIPH

(*WE lay our story in the East.*
Because 'tis Eastern? Not the least.
We place it there because we fear
To bring its parable too near,
And seem to touch with impious hand
Our dear, confiding native land.)

HAROUN ALRASCHID, in the days
He went about his vagrant ways,
And prowled at eve for good or bad
In lanes and alleys of BAGDAD,
Once found, at edge of the bazaar,
E'en where the poorest workers are,
A Carver.

(159)

At the Sign of the Lyre

Fair his work and fine
With mysteries of inlaced design,
And shapes of shut significance
To aught but an anointed glance,—
The dreams and visions that grow plain
In darkened chambers of the brain.
And all day busily he wrought
From dawn to eve, but no one bought;—
Save when some Jew with look askant,
Or keen-eyed Greek from the Levant,
Would pause awhile,—depreciate,—
Then buy a month's work by the weight,
Bearing it swiftly over seas
To garnish rich men's treasuries.

And now for long none bought at all,
So lay he sullen in his stall.
Him thus withdrawn the Caliph found,
And smote his staff upon the ground—
'Ho, there, within! Hast wares to sell?
Or slumber'st, having dined too well?'
'"Dined,"' quoth the man, with angry eyes,
'How should I dine when no one buys?'
'Nay,' said the other, answering low,—
'Nay, I but jested. Is it so?
Take then this coin, . . . but take beside
A counsel, friend, thou hast not tried.
This craft of thine, the mart to suit,
Is too refined,—remote, minute;
These small conceptions can but fail;
'Twere best to work on larger scale,
And rather choose such themes as wear
More of the earth and less of air:
The fisherman that hauls his net,—
The merchants in the market set,—

The couriers posting in the street,—
The gossips as they pass and greet,—
These—these are clear to all men's eyes,
Therefore with these they sympathize.
Further (neglect not this advice!)
Be sure to ask three times the price.'
The Carver sadly shook his head ;
He knew 'twas truth the Caliph said.
From that day forth his work was planned
So that the world might understand.
He carved it deeper, and more plain ;
He carved it thrice as large again ;
He sold it, too, for thrice the cost ;
—Ah, but the Artist that was lost !

1880.

TO AN UNKNOWN BUST IN THE BRITISH MUSEUM

' Sermons in stones.'

WHO were you once? Could we but guess,
   We might perchance more boldly
Define the patient weariness
   That sets your lips so coldly ;
You 'lived,' we know, for blame and fame ;
   But sure, to friend or foeman,
You bore some more distinctive name
   Than mere ' B. C.,'—and ' Roman ? '

Your pedestal should help us much.
   Thereon your acts, your title,
(Secure from cold Oblivion's touch !)
   Had doubtless due recital ;
Vain hope !—not even deeds can last !
   That stone, of which you're *minus*,
Maybe with all your virtues past
   Endows . . . a TIGELLINUS !

G   (161)

At the Sign of the Lyre

We seek it not; we should not find.
  But still, it needs no magic
To tell you wore, like most mankind,
  Your comic mask and tragic;
And held that things were false and true,
  Felt angry or forgiving,
As step by step you stumbled through
  This life-long task . . . of living!

You tried the *cul-de-sac* of Thought;
  The *montagne Russe* of Pleasure;
You found the best Ambition brought
  Was strangely short of measure;
You watched, at last, the fleet days fly,
  Till—drowsier and colder—
You felt MERCURIUS loitering by
  To touch you on the shoulder.

'Twas then (why not?) the whim would come
  That howso Time should garble
Those deeds of yours when you were dumb,
  At least you'd live—in Marble;
You smiled to think that after days,
  At least, in Bust or Statue,
(We all have sick-bed dreams!) would gaze,
  Not quite incurious, at you.

We gaze; *we* pity you, be sure!
  In truth, Death's worst inaction
Must be less tedious to endure
  Than nameless petrifaction;
Far better, in some nook unknown,
  To sleep for once—and soundly—
Than still survive in wistful stone,
  Forgotten more profoundly!

1879.

At the Sign of the Lyre

MOLLY TREFUSIS

' Now the Graces are four and the Venuses two,
And ten is the number of Muses;
For a Muse and a Grace and a Venus are you,—
My dear little Molly Trefusis!'

So he wrote, the old bard of an 'old Magazine':
   As a study it not without use is,
If we wonder a moment who she may have been,
   This same 'little Molly Trefusis!'

She was Cornish.   We know that at once by the 'Tre';
   Then of guessing it scarce an abuse is
If we say that where Bude bellows back to the sea
   Was the birthplace of Molly Trefusis.

And she lived in the era of patches and bows,
   Not knowing what rouge or ceruse is;
For they needed (I trust) but her natural rose,
   The lilies of Molly Trefusis.

And I somehow connect her (I frankly admit
   That the evidence hard to produce is)
With BATH in its hey-day of Fashion and Wit,—
   This dangerous Molly Trefusis.

I fancy her, radiant in ribbon and knot
   (How charming that old-fashioned puce is!),
All blooming in laces, fal-lals, and what not,
   At the PUMP ROOM,—Miss Molly Trefusis.

I fancy her reigning,—a Beauty,—a Toast,—
   Where BLADUD's medicinal cruse is;
And we know that at least of one Bard it could boast,—
   The Court of Queen Molly Trefusis.

He says she was 'VENUS.' I doubt it. Beside,
    (Your rhymer so hopelessly loose is !)
His 'little' could scarce be to Venus applied,
    If fitly to Molly Trefusis.

No, no. It was HEBE he had in his mind ;
    And fresh as the handmaid of Zeus is,
And rosy, and rounded, and dimpled—you'll find—
    Was certainly Molly Trefusis !

Then he calls her 'a MUSE.' To the charge I reply
    That we all of us know what a Muse is ;
It is something too awful,—too acid,—too dry,—
    For sunny-eyed Molly Trefusis.

But 'a GRACE.' There I grant he was probably right ;
    (The rest but a verse-making ruse is)
It was all that was graceful,—intangible,—light,—
    The beauty of Molly Trefusis !

Was she wooed ? Who can hesitate much about that
    Assuredly more than obtuse is ;
For how could the poet have written so pat
    '*My* dear little Molly Trefusis !'

And was wed ? That I think we must plainly infer,
    Since of suitors the common excuse is
To take to them Wives. So it happened to her,
    Of course,—'little Molly Trefusis !'

To the Bard ? 'Tis unlikely. Apollo, you see,
    In practical matters a goose is ;—
'Twas a Knight of the Shire, and a hunting J.P.,
    Who carried off Molly Trefusis !

And you'll find, I conclude, in the '*Gentleman's Mag.*,
    At the end, where the pick of the news is,
'*On the* (blank), *at* '*the Bath,*' *to Sir Hilary Bragg,*
    With a Fortune, MISS MOLLY TREFUSIS.'

Molly Trefusis

Thereupon ... But no farther the student may pry,
  Love's temple is dark as Eleusis;
So here, at the threshold we part, you and I,
  From 'dear little Molly Trefusis.'

   1878.

AT THE CONVENT GATE

WISTARIA blossoms trail and fall
Above the length of barrier wall,
    And softly, now and then,
The shy, staid-breasted doves will flit
From roof to gateway-top, and sit
    And watch the ways of men.

The gate's ajar.   If one might peep!
Ah, what a haunt of rest and sleep
    The shadowy garden seems!
And note how dimly to and fro
The grave, gray-hooded Sisters go,
    Like figures seen in dreams.

Look, there is one that tells her beads;
And yonder one apart that reads
    A tiny missal's page;
And see, beside the well, the two
That, kneeling, strive to lure anew
    The magpie to its cage!

Not beautiful—not all! But each
With that mild grace, outlying speech,
    Which comes of even mood;—
The Veil unseen that women wear
With heart-whole thought, and quiet care,
    And hope of higher good.

'A placid life—a peaceful life !
What need to these the name of Wife ?
   What gentler task (I said)—
What worthier—e'en your arts among—
Than tend the sick, and teach the young,
   And give the hungry bread ?'

'No worthier task !' re-echoes She,
Who (closelier clinging) turns with me
   To face the road again :
—And yet, in that warm heart of hers,
She means the doves', for she prefers
   To 'watch the ways of men.'

1879.

THE MILKMAID

A NEW SONG TO AN OLD TUNE

Across the grass I see her pass ;
  She comes with tripping pace,—
A maid I know,—and March winds blow
  Her hair across her face ;—
    With a hey, Dolly ! ho, Dolly !
     Dolly shall be mine,
    Before the spray is white with May,
     Or blooms the eglantine.

The March winds blow.   I watch her go :
  Her eye is brown and clear ;
Her cheek is brown, and soft as down,
  (To those who see it near !)—
    With a hey, Dolly ! ho, Dolly !
     Dolly shall be mine,
    Before the spray is white with May,
     Or blooms the eglantine.

The Milkmaid

What has she not that those have got,—
  The dames that walk in silk !
If she undo her 'kerchief blue,
  Her neck is white as milk.
    With a hey, Dolly ! ho, Dolly !
      Dolly shall be mine,
      Before the spray is white with May,
      Or blooms the eglantine.

Let those who will be proud and chill !
  For me, from June to June,
My Dolly's words are sweet as curds—
  Her laugh is like a tune ;—
    With a hey, Dolly ! ho, Dolly !
      Dolly shall be mine,
      Before the spray is white with May,
      Or blooms the eglantine.

Break, break to hear, O crocus-spear !
  O tall Lent-lilies flame !
There'll be a bride at Easter-tide,
  And Dolly is her name.
    With a hey, Dolly ! ho, Dolly !
      Dolly shall be mine,
      Before the spray is white with May,
      Or blooms the eglantine.

1883.

AN OLD FISH POND

GREEN growths of mosses drop and bead
   Around the granite brink ;
And 'twixt the isles of water-weed
   The wood-birds dip and drink.

Slow efts about the edges sleep ;
   Swift-darting water-flies
Shoot on the surface ; down the deep
   Fast-following bubbles rise.

Look down.   What groves that scarcely sway !
   What 'wood obscure,' profound !
What jungle !—where some beast of prey
   Might choose his vantage-ground !

   .   .   .   .   .   .

Who knows what lurks beneath the tide ?—
   Who knows what tale ?   Belike,
Those 'antres vast' and shadows hide
   Some patriarchal Pike ;—

Some tough old tyrant, wrinkle-jawed,
   To whom the sky, the earth,
Have but for aim to look on awed
   And see him wax in girth ;—

Hard ruler there by right of might ;
   An ageless Autocrat,
Whose 'good old rule' is 'Appetite,
   And subjects fresh and fat ;'—

While they—poor souls !—in wan despair
   Still watch for signs in him ;
And dying, hand from heir to heir
   The day undawned and dim,

An Old Fish Pond

When the pond's terror too must go;
   Or creeping in by stealth,
Some bolder brood, with common blow,
   Shall found a Commonwealth.

.   .   .   .   .   .

Or say,—perchance the liker this!—
   That these themselves are gone;
That Amurath *in minimis*,—
   Still hungry,—lingers on,

With dwindling trunk and wolfish jaw
   Revolving sullen things,
But most the blind unequal law
   That rules the food of Kings;—

The blot that makes the cosmic All
   A mere time-honoured cheat;—
That bids the Great to eat the Small,
   Yet lack the Small to eat!

.   .   .   .   .   .

Who knows! Meanwhile the mosses bead
   Around the granite brink;
And 'twixt the isles of water-weed
   The wood-birds dip and drink.

1877.

AN EASTERN APOLOGUE

(TO E. H. P.)

MELIK the Sultán, tired and wan,
Nodded at noon on his diván.

Beside the fountain lingered near
JAMÍL the bard, and the vizier—

Old YÚSUF, sour and hard to please;
Then JAMÍL sang, in words like these.

Slim is Butheina—slim is she
As boughs of the Aráka tree !

'Nay,' quoth the other, teeth between,
'Lean, if you will,—I call her lean.'

Sweet is Butheina—sweet as wine,
With smiles that like red bubbles shine !

'True,—by the Prophet !' YÚSUF said.
'She makes men wander in the head !'

Dear is Butheina—ah ! more dear
Than all the maidens of Kashmeer !

'Dear,' came the answer, quick as thought,
'Dear . . and yet always to be bought.'

So JAMÍL ceased.   But still Life's page
Shows diverse unto YOUTH and AGE :

And—be the song of ghouls or gods—
TIME, like the Sultán, sits . . and nods.

1881.

TO A MISSAL OF THE THIRTEENTH CENTURY

MISSAL of the Gothic age,
Missal with the blazoned page,
Whence, O Missal, hither come,
From what dim scriptorium ?

Whose the name that wrought thee thus,
Ambrose or Theophilus,
Bending, through the waning light,
O'er thy vellum scraped and white ;

To a Missal of the Thirteenth Century

Weaving 'twixt thy rubric lines
Sprays and leaves and quaint designs ;
Setting round thy border scrolled
Buds of purple and of gold ?

Ah !—a wondering brotherhood,
Doubtless, by that artist stood,
Raising o'er his careful ways
Little choruses of praise ;

Glad when his deft hand would paint
Strife of Sathanas and Saint,
Or in secret coign entwist
Jest of cloister humorist.

Well the worker earned his wage,
Bending o'er the blazoned page !
Tired the hand and tired the wit
Ere the final *Explicit !*

Not as ours the books of old—
Things that steam can stamp and fold,
Not as ours the books of yore—
Rows of type, and nothing more.

Then a book was still a Book,
Where a wistful man might look,
Finding something through the whole,
Beating,—like a human soul.

In that growth of day by day,
When to labour was to pray,
Surely something vital passed
To the patient page at last ;

Something that one still perceives
Vaguely present in the leaves ;
Something from the worker lent ;
Something mute—but eloquent !

1881.

A REVOLUTIONARY RELIC

OLD it is, and worn and battered,
   As I lift it from the stall;
And the leaves are frayed and tattered,
And the pendent sides are shattered,
   Pierced and blackened by a ball.

'Tis the tale of grief and gladness
   Told by sad St. Pierre of yore,
That in front of France's madness
Hangs a strange seductive sadness,
   Grown pathetic evermore.

And a perfume round it hovers,
   Which the pages half reveal,
For a folded corner covers,
Interlaced, two names of lovers,—
   A 'Savignac' and 'Lucile.'

As I read I marvel whether,
   In some pleasant old château,
Once they read this book together,
In the scented summer weather,
   With the shining Loire below?

Nooked—secluded from espial,
   Did Love slip and snare them so,
While the hours danced round the dial
To the sound of flute and viol,
   In that pleasant old château?

Did it happen that no single
   Word of mouth could either speak?
Did the brown and gold hair mingle,
Did the shamed skin thrill and tingle
   To the shock of cheek and cheek?

A Revolutionary Relic

Did they feel with that first flushing
　　Some new sudden power to feel,
Some new inner spring set gushing
At the names together rushing
　　Of 'Savignac' and 'Lucile'?

Did he drop on knee before her—
　　'*Son Amour, son Cœur, sa Reine*'—
In his high-flown way adore her,
Urgent, eloquent implore her,
　　Plead his pleasure and his pain?

Did she turn with sight swift-dimming,
　　And the quivering lip we know,
With the full, slow eyelid brimming,
With the languorous pupil swimming,
　　Like the love of Mirabeau?

Stretch her hand from cloudy frilling,
　　For his eager lips to press;
In a flash all fate fulfilling
Did he catch her, trembling, thrilling—
　　Crushing life to one caress?

Did they sit in that dim sweetness
　　Of attained love's after-calm,
Marking not the world—its meetness,
Marking Time not—nor his fleetness,
　　Only happy, palm to palm?

Till at last she,—sunlight smiting
　　Red on wrist and cheek and hair,—
Sought the page where love first lighting,
Fixed their fate, and, in this writing,
　　Fixed the record of it there.

.　　.　　.　　.　　.　　.

Did they marry midst the smother,
   Shame and slaughter of it all?
Did she wander like that other
Woful, wistful, wife and mother,
   Round and round his prison wall;—

Wander wailing, as the plover
   Waileth, wheeleth, desolate,
Heedless of the hawk above her,
While as yet the rushes cover,
   Waning fast, her wounded mate;—

Wander, till his love's eyes met hers,
   Fixed and wide in their despair?
Did he burst his prison fetters,
Did he write sweet, yearning letters
   ' *À Lucile,—en Angleterre* '?

Letters where the reader, reading,
   Halts him with a sudden stop,
For he feels a man's heart bleeding,
Draining out its pain's exceeding—
   Half a life, at every drop:

Letters where Love's iteration
   Seems to warble and to rave;
Letters where the pent sensation
Leaps to lyric exultation,
   Like a song-bird from a grave.

Where, through Passion's wild repeating,
   Peep the Pagan and the Gaul,
Politics and love competing,
Abelard and Cato greeting,
   Rousseau ramping over all.

A Revolutionary Relic

Yet your critic's right—you waive it,
　　Whirled along the fever-flood ;
And its touch of truth shall save it,
And its tender rain shall lave it,
For at least you read *Amavit*,
　　Written there in tears of blood.

.　　.　　.　　.　　.　　.　　.

Did they hunt him to his hiding,
　　Tracking traces in the snow ?
Did they tempt him out, confiding,
Shoot him ruthless down, deriding,
　　By the ruined old château ?

Left to lie, with thin lips resting
　　Frozen to a smile of scorn,
Just the bitter thought's suggesting,
At this excellent new jesting
　　Of the rabble Devil-born.

Till some ' tiger-monkey,' finding
　　These few words the covers bear,
Some swift rush of pity blinding,
Sent them in the shot-pierced binding
　　' *À Lucile, en Angleterre.*'

.　　.　　.　　.　　.　　.　　.

Fancies only !　Nought the covers,
　　Nothing more the leaves reveal,
Yet I love it for its lovers,
For the dream that round it hovers
　　Of ' Savignac ' and ' Lucile.'

1866.

A MADRIGAL

BEFORE me, careless lying,
Young Love his ware comes crying :
Full soon the elf untreasures
His pack of pains and pleasures,—
    With roguish eye,
    He bids me buy .
From out his pack of treasures.

His wallet's stuffed with blisses,
With true-love-knots and kisses,
With rings and rosy fetters,
And sugared vows and letters ;—
    He holds them out
    With boyish flout,
And bids me try the fetters.

Nay, Child (I cry), I know them ;
There's little need to show them !
Too well for new believing
I know their past deceiving,—
    I am too old
    (I say), and cold,
To-day, for new believing !

But still the wanton presses,
With honey-sweet caresses,
And still, to my undoing,
He wins me, with his wooing,
    To buy his ware
    With all its care,
Its sorrow and undoing.

1880.

A SONG TO THE LUTE

WHEN first I came to Court,
  Fa la !
When first I came to Court,
I deemed Dan Cupid but a boy,
And Love an idle sport,
A sport whereat a man might toy
With little hurt and mickle joy—
When first I came to Court !

Too soon I found my fault,
  Fa la !
Too soon I found my fault ;
The fairest of the fair brigade
Advanced to mine assault.
Alas ! against an adverse maid
Nor fosse can serve nor palisade—
Too soon I found my fault !

When SILVIA's eyes assail,
  Fa la !
When SILVIA's eyes assail,
No feint the arts of war can show,
No counterstroke avail ;
Naught skills but arms away to throw,
And kneel before that lovely foe,
When SILVIA's eyes assail !

Yet is all truce in vain,
  Fa la !
Yet is all truce in vain,
Since she that spares doth still pursue

(177)

To vanquish once again ;
And naught remains for man to do
But fight once more, to yield anew,
And so all truce is vain !

1887.

A GARDEN SONG

(TO W. E. H.)

HERE, in this sequestered close,
Bloom the hyacinth and rose ;
Here beside the modest stock
Flaunts the flaring hollyhock ;
Here, without a pang, one sees
Ranks, conditions, and degrees.

All the seasons run their race
In this quiet resting place ;
Peach, and apricot, and fig
Here will ripen, and grow big ;
Here is store and overplus,—
More had not Alcinoüs !

Here, in alleys cool and green,
Far ahead the thrush is seen ;
Here along the southern wall
Keeps the bee his festival ;
All is quiet else—afar
Sounds of toil and turmoil are.

Here be shadows large and long ;
Here be spaces meet for song ;
Grant, O garden-god, that I,
Now that none profane is nigh,—
Now that mood and moment please,—
Find the fair Pierides !

1885.

A CHAPTER OF FROISSART

(GRANDPAPA LOQUITUR)

You don't know Froissart now, young folks,
   This age, I think, prefers recitals
Of high-spiced crime, with 'slang' for jokes,
      And startling titles;

But, in my time, when still some few
   Loved 'old Montaigne,' and praised Pope's *Homer*
(Nay, thought to style him 'poet' too,
      Were scarce misnomer),

Sir John was less ignored. Indeed,
   I can recall how Some-one present
(Who spoils her grandson, Frank!) would read,
      And find him pleasant;

For,—by this copy,—hangs a Tale.
   Long since, in an old house in Surrey,
Where men knew more of 'morning ale'
      Than 'Lindley Murray,'

In a dim-lighted, whip-hung hall,
   'Neath Hogarth's 'Midnight Conversation,'
It stood; and oft 'twixt spring and fall,
      With fond elation,

I turned the brown old leaves. For there
   All through one hopeful happy summer,
At such a page (I well knew where),
      Some secret comer,

Whom I can picture, 'Trix, like you
   (Though scarcely such a colt unbroken),
Would sometimes place for private view
      A certain token;—

At the Sign of the Lyre

A rose-leaf, meaning 'Garden Wall,'
  An ivy-leaf for ' Orchard corner,'
A thorn to say ' Don't come at all,'—
        Unwelcome warner !—

Not that, in truth, our friends gainsaid ;
  But then Romance required dissembling,
(Ann Radcliffe taught us that !) which bred
        Some genuine trembling ;

Though, as a rule, all used to end
  In such kind confidential parley
As may to you kind Fortune send,
        You long-legged Charlie,

When your time comes.   How years slip on !
  We had our crosses like our betters ;
Fate sometimes looked askance upon
        Those floral letters ;

And once, for three long days disdained,
  The dust upon the folio settled ;
For some-one, in the right, was pained,
        And some one nettled,

That sure was in the wrong, but spake
  Of fixed intent and purpose stony
To serve King George, enlist and make
        Minced-meat of ' Boney,'

Who yet survived—ten years at least.
  And so, when she I mean came hither,
One day that need for letters ceased,
        She brought this with her !

Here is the leaf-stained Chapter :—*How*
  The English King laid siege to Calais ;
I think Gran. knows it even now,—
        Go ask her, Alice.

1874.

At the Sign of the Lyre

TO THE MAMMOTH-TORTOISE

OF THE MASCARENE ISLANDS

*'Tuque, Testudo, resonare septem
Callida nervis.'*—Hor. iii. II.

MONSTER Chelonian, you suggest
    To some, no doubt, the calm,—
The torpid ease of islets drest
    In fan-like fern and palm ;

To some your cumbrous ways, perchance,
    Darwinian dreams recall ;
And some your Rip-van-Winkle glance,
    And ancient youth appal ;

So widely varied views dispose :
    But not so mine,—for me
Your vasty vault but simply shows
    A LYRE immense, *per se,*

A LYRE to which the Muse might chant
    A truly 'Orphic tale,'
Could she but find that public want,
    A Bard—of equal scale !

Oh, for a Bard of awful words,
    And lungs serenely strong,
To sweep from your sonorous chords
    Niagaras of song,

Till, dinned by that tremendous strain,
    The grovelling world, aghast,
Should leave its paltry greed of gain,
    And mend its ways . . . at last !

1887.

At the Sign of the Lyre

A ROMAN ROUND-ROBIN

('HIS FRIENDS' TO QUINTUS HORATIUS FLACCUS)

' *Hæc decies repetita* [non] *placebit.*'—ARS POETICA.

FLACCUS, you write us charming songs:
    No bard we know possesses
In such perfection what belongs
    To brief and bright addresses;

No man can say that Life is short
    With mien so little fretful;
No man to Virtue's paths exhort
    In phrases less regretful;

Or touch, with more serene distress,
    On Fortune's ways erratic;
And then delightfully digress
    From Alp to Adriatic:

All this is well, no doubt, and tends
    Barbarian minds to soften;
But, HORACE—we, we are your friends—
    Why tell *us* this so often?

Why feign to spread a cheerful feast,
    And then thrust in our faces
These barren scraps (to say the least)
    Of Stoic common-places?

Recount, and welcome, your pursuits:
    Sing Lydë's lyre and hair;
Sing drums and Berecynthian flutes;
    Sing parsley-wreaths; but spare,—

A Roman Round-Robin

O, spare to sing, what none deny,
  That things we love decay ;
That Time and Gold have wings to fly ;—
  That all must Fate obey !

Or bid us dine—on this day week—
  And pour us, if you can,
As soft and sleek as girlish cheek,
  Your inmost Cæcuban ;—

Of that we fear not overplus ;
  But your didactic ' tap '—
Forgive us !—grows monotonous ;
  Nunc vale ! Verbum sap.

1875.

VERSES TO ORDER

(FOR A DRAWING BY E. A. ABBEY)

How weary 'twas to wait !   The year
  Went dragging slowly on ;
The red leaf to the running brook
  Dropped sadly, and was gone ;
December came, and locked in ice
  The plashing of the mill ;
The white snow filled the orchard up ;
  But she was waiting still.

Spring stirred and broke.   The rooks once more
  'Gan cawing in the loft ;
The young lambs' new-awakened cries
  Came trembling from the croft ;

(183)

At the Sign of the Lyre

The clumps of primrose filled again
  The hollows by the way ;
The pale wind-flowers blew ; but she
  Grew paler still than they.

How weary 'twas to wait !   With June,
  Through all the drowsy street,
Came distant murmurs of the war,
  And rumours of the fleet ;
The gossips, from the market-stalls,
  Cried news of Joe and Tim ;
But June shed all her leaves, and still
  There came no news of him.

And then, at last, at last, at last,
  One blessèd August morn,
Beneath the yellowing autumn elms,
  Pang-panging came the horn ;
The swift coach paused a creaking-space,
  Then flashed away, and passed ;
But she stood trembling yet, and dazed.
  The news had come—at last !

And thus the artist saw her stand,
  While all around her seems
As vague and shadowy as the shapes
  That flit from us in dreams ;
And naught in all the world is true,
  Save those few words which tell
That he she lost is found again—
  Is found again—and well !

1883.

A LEGACY

Aн, Postumus, we all must go:
  This keen North-Easter nips my shoulder;
My strength begins to fail; I know
  You find me older;

I've made my Will.   Dear, faithful friend—
  My Muse's friend and not my purse's!
Who still would hear and still commend
  My tedious verses,—

How will you live—of these deprived?
  I've learned your candid soul.   The venal,—
The sordid friend had scarce survived
  A test so penal;

But you—Nay, nay, 'tis so.   The rest
  Are not as you: you hide your merit;
You, more than all, deserve the best
  True friends inherit;—

Not gold,—that hearts like yours despise;
  Not 'spacious dirt' (your own expression),
No; but the rarer, dearer prize—
  The Life's Confession!

You catch my thought?   What!   Can't you guess?
  You, you alone, admired my Cantos;—
I've left you, P., my whole MS.,
  In three portmanteaus!

1873.

'LITTLE BLUE-RIBBONS'

'LITTLE Blue-Ribbons!' We call her that
From the ribbons she wears in her favourite hat;
For may not a person be only five,
And yet have the neatest of taste alive?—
As a matter of fact, this one has views
Of the strictest sort as to frocks and shoes;
And we never object to a sash or bow,
When 'little Blue-Ribbons' prefers it so.

'Little Blue-Ribbons' has eyes of blue,
And an arch little mouth, when the teeth peep through;
And her primitive look is wise and grave,
With a sense of the weight of the word 'behave';
Though now and again she may condescend
To a radiant smile for a private friend;
But to smile for ever is weak, you know,
And 'little Blue-Ribbons' regards it so.

She's a staid little woman! And so as well
Is her ladyship's doll, 'Miss Bonnibelle';
But I think what at present the most takes up
The thoughts of her heart is her last new cup;
For the object thereon,—be it understood,—
Is the 'Robin that buried the "Babes in the Wood"'—
It is not in the least like a robin, though,
But 'little Blue-Ribbons' declares it so.

'Little Blue-Ribbons' believes, I think,
That the rain comes down for the birds to drink;
Moreover, she holds, in a cab you'd get
To the spot where the suns of yesterday set;

And I know that she fully expects to meet
With a lion or wolf in Regent Street !
We may smile, and deny as we like—But, no,
For 'little Blue-Ribbons' still dreams it so.

Dear 'little Blue-Ribbons' ! She tells us all
That she never intends to be 'great' and 'tall';
(For how could she ever contrive to sit
In her 'own, own chair,' if she grew one bit !)
And, further, she says, she intends to stay
In her 'darling home' till she gets 'quite gray';
Alas ! we are gray ; and we doubt, you know,
But 'little Blue-Ribbons' will have it so !

1877.

LINES TO A STUPID PICTURE

'—the music of the moon
Sleeps in the plain eggs of the nightingale.'—AYLMER'S FIELD.

FIVE geese,—a landscape damp and wild,—
A stunted, not too pretty, child,
   Beneath a battered gingham ;
Such things, to say the least, require
A Muse of more-than-average Fire
   Effectively to sing 'em.

And yet—Why should they ? Souls of mark
Have sprung from such ;—e'en Joan of Arc
   Had scarce a grander duty ;
Not always ('tis a maxim trite)
From righteous sources comes the right,—
   From beautiful, the beauty.

At the Sign of the Lyre

Who shall decide where seed is sown?
Maybe some priceless germ was blown
   To this unwholesome marish;
(And what must grow will still increase,
Though cackled round by half the geese
   And ganders in the parish.)

Maybe this homely face may hide
A Staël before whose mannish pride
   Our frailer sex shall tremble;
Perchance this audience anserine
May hiss (O fluttering Muse of mine!)—
   May hiss—a future Kemble!

Or say the gingham shadows o'er
An undeveloped Hannah More!—
   A latent Mrs. Trimmer!!
Who shall affirm it?—who deny?—
Since of the truth nor you nor I
   Can catch the faintest glimmer?

So then—Caps off, my Masters all;
Reserve your final word,—recall
   Your all-too-hasty strictures;
Caps off, I say, for Wisdom sees
Undreamed potentialities
   In most unhopeful pictures.

1874.

At the Sign of the Lyre

A FAIRY TALE

' On court, hélas ! après la vérité ;
Ah ! croyez-moi, l'erreur a son mérite.'—VOLTAIRE.

CURLED in a maze of dolls and bricks,
I find Miss Mary, *aetat* six,
　　Blonde, blue-eyed, frank, capricious,
Absorbed in her first fairy book,
From which she scarce can pause to look,
　　Because it's '*so* delicious !'

'Such marvels, too.　A wondrous Boat,
In which they cross a magic Moat,
　　That's smooth as glass to row on—
A Cat that brings all kinds of things ;
And see, the Queen has angel wings—
　　Then OGRE comes '—and so on.

What trash it is !　How sad to find
(Dear Moralist !) the childish mind,
　　So active and so pliant,
Rejecting themes in which you mix
Fond truths with pleasing facts, to fix
　　On tales of Dwarf and Giant !

In merest prudence men should teach
That cats mellifluous in speech
　　Are painful contradictions ;
That science ranks as monstrous things
Two pairs of upper limbs ; so wings—
　　E'en angel's wings !—are fictions ;

That there's no giant now but Steam ;
That life, although 'an empty dream,'
　　Is scarce a 'land of Fairy.'
'Of course I said all this ?'　Why, no ;
I *did* a thing far wiser, though,—
　　I read the tale with Mary.

1876.

At the Sign of the Lyre

TO A CHILD

(FROM THE 'GARLAND OF RACHEL')

How shall I sing you, Child, for whom
    So many lyres are strung;
Or how the only tone assume
    That fits a Maid so young?

What rocks there are on either hand!
    Suppose—'tis on the cards—
You should grow up with quite a grand
    Platonic hate for bards!

How shall I then be shamed, undone,
    For ah! with what a scorn
Your eyes must greet that luckless One
    Who rhymed you, newly born,—

Who o'er your 'helpless cradle' bent,
    His idle verse to turn;
And twanged his tiresome instrument
    Above your unconcern!

Nay,—let my words be so discreet,
    That, keeping Chance in view,
Whatever after fate you meet
    A part may still be true.

Let others wish you mere good looks,—
    Your sex is always fair;
Or to be writ in fortune's books,—
    She's rich who has to spare:

I wish you but a heart that's kind,
    A head that's sound and clear;
(Yet let the heart be not too blind,
    The head not too severe!)

(190)

To a Child

A joy of life, a frank delight;
  A not-too-large desire;
And—if you fail to find a Knight—
  At least . . . a trusty Squire.

1881.

HOUSEHOLD ART

'MINE be a cot,' for the hours of play,
Of the kind that is built by Miss GREENAWAY;
Where the walls are low, and the roofs are red,
And the birds are gay in the blue o'erhead;
And the dear little figures, in frocks and frills,
Go roaming about at their own sweet wills,
And 'play with the pups,' and 'reprove the calves,'
And do nought in the world (but Work) by halves,
From 'Hunt the Slipper' and 'Riddle-me-ree'
To watching the cat in the apple-tree.

O Art of the Household! Men may prate
Of their ways 'intense' and Italianate,—
They may soar on their wings of sense, and float
To the *au delà* and the dim remote,—
Till the last sun sink in the last-lit West,
'Tis the Art at the Door that will please the best;
To the end of Time 'twill be still the same,
For the Earth first laughed when the children came

1883.

At the Sign of the Lyre

THE DISTRESSED POET

A SUGGESTION FROM HOGARTH

One knows the scene so well,—a touch,
  A word, brings back again
That room, not garnished overmuch,
  In gusty Drury Lane;

The empty safe, the child that cries,
  The kittens on the coat,
The good-wife with her patient eyes,
  The milkmaid's tuneless throat;

And last, in that mute woe sublime,
  The luckless verseman's air:
The 'Bysshe,' the foolscap and the rhyme,—
  The Rhyme . . . that is not there!

Poor Bard! to dream the verse inspired—
  With dews Castalian wet—
Is built from cold abstractions squired
  By 'Bysshe,' his epithet!

Ah! when she comes, the glad-eyed Muse,
  No step upon the stair
Betrays the guest we can't refuse,—
  She takes us unaware;

And tips with fire our lyric lips,
  And sets our hearts aflame,
And then, like Ariel, off she trips,
  And none knows how she came.

Only, henceforth, for right or wrong,
  By some dull sense grown keen,
Some blank hour blossomed into song,
  We feel that she has been.

1885.

JOCOSA LYRA

In our hearts is the Great One of Avon
   Engraven,
And we climb the cold summits once built on
   By Milton.

But at times not the air that is rarest
   Is fairest,
And we long in the valley to follow
   Apollo.

Then we drop from the heights atmospheric
   To Herrick,
Or we pour the Greek honey, grown blander,
   Of Landor;

Or our cosiest nook in the shade is
   Where Praed is,
Or we toss the light bells of the mocker
   With Locker.

Oh, the song where not one of the Graces
   Tight-laces,—
Where we woo the sweet Muses not starchly,
   But archly,—

Where the verse, like a piper a-Maying,
   Comes playing,
And the rhyme is as gay as a dancer,
   In answer,—

It will last till men weary of pleasure
   In measure!
It will last till men weary of laughter
   And after!

1881.

H   (193)

MY BOOKS

They dwell in the odour of camphor,
   They stand in a Sheraton shrine,
They are ' warranted early editions,'
   These worshipful tomes of mine ;—

In their creamiest ' Oxford vellum,'
   In their redolent ' crushed Levant,'
With their delicate watered linings,
   They are jewels of price, I grant ;—

Blind-tooled and morocco-jointed,
   They have Zaehnsdorf's daintiest dress,
They are graceful, attenuate, polished,
   But they gather the dust, no less ;—

For the row that I prize is yonder,
   Away on the unglazed shelves,
The bulged and the bruised *octavos*,
   The dear and the dumpy twelves,—

Montaigne with his sheepskin blistered,
   And Howell the worse for wear,
And the worm-drilled Jesuits' Horace,
   And the little old cropped Molière,

And the Burton I bought for a florin,
   And the Rabelais foxed and flea'd,—
For the others I never have opened,
   But those are the books I read.

1883.

THE COLLECTOR TO HIS LIBRARY

Brown Books of mine, who never yet
Have caused me anguish or regret,—
Save when some fiend in human shape
Has set your tender sides agape,
Or soiled with some unmanly smear
The candour of your margin clear,
Or writ you with some phrase inane,
The bantling of an idle brain,—
I love you : and because must end
This commerce between friend and friend,
I do implore each kindly Fate—
To each and all I supplicate—
That you, whom I have loved so long,
May not be vended 'for a song';—
That you, my dear desire and care,
May 'scape the common thoroughfare,
The dust, the eating rain, and all
The shame and squalor of the Stall.
Rather I trust your lot may touch
Some Croesus—if there should be such—
To buy you, and that you may so
From Croesus unto Croesus go
Till that inevitable day
When comes your moment of decay.

This, more than other good, I pray.

1887.

At the Sign of the Lyre

THE BOOK-PLATE'S PETITION

BY A GENTLEMAN OF THE TEMPLE

WHILE cynic CHARLES still trimm'd the vane
'Twixt *Querouaille* and *Castlemaine*,
In days that shocked JOHN EVELYN,
My First Possessor fixed me in.
In days of *Dutchmen* and of frost,
The narrow sea with JAMES I cross'd,
Returning when once more began
The Age of *Saturn* and of ANNE.
I am a part of all the past :
I knew the GEORGES, first and last ;
I have been oft where else was none
Save the great wig of ADDISON ;
And seen on shelves beneath me grope
The little eager form of POPE.
I lost the Third that owned me when
French NOAILLES fled at Dettingen ;
The year JAMES WOLFE surprised Quebec,
The Fourth in hunting broke his neck ;
The day that WILLIAM HOGARTH dy'd,
The Fifth one found me in Cheapside.
This was a *Scholar*, one of those
Whose *Greek* is sounder than their *hose ;*
He lov'd old Books and nappy ale,
So liv'd at Streatham, next to THRALE.
'Twas there this stain of grease I boast
Was made by Dr. JOHNSON's toast.
(He did it, as I think, for Spite ;
My Master call'd him *Jacobite !*)
And now that I so long to-day
Have rested *post discrimina*,

The Book-Plate's Petition

Safe in the brass-wir'd book-case where
I watch'd the Vicar's whit'ning hair,
Must I these travell'd bones inter
In some *Collector's* sepulchre!
Must I be torn herefrom and thrown
With *frontispiece* and *colophon*!
With vagrant *E's*, and *I's*, and *O's*,
The spoil of plunder'd *Folios*!
With scraps and snippets that to ME
Are naught but *kitchen company*!
Nay, rather, FRIEND, this favour grant me:
Tear me at once; *but don't transplant me.*

CHELTENHAM, *Sept.* 31, 1792.

1881.

THE WATER OF GOLD

'BUY,—who'll buy?' In the market-place,
   Out of the market din and clatter,
The quack with his puckered persuasive face
   Patters away in the ancient patter.

'Buy,—who'll buy? In this flask I hold—
   In this little flask that I tap with my stick, sir—
Is the famed, infallible Water of Gold,—
   The One, Original, True Elixir!

'Buy,—who'll buy? There's a maiden there,—
   She with the ell-long flaxen tresses,—
Here is a draught that will make you fair,
   Fit for an Emperor's own caresses!

'Buy,—who'll buy? Are you old and gray?
   Drink but of this, and in less than a minute,
Lo! you will dance like the flowers in May,
   Chirp and chirk like a new-fledged linnet!

'Buy,—who'll buy? Is a baby ill?
 Drop but a drop of this in his throttle,
Straight he will gossip and gorge his fill,
 Brisk as a burgher over a bottle!

'Here is wealth for your life,—if you will but ask;
 Here is health for your limb, without lint or lotion;
Here is all that you lack, in this tiny flask;
 And the price is a couple of silver groschen!

'Buy,—who'll buy?' So the tale runs on:
 And still in the Great World's market-places
The Quack, with his quack catholicon,
 Finds ever his crowd of upturned faces;

For he plays on our hearts with his pipe and drum,
 On our vague regret, on our weary yearning;
For he sells the thing that never can come,
 Or the thing that has vanished, past returning.

1887.

A FANCY FROM FONTENELLE

'*De mémoires de Roses on n'a point vu mourir le Jardinier.*'

THE Rose in the garden slipped her bud,
And she laughed in the pride of her youthful blood,
As she thought of the Gardener standing by—
'He is old,—so old! And he soon must die!'

The full Rose waxed in the warm June air,
And she spread and spread till her heart lay bare;
And she laughed once more as she heard his tread—
'He is older now! He will soon be dead!'

(198)

A Fancy from Fontenelle

But the breeze of the morning blew, and found
That the leaves of the blown Rose strewed the ground ;
And he came at noon, that Gardener old,
And he raked them gently under the mould.

And I wove the thing to a random rhyme,
For the Rose is Beauty, the Gardener, Time.

1885.

DON QUIXOTE

Behind thy pasteboard, on thy battered hack,
Thy lean cheek striped with plaster to and fro,
Thy long spear levelled at the unseen foe,
And doubtful Sancho trudging at thy back,
Thou wert a figure strange enough, good lack !
To make wiseacredom, both high and low,
Rub purblind eyes, and (having watched thee go)
Dispatch its Dogberrys upon thy track :
Alas ! poor Knight !   Alas ! poor soul possest !
Yet would to-day when Courtesy grows chill,
And life's fine loyalties are turned to jest,
Some fire of thine might burn within us still !
Ah, would but one might lay his lance in rest,
And charge in earnest . . . were it but a mill !

1882.

A BROKEN SWORD

(TO A. L.)

THE shopman shambled from the doorway out
  And twitched it down—
Snappèd in the blade! 'Twas scarcely dear, I doubt,
  At half-a-crown.

Useless enough! And yet can still be seen,
  In letters clear,
Traced on the metal's rusty damaskeen—
  ' *Povr Paruenyr.*'

Whose was it once?—Who manned it once in hope
  His fate to gain?
Who was it dreamed his oyster-world should ope
  To this—in vain?

Maybe with some stout Argonaut it sailed
  The Western Seas;
Maybe but to some paltry Nym availed
  For toasting cheese!

Or decked by Beauty on some morning lawn
  With silken knot,
Perchance, ere night, for Church and King 'twas drawn—
  Perchance 'twas not!

Who knows—or cares? To-day, 'mid foils and gloves
  Its hilt depends,
Flanked by the favours of forgotten loves,—
  Remembered friends;—

And oft its legend lends, in hours of stress,
  A word to aid;
Or like a warning comes, in puffed success,
  Its broken blade.

1886.

At the Sign of the Lyre

THE POET'S SEAT

AN IDYLL OF THE SUBURBS

' Ille terrarum mihi praeter omnes
Angulus RIDET.'—HOR. ii. 6.

It was an elm-tree root of yore,
　With lordly trunk, before they lopped it,
And weighty, said those five who bore
　Its bulk across the lawn, and dropped it
Not once or twice, before it lay,
　With two young pear-trees to protect it,
Safe where the Poet hoped some day
　The curious pilgrim would inspect it.

He saw him with his Poet's eye,
　The stately Maori, turned from etching
The ruin of St Paul's, to try
　Some object better worth the sketching :—
He saw him, and it nerved his strength
　What time he hacked and hewed and scraped it,
Until the monster grew at length
　The Master-piece to which he shaped it.

To wit—a goodly garden-seat,
　And fit alike for Shah or Sophy,
With shelf for cigarettes complete,
　And one, but lower down, for coffee ;
He planted pansies 'round its foot,—
　' Pansies for thoughts !' and rose and arum ;
The Motto (that he meant to put)
　Was ' *Ille angulus terrarum.*'

But 'Oh! the change' (as Milton sings)—
   'The heavy change!' When May departed,
When June with its 'delightful things'
   Had come and gone, the rough bark started,—
Began to lose its sylvan brown,
   Grew parched, and powdery, and spotted;
And, though the Poet nailed it down,
   It still flapped up, and dropped, and rotted.

Nor was this all. 'Twas next the scene
   Of vague (and viscous) vegetations;
Queer fissures gaped, with oozings green,
   And moist, unsavoury exhalations,—
Faint wafts of wood decayed and sick,
   Till, where he meant to carve his Motto,
Strange leathery fungi sprouted thick,
   And made it like an oyster grotto.

Briefly, it grew a seat of scorn,
   Bare,—shameless,—till, for fresh disaster,
From end to end, one April morn,
   'Twas riddled like a pepper caster,—
Drilled like a vellum of old time;
   And musing on this final mystery,
The Poet left off scribbling rhyme,
   And took to studying Natural History.

This was the turning of the tide;
   His five-act play is still unwritten;
The dreams that now his soul divide
   Are more of Lubbock than of Lytton;
'*Ballades*' are 'verses vain' to him
   Whose first ambition is to lecture
(So much is man the sport of whim!)
   On 'Insects and their Architecture.'

1892.

THE LOST ELIXIR

' One drop of ruddy human blood puts more life into the veins of a poem than all the delusive 'aurum potabile' that can be distilled out of the choicest library.'—LOWELL.

AH, yes, that ' drop of human blood !'—
    We had it once, may be,
When our young song's impetuous flood
    First poured its ecstasy ;
But now the shrunk poetic vein
Yields not that priceless drop again.

We toil,—as toiled we not of old ;
    Our patient hands distil
The shining spheres of chemic gold
    With hard-won, fruitless skill ;
But that red drop still seems to be
Beyond our utmost alchemy.

Perchance, but most in later age
    Time's after-gift, a tear,
Will strike a pathos on the page
    Beyond all art sincere ;
But that ' one drop of human blood '
Has gone with life's first leaf and bud.

1874.

MEMORIAL VERSES

A DIALOGUE

TO THE MEMORY OF MR. ALEXANDER POPE

' Non injussa cano.'—VIRG.

POET. I sing of POPE—

FRIEND. What, POPE, the *Twitnam* Bard,
Whom *Dennis, Cibber, Tibbald* push'd so hard!
POPE of the *Dunciad!* POPE who dar'd to woo,
And then to libel, *Wortley-Montagu!*
POPE of the *Ham-walks* story—

                             P. Scandals all!
Scandals that now I care not to recall.
Surely a little, in two hundred Years,
One may neglect Contemporary Sneers :—
Surely allowance for the Man may make
That had all *Grub Street* yelping in his Wake!
And who (I ask you) has been never Mean,
When urged by Envy, Anger or the Spleen?
No : I prefer to look on POPE as one
Not rightly happy till his Life was done ;
Whose whole Career, romance it as you please,
Was (what he call'd it) but a ' long Disease ' :
Think of his Lot,—his Pilgrimage of Pain,
His ' crazy Carcass ' and his restless Brain ;
Think of his Night-Hours with their Feet of Lead,
His dreary Vigil and his aching Head ;
Think of all this, and marvel then to find
The ' crooked Body with a crooked Mind!'
Nay rather, marvel that, in Fate's Despite,
You find so much to solace and delight,—

So much of Courage, and of Purpose high
In that unequal Struggle *not* to die.
I grant you freely that Pope played his Part
Sometimes ignobly—but he lov'd his Art;
I grant you freely that he sought his Ends
Not always wisely—but he lov'd his Friends;
And who of Friends a nobler Roll could show—
Swift, St. John, Bathurst, Marchmont, Peterb'ro',
Arbuthnot—

             Fr. Atticus?

                                P. Well (*entre nous*),
Most that he said of *Addison* was *true*.
Plain Truth, you know—

                              Fr. Is often not polite
(So *Hamlet* thought)—

                        P. And *Hamlet* (Sir) was right.
But leave Pope's Life. To-day, methinks, we touch
The Work too little and the Man too much.
Take up the *Lock*, the *Satires, Eloise*—
What Art supreme, what Elegance, what Ease!
How keen the Irony, the Wit how bright,
The Style how rapid, and the Verse how light!
Then read once more, and you shall wonder yet
At Skill, at Turn, at Point, at Epithet.
'True Wit is Nature to Advantage dress'd'—
Was ever Thought so pithily express'd?
'And ten low Words oft creep in one dull Line'—
Ah, what a Homily on Yours . . and Mine!
Or take—to choose at Random—take but This—
'Ten censure wrong for one that writes amiss.'

    Fr. Pack'd and precise, no Doubt. Yet surely those
Are but the Qualities we ask of Prose.
Was he a Poet?

A Dialogue

P. Yes : if that be what
Byron was certainly and *Bowles* was not ;
Or say you grant him, to come nearer Date,
What *Dryden* had, that was denied to *Tate*—

Fr. Which means, you claim for him the Spark divine,
Yet scarce would place him on the highest Line—

P. True, there are Classes.   Pope was most of all
Akin to *Horace, Persius, Juvenal;*
Pope was, like them, the Censor of his Age,
An Age more suited to Repose than Rage ;
When Rhyming turn'd from Freedom to the Schools,
And shock'd with Licence, shudder'd into Rules ;
When *Phœbus* touch'd the Poet's trembling Ear
With one supreme Commandment, *Be thou Clear ;*
When Thought meant less to reason than compile,
And the *Muse* labour'd . . chiefly with the File.
Beneath full Wigs no Lyric drew its Breath
As in the Days of great Elizabeth ;
And to the Bards of Anna was denied
The Note that *Wordsworth* heard on *Duddon*-side.
But Pope took up his Parable, and knit
The Woof of Wisdom with the Warp of Wit ;
He trimm'd the Measure on its equal Feet,
And smooth'd and fitted till the Line was neat ;
He taught the Pause with due Effect to fall ;
He taught the Epigram to come at Call ;
He wrote—

Fr. His *Iliad!*

P. Well, suppose you own
You like your *Iliad* in the Prose of *Bohn,*—
Tho' if you'd learn in Prose how *Homer* sang,
'Twere best to learn of *Butcher* and of *Lang,*—
Suppose you say your Worst of Pope, declare
His Jewels Paste, his Nature a Parterre,

(209)

His Art but Artifice—I ask once more
Where have you seen such Artifice before?
Where have you seen a Parterre better grac'd,
Or Gems that glitter like his Gems of Paste?
Where can you show, among your Names of Note,
So much to copy and so much to quote?
And where, in Fine, in all our English Verse,
A Style more trenchant and a Sense more terse?
So I, that love the old *Augustan* Days
Of formal Courtesies and formal Phrase;
That like along the finished Line to feel
The Ruffle's Flutter and the Flash of Steel;
That like my Couplet as compact as clear;
That like my Satire sparkling tho' severe,
Unmix'd with Bathos and unmarr'd by Trope,
I fling my Cap for Polish—and for POPE!

    1888.

A FAMILIAR EPISTLE

TO * * ESQ. OF * * WITH A LIFE OF THE LATE

INGENIOUS MR. WM. HOGARTH

DEAR Cosmopolitan,—I know
I *should* address you a *Rondeau*,
Or else announce what I've to say
At least *en Ballade fratrisée;*
But No: for once I leave Gymnasticks,
And take to simple *Hudibrasticks;*
Why should I choose another Way,
When this was good enough for GAY?

    You love, my FRIEND, with me, I think,
That Age of Lustre and of Link;
Of *Chelsea* China and long ' s 'es,
Of Bag-wigs and of flowered Dresses;

A Familiar Epistle

That Age of Folly and of Cards,
Of Hackney Chairs and Hackney Bards;
—No H—LTS, no K—G—N P—LS were then
Dispensing Competence to Men;
The gentle Trade was left to Churls,
Your frowsy TONSONS and your CURLLS;
Mere Wolves in Ambush to attack
The AUTHOR in a Sheep-skin Back;
Then SAVAGE and his Brother-Sinners
In *Porridge-Island* div'd for Dinners;
Or doz'd on *Covent Garden* Bulks,
And liken'd Letters to the Hulks;—
You know that by-gone Time, I say,
That aimless, easy-moral'd Day,
When rosy Morn found MADAM still
Wrangling at *Ombre* or *Quadrille;*
When good Sir JOHN reel'd Home to Bed,
From *Pontack's* or the *Shakespear's Head;*
When TRIP *convey'd* his Master's Cloaths,
And took his Titles and his Oaths;
While BETTY, in a cast *Brocade*,
Ogled MY LORD at Masquerade;
When GARRICK play'd the guilty *Richard*,
Or mouth'd *Macbeth* with MRS. PRITCHARD;
When FOOTE grimac'd his snarling Wit;
When CHURCHILL bullied in the Pit;
When the CUZZONI sang—
                                    But there!

The further Catalogue I spare,
Having no Purpose to eclipse
That tedious Tale of HOMER'S Ships;—
This is the MAN that drew it all
From *Pannier Alley* to the *Mall*,
Then turn'd and drew it once again
From *Bird-Cage Walk* to *Lewknor's Lane;*—

Its Rakes and Fools, its Rogues and Sots ;
Its bawling Quacks, its starveling Scots ;
Its Ups and Downs, its Rags and Garters,
Its HENLEYS, LOVATS, MALCOLMS, CHARTRES ;
Its Splendour, Squalor, Shame, Disease ;
Its *quicquid agunt Homines ;*—
Nor yet omitted to pourtray
Furens quid possit Foemina ;—
In short, held up to ev'ry Class
NATURE'S unflatt'ring looking-Glass ;
And, from his Canvass, spoke to All
The Message of a JUVENAL.

Take Him.   His Merits most aver ;
His weak Point is—his Chronicler !

NOVR. 1, 1879.
  1885.

HENRY FIELDING

(TO JAMES RUSSELL LOWELL)

NOT from the ranks of those we call
Philosopher or Admiral,—
Neither as LOCKE was, nor as BLAKE,
Is that Great Genius for whose sake
We keep this Autumn festival.

And yet in one sense, too, was he
A soldier—of humanity ;
And, surely, philosophic mind
Belonged to him whose brain designed
That teeming COMIC EPOS where,
As in CERVANTES and MOLIÈRE,
Jostles the medley of Mankind.

Henry Fielding

Our ENGLISH NOVEL's pioneer !
His was the eye that first saw clear
How, not in natures half-effaced
By cant of Fashion and of Taste,—
Not in the circles of the Great,
Faint-blooded and exanimate,—
Lay the true field of Jest and Whim,
Which we to-day reap after him.
No :—he stepped lower down and took
The piebald PEOPLE for his Book !

Ah, what a wealth of Life there is
In that large-laughing page of his !
What store and stock of Common-Sense,
Wit, Wisdom, Books, Experience !
How his keen Satire flashes through,
And cuts a sophistry in two !
How his ironic lightning plays
Around a rogue and all his ways !
Ah, how he knots his lash to see
That ancient cloak, Hypocrisy !

Whose are the characters that give
Such round reality?—that live
With such full pulse ?   Fair SOPHY yet
Sings *Bobbing Joan* at the spinet ;
We see AMELIA cooking still
That supper for the recreant WILL ;
We hear Squire WESTERN's headlong tones
Bawling 'Wut ha?—wut ha ?' to JONES.
Are they not present now to us,—
The Parson with his *Aeschylus?*
SLIPSLOP the frail, and NORTHERTON,
PARTRIDGE, and BATH, and HARRISON ?—
Are they not breathing, moving,—all
The motley, merry carnival
That FIELDING kept, in days agone ?

(213)

He was the first that dared to draw
Mankind the mixture that he saw ;
Not wholly good nor ill, but both,
With fine intricacies of growth.
He pulled the wraps of flesh apart,
And showed the working human heart ;
He scorned to drape the truthful nude
With smooth, decorous platitude !

He was too frank, may be ; and dared
Too boldly.   Those whose faults he bared,
Writhed in the ruthless grasp that brought
Into the light their secret thought.
Therefore the TARTUFFE-throng who say
' *Couvrez ce sein*,' and look that way,—
Therefore the Priests of Sentiment
Rose on him with their garments rent.
Therefore the gadfly swarm whose sting
Plies ever round some generous thing,
Buzzed of old bills and tavern-scores,
Old ' might-have-beens ' and ' heretofores ' ;—
Then, from that garbled record-list,
Made him his own Apologist.

And was he ?   Nay,—let who has known
Nor Youth nor Error, cast the stone !
If to have sense of Joy and Pain
Too keen,—to rise, to fall again,
To live too much,—be sin, why then,
This was no pattern among men.
But those who turn that later page,
The Journal of his middle-age,
Watch him serene in either fate,—
Philanthropist and Magistrate ;
Watch him as Husband, Father, Friend,
Faithful, and patient to the end ;

Grieving, as e'en the brave may grieve,
But for the loved ones he must leave :
These will admit—if any can—
That 'neath the green Estrella trees,
No artist merely, but a MAN,
Wrought on our noblest island-plan,
Sleeps with the alien Portuguese.

1883.

A POSTSCRIPT TO 'RETALIATION'

[*After the Fourth Edition of Doctor* GOLDSMITH's Retaliation *was printed, the Publisher received a supplementary Epitaph on the Wit and Punster* Caleb Whitefoord. *Though it is found appended to the later issues of the Poem, it has been suspected that* Whitefoord *wrote it himself. It may be that the following, which has recently come to light, is another forgery.*]

HERE JOHNSON is laid.   Have a care how you walk ;
If he stir in his sleep, in his sleep he will talk.
Ye gods ! how he talk'd !   What a torrent of sound,
His hearers invaded, encompass'd and—drown'd !
What a banquet of memory, fact, illustration,
In that innings-for-one that he call'd *conversation !*
Can't you hear his sonorous 'Why no, Sir !' and 'Stay, Sir !
Your premiss is wrong,' or 'You don't see your way, Sir !'
How he silenc'd a prig, or a slip-shod romancer !
How he pounc'd on a fool with a knock-me-down answer !

But peace to his slumbers !   Tho' rough in the rind,
The heart of the giant was gentle and kind :
What signifies now, if in bouts with a friend,
When his pistol miss'd fire, he would use the butt-end ?

Memorial Verses

If he trampled your flow'rs, like a bull in a garden,
What matter for that? he was sure to ask pardon;
And you felt on the whole, tho' he'd toss'd you and gor'd
    you,
It was something, at least, that he had not ignor'd you.
Yes! the outside was rugged. But test him within,
You found he had nought of the bear but the skin;
And for bottom and base to his *anfractuosity*,
A fund of fine feeling, good taste, generosity.
He was true to his conscience, his King, and his duty;
And he hated the *Whigs*, and he soften'd to Beauty.

Turn now to his Writings. I grant, in his tales,
That he made little fishes talk vastly like whales;
I grant that his language was rather emphatic,
Nay, even—to put the thing plainly—dogmatic;
But read him for Style,—and dismiss from your thoughts,
The crowd of compilers who copied his faults,—
Say, where is there English so full and so clear,
So weighty, so dignified, manly, sincere?
So strong in expression, conviction, persuasion?
So prompt to take colour from place and occasion?
So widely remov'd from the doubtful, the tentative;
So truly—and in the best sense—argumentative?
You may talk of your BURKES and your GIBBONS so clever,
But I hark back to him with a 'JOHNSON for ever!'
And I feel as I muse on his ponderous figure,
Tho' he's great in this age, in the next he'll grow bigger;
And still while . . . [*Cætera desunt.*]

   1896.

Memorial Verses

HENRY WADSWORTH LONGFELLOW

' Nec turpem senectam
Degere, nec cithara carentem.'—HOR. i. 31.

' NOT to be tuneless in old age ! '
Ah ! surely blest his pilgrimage,
   Who, in his Winter's snow,
Still sings with note as sweet and clear
As in the morning of the year
   When the first violets blow !

Blest !—but more blest, whom Summer's heat,
Whom Spring's impulsive stir and beat,
   Have taught no feverish lure ;
Whose Muse, benignant and serene,
Still keeps his Autumn chaplet green
   Because his verse is pure !

Lie calm, O white and laureate head !
Lie calm, O Dead, that art not dead,
   Since from the voiceless grave,
Thy voice shall speak to old and young
While song yet speaks an English tongue
   By Charles' or Thamis' wave !

1882.

Memorial Verses

CHARLES GEORGE GORDON

' RATHER be dead than praised,' he said,
That hero, like a hero dead,
In this slack-sinewed age endued
With more than antique fortitude !

' Rather be dead than praised !' Shall we,
Who loved thee, now that Death sets free
Thine eager soul, with word and line
Profane that empty house of thine ?

Nay,—let us hold, be mute.   Our pain
Will not be less that we refrain ;
And this our silence shall but be
A larger monument to thee.

1885.

VICTOR HUGO

HE set the trumpet to his lips, and lo !
The clash of waves, the roar of winds that blow,
The strife and stress of Nature's warring things,
Rose like a storm cloud, upon angry wings.

He set the reed pipe to his lips, and lo !
The wreck of landscape took a rosy glow,
And Life, and Love, and gladness that Love brings
Laughed in the music, like a child that sings.

Master of each, Arch-Master !   We that still
Wait in the verge and outskirt of the Hill,
Look upward lonely—lonely to the height
Where thou hast climbed, for ever, out of sight !

1885.

Memorial Verses

ALFRED, LORD TENNYSON

EMIGRAVIT, OCTOBER VI., MDCCCXCII

GRIEF there will be, and may,
When King Apollo's bay
Is cut midwise;
Grief that a song is stilled,
Grief for the unfulfilled
Singer that dies.

Not so we mourn thee now,
Not so we grieve that thou,
MASTER, art passed,
Since thou thy song didst raise,
Through the full round of days,
E'en to the last.

Grief there may be, and will,
When that the singer still
Sinks in the song;
When that the wingèd rhyme
Fails of the promised prime,
Ruined and wrong.

Not thus we mourn thee—we—
Not thus we grieve for thee,
MASTER and Friend;
Since, like a clearing flame,
Clearer thy pure song came
E'en to the end.

Nay—nor for thee we grieve
E'en as for those that leave
Life without name;
Lost as the stars that set,
Empty of men's regret,
Empty of fame.

Memorial Verses

Rather we count thee one
Who, when his race is run,
Layeth him down,
Calm—through all coming days,
Filled with a nation's praise,
Filled with renown.

1892.

FABLES OF LITERATURE
AND ART

THE POET AND THE CRITICS

If those who wield the Rod forget,
'Tis truly—*Quis custodiet?*

A certain Bard (as Bards will do)
Dressed up his Poems for Review.
His Type was plain, his Title clear;
His Frontispiece by FOURDRINIER.
Moreover, he had on the Back
A sort of sheepskin Zodiac;—
A Mask, a Harp, an Owl,—in fine,
A neat and 'classical' Design.
But the *in*-Side?—Well, good or bad,
The Inside was the best he had:
Much Memory,—more Imitation;—
Some Accidents of Inspiration;—
Some Essays in that finer Fashion
Where Fancy takes the place of Passion;—
And some (of course) more roughly wrought
To catch the Advocates of Thought.

In the less-crowded Age of ANNE,
Our Bard had been a favoured Man;
Fortune, more chary with the Sickle,
Had ranked him next to GARTH or TICKELL;—
He might have even dared to hope
A Line's Malignity from POPE!
But now, when Folks are hard to please,
And Poets are as thick as—Peas,
The Fates are not so prone to flatter,
Unless, indeed, a Friend . . . No Matter.

Fables of Literature and Art

The Book, then, had a minor Credit:
The Critics took, and doubtless read it.
Said A.—*These little Songs display*
No lyric Gift; but still a Ray,—
A Promise. They will do no Harm.
'Twas kindly, if not *very* warm.
Said B.—*The Author may, in Time,*
Acquire the Rudiments of Rhyme:
His Efforts now are scarcely Verse.
This, certainly, could not be worse.

Sorely discomfited, our Bard
Worked for another ten Years—hard.
Meanwhile the World, unmoved, went on;
New Stars shot up, shone out, were gone;
Before his second Volume came
His Critics had forgot his Name:
And who, forsooth, is bound to know
Each Laureate *in embryo!*
They tried and tested him, no less,—
The sworn Assayers of the Press.
Said A.—*The Author may, in Time* . . . .
Or much what B. had said of Rhyme.
Then B.—*These little Songs display* . . . .
And so forth, in the sense of A.
Over the Bard I throw a Veil.

There is no MORAL to this Tale.

1879.

THE TOYMAN

WITH Verse, is Form the first, or Sense?
Hereon men waste their Eloquence.

' Sense (cry the one Side), Sense, of course.
How can you lend your Theme its Force?
How can you be direct and clear,
Concise, and (best of all) sincere,
If you must pen your Strain sublime
In Bonds of Measure and of Rhyme?
Who ever heard true Grief relate
Its artless Woes in ' six ' and ' eight '?
Or felt his manly Bosom swell
Beneath a French-made *Villanelle?*
How can your *Mens divinior* sing
Within the Sonnet's scanty Ring,
Where she must chant her Orphic Tale
In just so many Lines, or fail? . . .'

' Form is the first (the Others bawl);
If not, why write in Verse at all?
Why not your throbbing Thoughts expose
(If Verse be such Restraint) in Prose?
For surely if you speak your Soul
Most freely where there 's least Control,
It follows you must speak it best
By Rhyme (or Reason) unreprest.
Blest Hour! be not delayed too long,
When Britain frees her Slaves of Song;
And barred no more by Lack of Skill,
The Mob may crowd *Parnassus* Hill! . . .'

Just at this Point—for you must know,
All this was but the To-and-fro
Of MATT and DICK, who played with Thought,
And lingered longer than they ought
(So pleasant 'tis to tap one's Box
And trifle round a Paradox!)—
There came—but I forgot to say,
'Twas in the Mall, the Month was May—
There came a Fellow where they sat,
His Elf-locks peeping through his Hat,
Who bore a Basket.   Straight his Load
He set upon the Ground, and showed
His newest Toy—a Card with Strings.
On this side was a Bird with Wings,
On that, a Cage.   You twirled, and lo!
The twain were one.

     Said MATT, 'E'en so
Here's the Solution in a Word:—
Form is the Cage and Sense the Bird.
The Poet twirls them in his Mind,
And wins the Trick with both combined.'

1889.

THE SUCCESSFUL AUTHOR

WHEN Fate presents us with the Bays,
We prize the Praiser, not the Praise.
We scarcely think our Fame eternal
If vouched for by the *Farthing Journal;*
But when the *Craftsman's* self has spoken
We take it for a certain Token.
This an Example best will show,
Derived from DENNIS DIDEROT.

A hackney Author, who'd essayed
All Hazards of the scribbling Trade,

The Successful Author

And failed to live by every Mode,
From *Persian Tale* to *Birthday Ode ;*
Embarked at last, thro' pure Starvation,
In Theologic Speculation.
'Tis commonly affirmed his Pen
Had been most orthodox till then ;
But oft, as SOCRATES has said,
The Stomach's stronger than the Head ;
And, for a sudden Change of Creed,
There is no *Jesuit* like Need.
Then, too, 'twas cheap ; he took it all,
By force of Habit, from the Gaul.
He showed (the Trick is nowise new)
That Nothing we believe is true ;
But chiefly that Mistake is rife
Touching the point of *After-life ;*
Here all were wrong from PLATO down :
His Price (in Boards) was Half-a-Crown.
The Thing created quite a Scare :—
He got a Letter from VOLTAIRE,
Naming him *Ami* and *Confrère ;*
Besides two most attractive Offers
Of Chaplaincies from noted Scoffers.
He fell forthwith his Head to lift,
To talk of ' I and Dr. Sw—FT ' ;
And brag, at Clubs, as one who spoke
On equal Terms with BOLINGBROKE.
But, at the last, a Missive came
That put the Copestone to his Fame.
The Boy who brought it would not wait :
It bore a *Covent-Garden* Date ;—
A woful Sheet with doubtful Ink,
And Air of *Bridewell* or the *Clink.*
It ran in this wise :—*Learned Sir !*
We, whose Subscriptions follow here,
Desire to state our Fellow-feeling

I 2

In this Religion you're revealing.
You make it plain that if so be
We 'scape on Earth from Tyburn Tree,
There's nothing left for us to fear
In this—or any other Sphere.
We offer you our Thanks; and hope
Your Honor, too, may cheat the Rope!
With that came all the Names beneath,
As BLUESKIN, JERRY CLINCH, MACHEATH,
BET CARELESS, and the Rest— a Score
Of Rogues and *Bona Robas* more.

This *Newgate Calendar* he read:
'Tis not recorded what he said.

1880.

THE DILETTANT

THE most oppressive Form of Cant
Is that of your Art-Dilettant :—
Or rather 'was.' The Race, I own,
To-day is, happily, unknown.

A Painter, now by Fame forgot,
Had painted—'tis no matter what;
Enough that he resolved to try
The Verdict of a critic Eye.
The Friend he sought made no Pretence
To more than candid Common-sense,
Nor held himself from Fault exempt.
He praised, it seems, the whole Attempt.
Then, pausing long, showed here and there
That Parts required a nicer Care,—
A closer Thought. The Artist heard,
Expostulated, chafed, demurred.

(228)

The Dilettant

Just then popped in a passing Beau,
Half Pertness, half Pulvilio ;—
One of those Mushroom Growths that spring
From *Grand Tours* and from Tailoring ;—
And dealing much in terms of Art
Picked up at Sale and auction Mart.

Straight to the Masterpiece he ran
With lifted Glass, and thus began,
Mumbling as fast as he could speak :—
' Sublime !—prodigious !—truly Greek !
That " Air of Head " is just divine ;
That contour GUIDO, every line ;
That Forearm, too, has quite the *Gusto*
Of the third Manner of ROBUSTO. . . .'
Then, with a Simper and a Cough,
He skipped a little farther off :—
' The middle Distance, too, is placed
Quite in the best Italian Taste ;
And Nothing could be more effective
Than the *Ordonnance* and Perspective . . .
You've sold it ?—No ?—Then take my word,
I shall speak of it to MY LORD.
What !—I insist.   Don't stir, I beg.
Adieu ! ' With that he made a Leg,
Offered on either Side his Box,—
So took his *Virtú* off to COCK's.

The Critic, with a Shrug, once more
Turned to the Canvas as before.
' Nay,'—said the Painter—' I allow
The Worst that you can tell me now.
'Tis plain my Art must go to School,
To win such Praises—from a FOOL !

1880.

Fables of Literature and Art

THE TWO PAINTERS

In Art some hold Themselves content
If they but compass what they meant;
Others prefer, their Purpose gained,
Still to find Something unattained—
Something whereto they vaguely grope
With no more Aid than that of Hope.
Which are the Wiser? Who shall say!
The prudent Follower of Gay
Declines to speak for either View,
But sets his Fable 'twixt the two.

Once—'twas in good Queen Anna's Time—
While yet in this benighted Clime
The Genius of the Arts (now known
On mouldy Pediments alone)
Protected all the Men of Mark,
Two Painters met Her in the Park.
Whether She wore the Robe of Air
Portrayed by Verrio and Laguerre;
Or, like Belinda, trod this Earth,
Equipped with Hoop of monstrous Girth,
And armed at every Point for Slaughter
With Essences and Orange-water,
I know not: but it seems that then,
After some talk of Brush and Pen,—
Some chat of Art both High and Low,
Of Van's 'Goose-Pie' and Kneller's ' *Mot*,'—
The Lady, as a Goddess should,
Bade Them ask of Her what They would.
'Then, Madam, my request,' says Brisk,
Giving his *Ramillie* a whisk,
' Is that your Majesty will crown
My humble Efforts with Renown.
Let me, I beg it—Thanks to You—

Be praised for Everything I do,
Whether I paint a Man of Note,
Or only plan a Petticoat.'
'Nay,' quoth the other, 'I confess'
(This One was plainer in his Dress,
And even poorly clad), 'for me,
I scorn Your Popularity.
Why should I care to catch at once
The Point of View of every Dunce?
Let me do well, indeed, but find
The Fancy first, the Work behind;
Nor wholly touch the thing I wanted . . .'
The goddess both Petitions granted.

Each in his Way, achieved Success;
But One grew Great. And which One? Guess.

1882.

THE CLAIMS OF THE MUSE

Too oft we hide our Frailties' Blame
Beneath some simple-sounding Name!
So Folks, who in gilt Coaches ride,
Will call Display but *Proper Pride ;*
So Spendthrifts, who their Acres lose,
Curse not their Folly but the *Jews ;*
So *Madam*, when her Roses faint,
Resorts to . . . anything but *Paint*.

An honest Uncle, who had plied
His Trade of Mercer in *Cheapside*,
Until his Name on *'Change* was found
Good for some Thirty Thousand Pound,
Was burdened with an Heir inclined
To thoughts of quite a different Kind.
His Nephew dreamed of Naught but Verse
From Morn to Night, and, what was worse,

He quitted all at length to follow
That 'sneaking, whey-faced god, APOLLO.'
In plainer Words, he ran up Bills
At *Child's*, at *Batson's*, and at *Will's;*
Discussed the Claims of rival Bards
At Midnight,—with a Pack of Cards;
Or made excuse for 't'other Bottle'
Over a point in ARISTOTLE.
This could not last, and like his Betters
He found, too soon, the *Cost* of Letters.
Back to his Uncle's House he flew,
Confessing that he'd not a *Sou.*
'Tis true, his Reasons, if sincere,
Were more poetical than clear:
'Alas!' he said, 'I name no Names:
The *Muse*, dear Sir, the *Muse* has claims.'
His Uncle, who, behind his Till,
Knew less of *Pindus* than *Snow-Hill*,
Looked grave, but thinking (as Men say)
That Youth but once can have its Day,
Equipped anew his *Pride* and *Hope*
To frisk it on *Parnassus* Slope.
In one short Month he sought the Door
More shorn and ragged than before.
This Time he showed but small Contrition,
And gloried in his mean Condition.
'The greatest of our Race,' he said,
'Through *Asian* Cities begged his Bread.
The *Muse*—the *Muse* delights to see
Not *Broadcloth* but *Philosophy!*
Who doubts of this her Honour shames,
But (as you know) she has her Claims. . . .'
'Friend,' quoth his Uncle then, 'I doubt
This scurvy Craft that you're about
Will lead your *philosophic* Feet
Either to *Bedlam* or the *Fleet.*

The Claims of the Muse

Still, as I would not have you lack,
Go get some *Broadcloth* to your Back,
And—if it please this precious *Muse*—
'Twere well to purchase decent Shoes.
Though harkye, Sir . . . .' The Youth was gone,
Before the good Man could go on.
And yet ere long again was seen
That Votary of *Hippocrene*.
As along *Cheap* his Way he took,
His Uncle spied him by a Brook,
Not such as *Nymphs Castalian* pour,—
'Twas but the Kennel, nothing more.
His Plight was plain by every Sign
Of Idiot Smile and Stains of Wine.
He strove to rise, and wagged his Head—
'The *Muse*, dear Sir, the *Muse*—' he said.
'*Muse!*' quoth the Other, in a Fury,
'The *Muse* shan't serve you, I assure ye.
She's just some wanton, idle *Jade*
That makes young Fools forget their Trade,—
Who should be whipped, if I'd my Will,
From *Charing Cross* to *Ludgate Hill*.
She's just. . . .' But he began to stutter,
So left Sir GRACELESS in the Gutter.

1880.

THE 'SQUIRE AT VAUXHALL

NOTHING so idle as to waste
This Life disputing upon *Taste*;
And most—let that sad Truth be written—
In this contentious Land of *Britain*,
Where each one holds 'it seems to me'
Equivalent to *Q. E. D.*,
And if you dare to doubt his Word
Proclaims you Blockhead and absurd.

And then, too often, the Debate
Is not 'twixt First and Second-rate,
Some narrow Issue, where a Touch
Of more or less can't matter much,
But, and this makes the Case so sad,
Betwixt undoubted Good and Bad.
Nay,—there are some so strangely wrought,—
So warped and twisted in their Thought,—
That, if the Fact be but confest,
They like the baser Thing the best.
Take Bottom, who for one, 'tis clear,
Possessed a ' reasonable Ear ' ;
He might have had at his Command
The Symphonies of *Fairy-Land ;*
Well, our immortal Shakespear owns
The Oaf preferred the ' Tongs and Bones ! '

'Squire Homespun from *Clod-Hall* rode down,
As the Phrase is—' to see the Town ' ;
(The Town, in those Days, mostly lay
Between the *Tavern* and the *Play.*)
Like all their Worships the J. P.'s,
He put up at the *Hercules ;*
Then sallied forth on Shanks his Mare,
Rather than jolt it in a Chair,—
A curst, new-fangled *Little-Ease,*
That knocks your Nose against your Knees.
For the good 'Squire was Country-bred,
And had strange Notions in his Head,
Which made him see in every Cur
The starveling Breed of *Hanover ;*
He classed your Kickshaws and *Ragoos*
With Popery and Wooden Shoes ;
Railed at all Foreign Tongues as Lingo,
And sighed o'er *Chaos* Wine for Stingo.

Hence, as he wandered to and fro,

The 'Squire at Vauxhall

Nothing could please him, high or low.
As *Savages* at *Ships of War*
He looked unawed on *Temple-Bar*;
Scarce could conceal his Discontent
With *Fish-Street* and the *Monument*;
And might (except at Feeding-Hour)
Have scorned the Lion in the *Tower*,
But that the Lion's Race was run,
And—for the Moment—there was none.

At length, blind Fate, that drives us all,
Brought him at Even to *Vauxhall*,
What Time the eager Matron jerks
Her slow Spouse to the *Water-Works*,
And the coy Spinster, half-afraid,
Consults the *Hermit* in the Shade.
Dazed with the Din and Crowd, the 'Squire
Sank in a Seat before the Choir.
The FAUSTINETTA, fair and showy,
Warbled an Air from *Arsinoë*,
Playing her Bosom and her Eyes
As Swans do when they agonize.
Alas! to some a Mug of Ale
Is better than an *Orphic Tale!*
The 'Squire grew dull, the 'Squire grew bored;
His chin dropt down; he slept; he snored.
Then, straying thro' the 'poppied Reign,'
He dreamed him at *Clod-Hall* again;
He heard once more the well-known Sounds,
The Crack of Whip, the Cry of Hounds.
He rubbed his Eyes, woke up, and lo!
A Change had come upon the Show.
Where late the Singer stood, a Fellow,
Clad in a Jockey's Coat of Yellow,
Was mimicking a Cock that crew.
Then came the Cry of Hounds anew,

Yoicks ! Stole Away ! and harking back ;
Then Ringwood leading up the Pack.
The 'Squire in Transport slapped his Knee
At this most hugeous Pleasantry.
The sawn Wood followed ; last of all
The Man brought something in a Shawl,—
Something that struggled, scraped, and squeaked
As Porkers do, whose tails are tweaked.
Our honest 'Squire could scarcely sit,
So excellent he thought the Wit.
But when *Sir Wag* drew off the Sheath
And showed there was no Pig beneath,
His pent-up Wonder, Pleasure, Awe,
Exploded in a long Guffaw :
And, to his dying Day, he'd swear
That Naught in Town the Bell could bear
From ' Jockey wi' the Yellow Coat
That had a Farm-Yard in his Throat ! '

Moral the First you may discover :
The 'Squire was like Titania's lover ;
He put a squeaking Pig before
The Harmony of Clayton's Score.

Moral the Second—not so clear ;
But still it shall be added here :
He praised the Thing he understood ;
'Twere well if every Critic would.

1884.

THE CLIMACTERIC

WHEN do the reasoning Powers decline?
The Ancients said at Forty-Nine.
At Forty-Nine behoves it then
To quit the Inkhorn and the Pen,
Since ARISTOTLE so decreed.
Premising thus, we now proceed.

In that thrice-favoured Northern Land,
Where most the Flowers of Thought expand,
And all things nebulous grow clear
Through Spectacles and Lager-Beer,
There lived, at *Dumpelsheim* the Lesser,
A certain High-Dutch Herr Professor.
Than GROTIUS more alert and quick,
More logical than BURGERSDYCK,
His Lectures both so much transcended,
That far and wide his Fame extended,
Proclaiming him to every clime
Within a Mile of *Dumpelsheim.*
But chief he taught, by Day and Night,
The Doctrine of the Stagirite,
Proving it fixed beyond Dispute,
In Ways that none could well refute ;
For if by Chance 'twas urged that Men
O'er-stepped the Limit now and then,
He'd show unanswerably still
Either that all they did was ' Nil,'
Or else 'twas marked by Indication
Of grievous mental Degradation :
Nay—he could even trace, they say,
That Degradation to a Day.

(237)

The Years rolled on, and as they flew,
More famed the Herr Professor grew,
His ' *Locus* of the Pineal Gland '
(A Masterpiece he long had planned)
Had reached the End of Book Eleven,
And he was nearing Forty-Seven.
Admirers had not long to wait ;
The last Book came at Forty-Eight,
And should have been the Heart and Soul—
The Crown and Summit—of the whole.
But now the oddest Thing ensued ;
'Twas so insufferably crude,
So feeble and so poor, 'twas plain
The Writer's Mind was on the wane.
Nothing could possibly be said ;
E'en Friendship's self must hang the head,
While jealous Rivals, scarce so civil,
Denounced it openly as ' Drivel.'
Never was such Collapse.   In brief,
The poor Professor died of Grief.

With fitting mortuary Rhyme
They buried him at *Dumpelsheim*,
And as they sorrowing set about
A ' Short Memoir,' the Truth came out.
He had been older than he knew.
The Parish Clerk had put a ' 2 '
In place of ' Nought,' and made his Date
Of Birth a Brace of Years too late.
When he had written Book the Last,
His true Climacteric had past !

MORAL.—To estimate your Worth,
Be certain as to date of Birth.

1889.

TALES IN RHYME

THE VIRGIN WITH THE BELLS

MUCH strange is true.   And yet so much
Dan Time thereto of doubtful lays
He blurs them both beneath his touch :—

In this our tale his part he plays.
At Florence, so the legend tells,
There stood a church that men would praise

(Even where Art the most excels)
For works of price ; but chief for one
They called the ‘ Virgin with the Bells.’

Gracious she was, and featly done,
With crown of gold about the hair,
And robe of blue with stars thereon,

And sceptre in her hand did bear ;
And o’er her, in an almond tree,
Three little golden bells there were,

Writ with Faith, Hope, and Charity.
None knew from whence she came of old,
Nor whose the sculptor’s name should be

Of great or small.   But this they told :—
That once from out the blaze of square,
And bickering folk that bought and sold,

More moved no doubt of heat than prayer,
Came to the church an Umbrian,
Lord of much gold and champaign fair,

But, for all this, a hard, haught man,
To whom the priests, in humbleness,
At once to beg for alms began,

Praying him grant of his excess
Such as for poor men's bread might pay,
Or give their saint a gala-dress.

Thereat with scorn he answered—'Nay,
Most Reverend!   Far too well ye know,
By guile and wile, the fox's way

'To swell the Church's overflow.
But ere from me the least carline
Ye win, this summer's sky shall snow;

'Or, likelier still, your doll's-eyed queen
Shall ring her bells . . but not of craft,
By Bacchus! ye are none too lean

'For fasting folk!'   With that he laughed,
And so, across the porphyry floor,
His hand upon his dagger-haft,

Strode, and of these was seen no more.
Nor, of a truth, much marvelled they
At those his words, since gear and store

Oft dower shrunk souls.   But, on a day,
While yet again throughout the square,
The buyers in their noisy way

Chaffered around the basket ware,
It chanced (I but the tale reveal,
Nor true nor false therein declare)—

It chanced that when the priest would kneel
Before the taper's flickering flame,
Sudden a little tremulous peal

The Virgin with the Bells

From out the Virgin's altar came.
And they that heard must fain recall
The Umbrian, and the words of shame

Spoke in his pride, and therewithal
Came news how, at that very date
And hour of time, was fixed his fall,

Who, of the Duke, was banned the State,
And all his goods, and lands as well,
To Holy Church were confiscate.

Such is the tale the Frati tell.

1881.

A TALE OF POLYPHEME

'THERE's nothing new'—Not that I go so far
    As he who also said 'There's nothing true,'
Since, on the contrary, I hold there are
    Surviving still a verity or two ;
But, as to novelty, in my conviction,
There's nothing new,—especially in fiction.

Hence, at the outset, I make no apology,
    If this *my* story is as old as Time,
Being, indeed, that idyll of mythology,—
    The Cyclops' love,—which, somewhat varied, I'm
To tell once more, the adverse Muse permitting,
In easy rhyme, and phrases neatly fitting.

'Once on a time'—there's nothing new, I said—
    It may be fifty years ago or more,
Beside a lonely posting-road that led
    Seaward from Town, there used to stand of yore,
With low-built bar and old bow-window shady,
An ancient Inn, the 'Dragon and the Lady.'

Tales in Rhyme

Say that by chance, wayfaring Reader mine,
  You cast a shoe, and at this dusty Dragon,
Where beast and man were equal on the sign,
  Inquired at once for Blacksmith and for flagon :
The landlord showed you, while you drank your hops,
A road-side break beyond the straggling shops.

And so directed, thereupon you led
  Your halting roadster to a kind of pass ;
This you descended with a crumbling tread,
  And found the sea beneath you like a glass ;
And soon, beside a building partly walled—
Half hut, half cave—you raised your voice and called.

Then a dog growled ; and straightway there began
  Tumult within—for, bleating with affright,
A goat burst out, escaping from the can ;
  And, following close, slowly rose into sight—
Blind of one eye, and black with toil and tan—
An uncouth, limping, heavy-shouldered man.

Part smith, part seaman, and part shepherd too :
  You scarce knew which, as, pausing with the pail
Half-filled with goat's milk, silently he drew
  An anvil forth, and reaching shoe and nail,
Bared a red forearm, bringing into view
Anchors and hearts in shadowy tattoo.

And then he lit his fire . . . . But I dispense
  Henceforth with you, my Reader, and your horse,
As being but a colourable pretence
  To bring an awkward hero in perforce ;
Since this our smith, for reasons never known,
To most society preferred his own.

A Tale of Polypheme

Women declared that he'd an 'Evil Eye,'—
  This in a sense was true—he had but one ;
Men, on the other hand, alleged him shy :
  We sometimes say so of the friends we shun ;
But, wrong or right, suffices to affirm it—
The Cyclops lived a veritable hermit,—

Dwelling below the cliff, beside the sea,
  Caved like an ancient British Troglodyte,
Milking his goat at eve, and it may be,
  Spearing the fish along the flats at night,
Until, at last, one April evening mild,
Came to the Inn a Lady and a Child.

The Lady was a nullity ; the Child
  One of those bright bewitching little creatures,
Who, if she once but shyly looked and smiled,
  Would soften out the ruggedest of features ;
Fragile and slight,—a very fay for size,—
With pale town-cheeks, and 'clear germander eyes.'

Nurses, no doubt, might name her 'somewhat wild' ;
  And pedants, possibly, pronounce her 'slow' ;
Or corset-makers add, that for a child,
  She needed 'cultivation' ;—all I know
Is that whene'er she spoke, or laughed, or romped, you
Felt in each act the beauty of impromptu.

The Lady was a nullity—a pale,
  Nerveless and pulseless quasi-invalid,
Who, lest the ozone should in aught avail,
  Remained religiously indoors to read ;
So that, in wandering at her will, the Child
Did, in reality, run 'somewhat wild.'

Tales in Rhyme

At first but peering at the sanded floor
   And great shark jaw-bone in the cosy bar ;
Then watching idly from the dusky door,
   The noisy advent of a coach or car ;
.Then stealing out to wonder at the fate
Of blistered Ajax by the garden gate,—

Some old ship's figure-head—until at last,
   Straying with each excursion more and more,
She reached the limits of the road, and passed,
   Plucking the pansies, downward to the shore,
And so, as you, respected Reader, showed,
Came to the smith's ' desirable abode.'

There by the cave the occupant she found,
   Weaving a crate ; and, with a gladsome cry,
The dog frisked out, although the Cyclops frowned
   With all the terrors of his single eye ;
Then from a mound came running, too, the goat,
Uttering her plaintive, desultory note.

The Child stood wondering at the silent man,
   Doubtful to go or stay, when presently
She felt a plucking, for the goat began
   To crop the trail of twining briony
She held behind her ; so that, laughing, she
Turned her light steps, retreating, to the sea.

But the goat followed her on eager feet,
   And therewithal an air so grave and mild,
Coupled with such a deprecatory bleat
   Of injured confidence, that soon the Child
Filled the lone shore with louder merriment,
And e'en the Cyclops' heavy brow unbent.

A Tale of Polypheme

Thus grew acquaintanceship between the pair
　　The girl and goat;—for thenceforth, day by day
The Child would bring her four-foot friend such fare
　　As might be gathered on the downward way —
Foxglove or broom, and 'yellow cytisus,'
Dear to all goats since Greek Theocritus.

But, for the Cyclops, that misogynist
　　Having, by stress of circumstances, smiled,
Felt it at least incumbent to resist
　　Further encroachment, and as one beguiled
By adverse fortune, with the half-door shut,
Dwelt in the dim seclusion of his hut.

And yet not less from thence he still must see
　　That daily coming, and must hear the goat
Bleating her welcome; then, towards the sea,
　　The happy voices of the playmates float;
Until at last, enduring it no more,
He took his wonted station by the door.

Here was, of course, a pitiful surrender;
　　For soon the Child, on whom the Evil Eye
Seemed to exert an influence but slender,
　　Would run to question him, till, by and by,
His moody humour like a cloud dispersing,
He found himself uneasily conversing.

That was a sow's-ear, that an egg of skate,
　　And this an agate rounded by the wave.
Then came inquiries still more intimate
　　About himself, the anvil, and the cave;
And then, at last, the Child, without alarm,
Would even spell the letters on his arm.

'G—a—l—*Galatea.*'   So there grew
   On his part, like some half-remembered tale,
The new-found memory of an icebound crew,
   And vague garrulities of spouting whale,—
Of sea-cow basking upon berg and floe,
And Polar light, and stunted Eskimo.

Till, in his heart, which hitherto had been
   Locked as those frozen barriers of the North,
There came once more the season of the green,—
   The tender bud-time and the putting forth ;
So that the man, before the new sensation,
Felt for the child a kind of adoration ;—

Rising by night, to search for shell and flower,
   To lay in places where she found them first ;
Hoarding his cherished goat's milk for the hour
   When those young lips might feel the summer's thirst ;
Holding himself for all devotion paid
By that clear laughter of the little maid.

Dwelling, alas ! in that fond Paradise
   Where no to-morrow quivers in suspense,—
Where scarce the changes of the sky suffice
   To break the soft forgetfulness of sense,—
Where dreams become realities ; and where
I willingly would leave him—did I dare.

Yet for a little space it still endured,
   Until, upon a day when least of all
The softened Cyclops, by his hopes assured,
   Dreamed the inevitable blow could fall,
Came the stern moment that should all destroy
Bringing a pert young cockerel of a Boy.

A Tale of Polypheme

Middy, I think—he'd ' *Acis* ' on his box :—
   A black-eyed, sun-burnt, mischief-making imp,
Pet of the mess,—a Puck with curling locks,
   Who straightway travestied the Cyclops' limp,
And marvelled how his cousin so could care
For such a ' one-eyed, melancholy Bear.'

Thus there was war at once ; not overt yet,
   For still the Child, unwilling, would not break
The new acquaintanceship, nor quite forget
   The pleasant past ; while, for his treasure's sake,
The boding smith with clumsy efforts tried
To win the laughing scorner to his side.

There are some sights pathetic ; none I know
   More sad than this : to watch a slow-wrought mind
Humbling itself, for love, to come and go
   Before some petty tyrant of its kind ;
Saddest, ah !—saddest far,—when it can do
Naught to advance the end it has in view.

This was at least the Cyclops' case, until,
   Whether the boy beguiled the Child away,
Or whether that limp Matron on the Hill
   Woke from her novel-reading trance, one day
He waited long and wearily in vain,—
But, from that hour, they never came again.

Yet still he waited, hoping—wondering if
   They still might come, or dreaming that he heard
The sound of far-off voices on the cliff,
   Or starting strangely when the she-goat stirred ;
But nothing broke the silence of the shore,
And, from that hour, the Child returned no more.

Therefore our Cyclops sorrowed,—not as one
  Who can command the gamut of despair;
But as a man who feels his days are done,
  So dead they seem,—so desolately bare;
For, though he'd lived a hermit, 'twas but only
Now he discovered that his life was lonely.

The very sea seemed altered, and the shore;
  The very voices of the air were dumb;
Time was an emptiness that o'er and o'er
  Ticked with the dull pulsation 'Will she come?'
So that he sat 'consuming in a dream,'
Much like his old forerunner Polypheme.

Until there came the question, 'Is she gone?'
  With such sad sick persistence that at last,
Urged by the hungry thought which drove him on,
  Along the steep declivity he passed,
And by the summit panting stood, and still,
Just as the horn was sounding on the hill.

Then, in a dream, beside the 'Dragon' door,
  The smith saw travellers standing in the sun;
Then came the horn again, and three or four
  Looked idly at him from the roof, but One,—
A Child within,—suffused with sudden shame,
Thrust forth a hand, and called to him by name.

Thus the coach vanished from his sight, but he
  Limped back with bitter pleasure in his pain;
He was not all forgotten—could it be?
  And yet the knowledge made the memory vain;
And then—he felt a pressure in his throat,
So, for that night, forgot to milk his goat.

What then might come of silent misery,
   What new resolvings then might intervene,
I know not.   Only, with the morning sky,
   The goat stood tethered on the 'Dragon' green,
And those who, wondering, questioned thereupon,
Found the hut empty,—for the man was gone.

1876.

A STORY FROM A DICTIONARY

> *'Sic visum Veneri : cui placet impares*
> *Formas atque animos sub juga aënea*
>   *Saevo mittere cum joco.'*—HOR. i. 33.

'LOVE mocks us all'—as Horace said of old :
   From sheer perversity, that arch-offender
Still yokes unequally the hot and cold,
   The short and tall, the hardened and the tender ;
He bids a Socrates espouse a scold,
   And makes a Hercules forget his gender :—
Sic visum Veneri !   Lest samples fail,
I add a fresh one from the page of BAYLE.

It was in Athens that the thing occurred,
   In the last days of Alexander's rule,
While yet in Grove or Portico was heard
   The studious murmur of its learned school ;—
Nay, 'tis one favoured of Minerva's bird
   Who plays therein the hero (or the fool)
With a Megarian, who must then have been
A maid, and beautiful, and just eighteen.

I shan't describe her.   Beauty is the same
   In Anno Domini as erst B.C. ;
The type is still that witching One who came,
   Between the furrows, from the bitter sea ;

Tis but to shift accessories and frame,
    And this our heroine in a trice would be,
Save that she wore a *peplum* and a *chiton*,
Like any modern on the beach at Brighton.

Stay, I forget! Of course the sequel shows
    She had some qualities of disposition,
To which, in general, her sex are foes,—
    As strange proclivities to erudition,
And lore unfeminine, reserved for those
    Who nowadays descant on 'Woman's Mission,'
Or tread instead that 'primrose path' to knowledge,
That milder Academe—the Girton College.

The truth is, she admired . . . a learned man.
    There were no curates in that sunny Greece,
For whom the mind emotional could plan
    Fine-art habiliments in gold and fleece;
(This was ere chasuble or cope began
    To shake the centres of domestic peace;)
So that 'admiring,' such as maids give way to,
Turned to the ranks of Zeno and of Plato.

The 'object' here was mildly prepossessing,
    At least, regarded in a woman's sense;
His *forte*, it seems, lay chiefly in expressing
    Disputed fact in Attic eloquence;
His ways were primitive; and as to dressing,
    His toilet was a negative pretence;
He kept, besides, the *régime* of the Stoic;
In short, was not, by any means, 'heroic.'

Sic visum Veneri !—The thing is clear.
    Her friends were furious, her lovers nettled;
'Twas much as though the Lady Vere de Vere
    On some hedge-schoolmaster her heart had settled.

A Story from a Dictionary

Unheard! Intolerable!—a lumbering steer
　　To plod the upland with a mare high-mettled!—
They would, no doubt, with far more pleasure hand her
To curled Euphorion or Anaximander.

And so they used due discipline, of course,
　　To lead to reason this most erring daughter,
Proceeding even to extremes of force,—
　　Confinement (solitary), and bread and water;
Then, having lectured her till they were hoarse,
　　Finding that this to no submission brought her
At last, (unwisely [1]) to the man they sent,
That he might combat her by argument,

Being, they fancied, but a bloodless thing;
　　Or else too well forewarned of that commotion
Which poets feign inseparable from Spring
　　To suffer danger from a school-girl notion;
Also they hoped that she might find her king,
　　On close inspection, clumsy and Bœotian:—
This was acute enough, and yet, between us,
I think they thought too little about Venus.

Something, I know, of this sort is related
　　In Garrick's life.   However, the man came,
And taking first his mission's end as stated,
　　Began at once her sentiments to tame,
Working discreetly to the point debated
　　By steps rhetorical I spare to name;
In other words,—he broke the matter gently.
Meanwhile, the lady looked at him intently,

---

[1] 'Unwisely,' surely.   But 'tis well to mention
That this particular is *not* invention.

Wistfully, sadly,—and it put him out,
  Although he went on steadily, but faster.
There were some maladies he'd read about
  Which seemed, at first, most difficult to master ;
They looked intractable at times, no doubt,
  But all they needed was a little plaster ;
This was a thing physicians long had pondered,
Considered, weighed . . . and then . . . and then he wandered.

('Tis so embarrassing to have before you
  A silent auditor, with candid eyes ;
With lips that speak no sentence to restore you,
  And aspect, generally, of pained surprise ;
Then, if we add that all these things adore you,
  'Tis really difficult to syllogize :—
Of course it mattered not to him a feather,
But still he wished . . . they'd not been left together.)

' Of one,' he said, continuing, ' of these
  The young especially should be suspicious ;
Seeing no ailment in Hippocrates
  Could be at once so tedious and capricious ;
No seeming apple of Hesperides
  More fatal, deadlier, and more delicious—
Pernicious,—he should say,—for all its seeming . . .'
It seemed to him he simply was blaspheming.

If she had only turned askance, or uttered
  Word in reply, or trifled with her brooch,
Or sighed, or cried, grown petulant, or fluttered,
  He might (in metaphor) have ' called his coach ' ;
Yet still, while patiently he hemmed and stuttered,
  She wore her look of wondering reproach ;
(And those who read the ' Shakespeare of Romances '
Know of what stuff a girl's ' dynamic glance ' is.)

A Story from a Dictionary

' But there was still a cure, the wise insisted,
  In Love,—or rather, in Philosophy.
Philosophy—no, Love—at best existed
  But as an ill for that to remedy :
There was no knot so intricately twisted,
  There was no riddle but at last should be
By Love—he meant Philosophy—resolved . . .'
The truth is, he was getting quite involved.

O sovran Love ! how far thy power surpasses
  Aught that is taught of Logic or the Schools !
Here was a man, ' far seen ' in all the classes,
  Strengthened of precept, fortified of rules,
Mute as the least articulate of asses ;
  Nay, at an age when every passion cools,
Conscious of nothing but a sudden yearning
Stronger by far than any force of learning !

Therefore he changed his tone, flung down his wallet,
  Described his lot, how pitiable and poor ;
The hut of mud,—the miserable pallet,—
  The alms solicited from door to door ;
The scanty fare of bitter bread and sallet,—
  Could she this shame,—this poverty endure ?
I scarcely think he knew what he was doing,
But that last line had quite a touch of wooing.

And so she answered him,—those early Greeks
  Took little care to keep concealment preying
At any length upon their damask cheeks,—
  She answered him by very simply saying,
She could and would :—and said it as one speaks
  Who takes no course without much careful weighing. . . .
Was this, perchance, the answer that he hoped ?
It might, or might not be.   But they eloped,

Sought the free pine-wood and the larger air,—
   The leafy sanctuaries, remote and inner,
Where the great heart of nature, beating bare,
   Receives benignantly both saint and sinner ;—
Leaving propriety to gasp and stare,
   And shake its head, like Burleigh, after dinner,
From pure incompetence to mar or mend them :
They fled and wed ;—though, mind, I don't defend them.

I don't defend them. 'Twas a serious act,
   No doubt too much determined by the senses ;
(Alas ! when these affinities attract,
   We lose the future in the present tenses !)
Besides, the least establishment 's a fact
   Involving nice adjustment of expenses ;
Moreover, too, reflection should reveal
That not remote contingent—*la famille*.

Yet these, maybe, were happy in their lot.
   Milton has said (and surely Milton knows)
That, after all, philosophy is 'not,—
   Not harsh and crabbed, as dull fools suppose';
And some, no doubt, for Love's sake have forgot
   Much that is needful in this world of prose :—
Perchance 'twas so with these. But who shall say ?
Time has long since swept them and theirs away.

   1880.

THE WATER-CURE

A TALE: IN THE MANNER OF PRIOR

'—*portentaque Thessala rides?*'—HOR.
'—*Thessalian portents do you flout?*'

CARDENIO'S fortunes ne'er miscarried
Until the day CARDENIO married.
What then? the Nymph no doubt was young?
She was: but yet—she had a tongue!
Most women have, you seem to say.
I grant it—in a different way.

'Twas not that organ half-divine,
With which, Dear Friend, your spouse or mine,
What time we seek our nightly pillows,
Rebukes our easy peccadilloes:
'Twas not so tuneful, so composing;
'Twas louder and less often dozing;
At *Ombre, Basset, Loo, Quadrille,*
You heard it resonant and shrill;
You heard it rising, rising yet
Beyond SELINDA'S parroquet;
You heard it rival and outdo
The chair-men and the link-boy too;
In short, wherever lungs perform,
Like MARLBOROUGH, it rode the storm.

So uncontrolled it came to be
CARDENIO feared his *chère amie*
(Like ECHO by *Cephissus* shore)
Would turn to voice and nothing more.

K (257)

Tales in Rhyme

That ('tis conceded) must be cured
Which can't by practice be endured.
CARDENIO, though he loved the maid,
Grew daily more and more afraid;
And since advice could not prevail
(Reproof but seemed to fan the gale),
A prudent man, he cast about
To find some fitting nostrum out.
What need to say that priceless drug
Had not in any mine been dug?
What need to say no skilful leech
Could check that plethora of speech?
Suffice it, that one lucky day
CARDENIO tried—another way.

A Hermit (there were hermits then;
The most accessible of men!)
Near *Vauxhall's* sacred shade resided;
In him, at length, our friend confided.
(Simples, for show, he used to sell;
But cast *Nativities* as well.)
Consulted, he looked wondrous wise;
Then undertook the enterprise.

What that might be, the Muse must spare:
To tell the truth, she was not there.
She scorns to patch what she ignores
With *Similes* and *Metaphors;*
And so, in short, to change the scene,
She slips a fortnight in between.

Behold our pair then (quite by chance!)
In *Vauxhall's* garden of romance,—
That paradise of nymphs and grottoes,
Of fans, and fiddles, and ridottoes!

The Water-Cure

What wonder if, the lamps reviewed,
The song encored, the maze pursued,
No further feat could seem more pat
Than seek the Hermit after that?
Who then more keen her fate to see
Than this, the new LEUCONOË,
On fire to learn the lore forbidden
In Babylonian numbers hidden?
Forthwith they took the darkling road
To ALBUMAZAR his abode.

   Arriving, they beheld the sage
Intent on hieroglyphic page,
In high *Armenian* cap arrayed,
And girt with engines of his trade;
(As *Skeletons*, and *Spheres*, and *Cubes*;
As *Amulets* and *Optic tubes*;)
With dusky depths behind revealing
Strange shapes that dangled from the ceiling;
While more to palsy the beholder
A Black Cat sat upon his shoulder.

   The Hermit eyed the Lady o'er
As one whose face he'd seen before;
And then, with agitated looks,
He fell to fumbling at his books.

   CARDENIO felt his spouse was frightened,
Her grasp upon his arm had tightened;
Judge then her horror and her dread
When 'Vox Stellarum' shook his head;
Then darkly spake in phrase forlorn
Of *Taurus* and of *Capricorn;*
Of stars averse, and stars ascendant,
And stars entirely independent;

In fact, it seemed that all the Heavens
Were set at sixes and at sevens,
Portending, in her case, some fate
Too fearful to prognosticate.

Meanwhile the Dame was well-nigh dead.
'But is there naught,' CARDENIO said,
'No sign or token, Sage, to show
From whence, or what, this dismal woe?'

The Sage, with circle and with plane,
Betook him to his charts again.
'It vaguely seems to threaten Speech:
No more (he said) the signs can teach.'

But still CARDENIO tried once more:
'Is there no potion in your store,
No charm by *Chaldee* mage concerted
By which this doom can be averted?'

The Sage, with motion doubly mystic,
Resumed his juggling cabalistic.
The aspects here again were various;
But seemed to indicate *Aquarius*.
Thereat portentously he frowned;
Then frowned again, then smiled;—'twas found!
But 'twas too simple to be tried.
'What is it, then?' at once they cried.

'Whene'er by chance you feel incited
To speak at length, or uninvited;
Whene'er you feel your tones grow shrill
(At times, we know, the softest will!),
This word oracular, my Daughter,
Bids you to fill your mouth with water:
Further, to hold it firm and fast,
Until the danger be o'erpast.'

The Water-Cure

The Dame, by this in part relieved,
The prospect of escape perceived,
Rebelled a little at the diet.
CARDENIO said discreetly, 'Try it,
Try it, my Own.   You have no choice,
What if you lose your charming voice!'
She tried, it seems.   And whether then
Some god stepped in, benign to men;
Or Modesty, too long outlawed,
Contrived to aid the pious fraud,
I know not:—but from that same day
She talked in quite a different way.

1879.

THE NOBLE PATRON

'Ce sont les amours
Qui font les beaux jours.'

WHAT is a *Patron?*   JOHNSON knew,
And well that lifelike portrait drew.
He is a Patron who looks down
With careless eye on men who drown;
But if they chance to reach the land,
Encumbers them with helping hand.
Ah! happy we whose artless rhyme
No longer now must creep to climb!
Ah! happy we of later days,
Who 'scape those *Caudine Forks* of praise!
Whose votive page may dare commend
A Brother, or a private Friend!
Not so it fared with scribbling man,
As POPE says, 'under My Queen ANNE.'

(261)

Tales in Rhyme

DICK DOVECOT (this was long, be sure,
Ere he attained his *Wiltshire* cure,
And settled down, like humbler folks,
To cowslip wine and country jokes)
Once hoped—as who will not?—for fame,
And dreamed of honours and a Name.
A fresh-cheeked lad, he came to Town
In homespun hose and russet brown,
But armed at point with every view
Enforced in RAPIN and BOSSU,
Besides a stout portfolio ripe
For LINTOT'S or for TONSON'S type.
He went the rounds, saw all the sights,
Dropped in at *Will's* and *Tom's* o' nights;
Heard BURNET preach, saw BICKNELL dance,
E'en gained from ADDISON a glance;
Nay, once, to make his bliss complete,
He supped with STEELE in *Bury Street*.
('Tis true the feast was half by stealth:
PRUE was in bed: they drank her health.)

By this his purse was running low,
And he must either print or go.
He went to TONSON.   TONSON said—
Well!   TONSON hummed and shook his head;
Deplored the times; abused the Town;
But thought—at length—it might go down;
With aid, of course, of *Elzevir*,
And *Prologue* to a Prince, or Peer.
Dick winced at this, for adulation
Was scarce that candid youth's vocation:
Nor did he deem his rustic lays
Required a *Coronet* for *Bays*.
But there—the choice was that, or none.
The lord was found; the thing was done.

(262)

The Noble Patron

With HORACE and with TOOKE'S *Pantheon*,
He penned his tributary pæan;
Dispatched his gift, nor waited long
The meed of his ingenuous song.

Ere two days passed, a hackney chair
Brought a pert spark with languid air,
A lace cravat about his throat,—
Brocaded gown,—*en papillotes*,
('My Lord himself,' quoth DICK, 'at least!'
But no, 'twas that 'inferior priest,'
His Lordship's man.)   He held a card:
My Lord (it said) would see the Bard.

The day arrived; Dick went, was shown
Into an ante-room, alone—
A great gilt room with mirrored door,
Festoons of flowers and marble floor,
Whose lavish splendours made him look
More shabby than a sheepskin book.
(His own book—by the way—he spied
On a far table, toss'd aside.)

DICK waited, as they only wait
Who haunt the chambers of the Great.
He heard the chairmen come and go;
He heard the Porter yawn below;
Beyond him, in the Grand Saloon,
He heard the silver stroke of noon,
And thought how at this very time
The old church clock at home would chime.
Dear heart, how plain he saw it all!
The lich-gate and the crumbling wall,
The stream, the pathway to the wood,
The bridge where they so oft had stood.
Then, in a trice, both church and clock
Vanished before . . . a shuttlecock.

A shuttlecock ! And following slow
The zigzag of its to-and-fro,
And so intent upon its flight
She neither looked to left nor right,
Came a tall girl with floating hair,
Light as a wood-nymph, and as fair.

O Dea certé !—thought poor DICK,
And thereupon his memories quick
Ran back to her who flung the ball
In HOMER'S page, and next to all
The dancing maids that bards have sung,
Lastly to One at home, as young,
As fresh, as light of foot, and glad,
Who, when he went, had seemed so sad.
O Dea certé ! (Still, he stirred
Nor hand nor foot, nor uttered word.)

Meanwhile the shuttlecock in air
Went darting gaily here and there ;
Now crossed a mirror's face, and next
Shot up amidst the sprawled, perplexed
Olympus overhead.   At last,
Jerked sidelong by a random cast,
The striker missed it, and it fell
Plump on the book DICK knew so well.

(If he had thought to speak or bow,
Judge if he moved a muscle now !)
The player paused, bent down to look,
Lifted a cover of the book ;
Poohed at the Prologue, passed it o'er,
Went forward for a page or more
(*Asem and Asa:* DICK could trace
Almost the passage and the place) ;
Then for a moment with bent head
Rested upon her hand and read.

The Noble Patron

(DICK thought once more how Cousin CIS
Used when she read to lean like this ;—
' Used when she *read*,'—why, CIS could *say*
All he had written,—any day !)

Sudden was heard a hurrying tread ;
The great doors creaked.   The reader fled.
Forth came a crowd with muffled laughter,
A waft of Bergamot, and after,
With wine-bag cheeks and vacant face,
A portly shape in stars and lace—
My Lord himself in all his pride,
His Chaplain smirking at his side.

DICK bowed and smiled.   The Great Man stared,
With look half puzzled and half scared ;
Then seemed to recollect, turned round,
And mumbled some imperfect sound :
A moment more, his coach of state
Dipped on its springs beneath his weight ;
And DICK, who followed at his heels,
Heard but the din of rolling wheels.

Away, too, all his dreams had rolled ;
And yet they left him half consoled :
Fame, after all, he thought, might wait.
Would CIS ? Suppose he were too late !
Ten months he'd lost in Town—an age !

Next day he took the *Wiltshire* Stage.

1889.

VERS DE SOCIÉTÉ

'Apollinea bellum puerile pharetra.'

A CITY FLOWER

' *Il y a des fleurs animées.*'—POLITE COLLOQUIALISM.

To and fro in the City I go,
Tired of the ceaseless ebb and flow,
　　Sick of the crowded mart ;
Tired of the din and rattle of wheels,
Sick of the dust as one who feels
　　The dust is over his heart.

And again and again, as the sunlight wanes,
I think of the lights in the leafy lanes,
　　With the bits of blue between ;
And when about Rimmel's the perfumes play,
I smell no vapours of ' Ess Bouquet,'
　　But violets hid in the green ;
And I love—how I love—the plants that fill
The pots on my dust-dry window-sill,—
　　A sensitive sickly crop,—
But a flower that charms me more, I think,
Than cowslip, or crocus, or rose, or pink,
　　Blooms—in a milliner's shop.

Hazel eyes that wickedly peep,
Flash, abash, and suddenly sleep
　　Under the lids drawn in ;
Ripple of hair that rioteth out,
Mouth with a half-born smile and a pout,
　　And a baby breadth of chin ;
Hands that light as the lighting bird,
On the bloom-bent bough, and the bough is stirred
　　With a delicate ecstasy ;

Vers de Société

Fingers tipped with a roseate flush,
Flicking and flirting a feathery brush
    Over the papery bonnetry ;—
Till the gauzy rose begins to glow,
And the gauzy hyacinths break and blow,
    And the dusty grape grows red ;
And the flaunting grasses seem to say,
' Do we look like ornaments—tell us, we pray—
    Fit for a lady's head ? '
And the butterfly wakes to a wiry life,
Like an elderly gentleman taking a wife,
    Knowing he must be gay,
And all the bonnets nid-noddle about,
Like chattering chaperons set at a rout,
    Quarrelling over their play.

How can I otherwise choose than look
At the beautiful face like a beautiful book,
    And learn a tiny part ?
So I feel somehow that every day
Some flake of the dust is brushed away
    That had settled over my heart.

1864.

INCOGNITA

JUST for a space that I met her—
    Just for a day in the train !
It began when she feared it would wet her,
    That tiniest spurtle of rain :
So we tucked a great rug in the sashes,
    And carefully padded the pane ;
And I sorrow in sackcloth and ashes,
    Longing to do it again !

Incognita

Then it grew when she begged me to reach her
 A dressing-case under the seat;
She was ‘really so tiny a creature,
 That she needed a stool for her feet!’
Which was promptly arranged to her order
 With a care that was even minute,
And a glimpse—of an open-work border,
 And a glance—of the fairyest boot.

Then it drooped, and revived at some hovels—
 ‘Were they houses for men or for pigs?’
Then it shifted to muscular novels,
 With a little digression on prigs:
She thought ‘Wives and Daughters’ ‘so jolly’;
 ‘Had I read it?’ She knew when I had,
Like the rest, I should dote upon ‘Molly’;
 And ‘poor Mrs. Gaskell—how sad!’

‘Like Browning?’ ‘But so-so.’ His proof lay
 Too deep for her frivolous mood,
That preferred your mere metrical *soufflé*
 To the stronger poetical food;
Yet at times he was good—‘as a tonic’:
 Was Tennyson writing just now?
And was this new poet Byronic
 And clever, and naughty, or how?

Then we trifled with concerts and croquet;
 Then she daintily dusted her face;
Then she sprinkled herself with ‘Ess Bouquet,’
 Fished out from the foregoing case;
And we chattered of Gassier and Grisi,
 And voted Aunt Sally a bore;
Discussed if the tight rope were easy,
 Or Chopin much harder than Spohr.

Vers de Société

And oh! the odd things that she quoted,
　　With the prettiest possible look,
And the price of two buns that she noted
　　In the prettiest possible book;
While her talk like a musical rillet
　　Flashed on with the hours that flew;
And the carriage, her smile seemed to fill it
　　With just enough summer—for Two.

Till at last in her corner, peeping
　　From a nest of rugs and of furs,
With the white shut eyelids sleeping
　　On those dangerous looks of hers,
She seemed like a snow-drop breaking,
　　Not wholly alive nor dead,
But with one blind impulse making
　　To the sounds of the spring overhead;

And I watched in the lamplight's swerving
　　The shade of the down-dropt lid,
And the lip-line's delicate curving,
　　Where a slumbering smile lay hid,
Till I longed that, rather than sever,
　　The train should shriek into space,
And carry us onward—for ever,—
　　Me and that beautiful face.

But she suddenly woke in a fidget,
　　With fears she was 'nearly at home,'
And talk of a certain Aunt Bridget,
　　Whom I mentally wished—well, at Rome;
Got out at the very next station,
　　Looking back with a merry *Bon Soir*;
Adding, too, to my utter vexation,
　　A surplus, unkind *Au Revoir*.

Incognita

So left me to muse on her graces,
  To doze and to muse, till I dreamed
That we sailed through the sunniest places
  In a glorified galley, it seemed;
But the cabin was made of a carriage,
  And the ocean was Eau-de-Cologne,
And we split on a rock labelled MARRIAGE,
  And I woke,—as cold as a stone.

And that's how I lost her—a jewel,
  Incognita—one in a crowd,
Not prudent enough to be cruel,
  Not worldly enough to be proud.
It was just a shut lid and its lashes,
  Just a few hours in a train,
And I sorrow in sackcloth and ashes,
  Longing to see her again.

1866.

DORA *VERSUS* ROSE

' The Case is proceeding.'

FROM the tragic-est novels at Mudie's—
  At least, on a practical plan—
To the tales of mere Hodges and Judys,
  One love is enough for a man.
But no case that I ever yet met is
  Like mine : I am equally fond
Of Rose, who a charming brunette is,
            And Dora, a blonde.

Each rivals the other in powers—
  Each waltzes, each warbles, each paints—
Miss Rose, chiefly tumble-down towers;
  Miss Do., perpendicular saints.

Vers de Société

In short, to distinguish is folly;
  'Twixt the pair I am come to the pass
Of Macheath, between Lucy and Polly,—
            Or Buridan's ass.

If it happens that Rosa I've singled
  For a soft celebration in rhyme,
Then the ringlets of Dora get mingled
  Somehow with the tune and the time;
Or I painfully pen me a sonnet
  To an eyebrow intended for Do.'s,
And behold I am writing upon it
            The legend 'To Rose.'

Or I try to draw Dora (my blotter
  Is all overscrawled with her head),
If I fancy at last that I've got her,
  It turns to her rival instead;
Or I find myself placidly adding
  To the rapturous tresses of Rose
Miss Dora's bud-mouth, and her madding,
            Ineffable nose.

Was there ever so sad a dilemma?
  For Rose I would perish (*pro tem.*);
For Dora I'd willingly stem a—
  (Whatever might offer to stem);
But to make the invidious election,—
  To declare that on either one's side
I've a scruple,—a grain, more affection,
            I *cannot* decide.

And, as either so hopelessly nice is,
  My sole and my final resource
Is to wait some indefinite crisis,—
  Some feat of molecular force,

Dora Versus Rose

To solve me this riddle conducive
    By no means to peace or repose,
Since the issue can scarce be inclusive
        Of Dora *and* Rose.

(*Afterthought.*)

But, perhaps, if a third (say a Norah),
    Not quite so delightful as Rose,—
Not wholly so charming as Dora,—
    Should appear, is it wrong to suppose,—
As the claims of the others are equal,—
    And flight—in the main—is the best,—
That I might . . . But no matter,—the sequel
        Is easily guessed.

1874.

AD ROSAM

'*Mitte sectari*, ROSA *quo locorum
        Serà moretur.*'—HOR. i. 38.

I HAD a vacant dwelling—
    Where situated, I,
As naught can serve the telling,
    Decline to specify ;—
Enough 'twas neither haunted,
    Entailed, nor out of date ;
I put up ' Tenant Wanted,'
    And left the rest to Fate.

Then, Rose, you passed the window,—
    I see you passing yet,—
Ah, what could I within do,
    When, Rose, our glances met !

Vers de Société

You snared me, Rose, with ribbons,
    Your rose-mouth made me thrall,
Brief—briefer far than Gibbon's,
    Was my ' Decline and Fall.'

I heard the summons spoken
    That all hear—king and clown :
You smiled—the ice was broken ;
    You stopped—the bill was down.
How blind we are ! It never
    Occurred to me to seek
If you had come for ever,
    Or only for a week.

The words your voice neglected,
    Seemed written in your eyes ;
The thought your heart protected,
    Your cheek told, missal-wise ;—
I read the rubric plainly
    As any Expert could ;
In short, we dreamed,—insanely,
    As only lovers should.

I broke the tall Œnone,
    That then my chambers graced,
Because she seemed ' too bony,'
    To suit your purist taste ;
And you, without vexation,
    May certainly confess
Some graceful approbation,
    Designed *à mon adresse.*

You liked me then, *carina,*—
    You liked me then, I think ;
For your sake gall had been a
    Mere tonic-cup to drink ;

Ad Rosam

For your sake, bonds were trivial,
    The rack, a *tour-de-force* ;
And banishment, convivial,—
    You coming too, of course.

Then, Rose, a word in jest meant
    Would throw you in a state
That no well-timed investment
    Could quite alleviate ;
Beyond a Paris trousseau
    You prized my smile, I know :
I, yours—ah, more than Rousseau
    The lip of d'Houdetot.

Then, Rose,—But why pursue it ?
    When Fate begins to frown,
Best write the final '*fuit*,'
    And gulp the physic down.
And yet,—and yet, that only,
    The song should end with this :—
You left me,—left me lonely,
    Rosa mutabilis !

Left me, with Time for Mentor,
    (A dreary *tête-à-tête !*)
To pen my 'Last Lament,' or
    Extemporize to Fate,
In blankest verse disclosing
    My bitterness of mind,—
Which is, I learn, composing
    In cases of the kind.

No, Rose.   Though you refuse me,
    Culture the pang prevents ;
'I am not made'—excuse me—
    'Of so slight elements' ;

Vers de Société

I leave to common lovers
    The hemlock or the hood ;
My rarer soul recovers
    In dreams of public good.

The Roses of this nation—
    Or so I understand
From careful computation—
    Exceed the gross demand ;
And, therefore, in civility
    To maids that can't be matched,
No man of sensibility
    Should linger unattached.

So, without further fashion—
    A modern Curtius,
Plunging, from pure compassion,
    To aid the overplus,—
I sit down, sad—not daunted,
    And, in my weeds, begin
A new card—' Tenant Wanted,
    Particulars within.'

1869.

OUTWARD BOUND

(HORACE, III. 7)

' Quid fles, Asterie, quem tibi candidi
Primo restituent vere Favonii . . .
*   Gygen ?'*

COME, Laura, patience.   Time and Spring
Your absent Arthur back shall bring,
Enriched with many an Indian thing
    Once more to woo you ;
Him neither wind nor wave can check,
Who, cramped beneath the ' Simla's ' deck,
Still constant, though with stiffened neck,
    Makes verses to you.

(278)

Outward Bound

Would it were wave and wind alone!
The terrors of the torrid zone,
The indiscriminate cyclone,
      A man might parry;
But only faith, or 'triple brass,'
Can help the 'outward-bound' to pass
Safe through that eastward-faring class
      Who sail to marry.

For him fond mothers, stout and fair,
Ascend the tortuous cabin stair
Only to hold around his chair
      Insidious sessions;
For him the eyes of daughters droop
Across the plate of handed soup,
Suggesting seats upon the poop,
      And soft confessions.

Nor are these all his pains, nor most.
Romancing captains cease to boast—
Loud majors leave their whist—to roast
      The youthful griffin;
All, all with pleased persistence show
His fate,—'remote, unfriended, slow,'—
His 'melancholy' bungalow,—
      His lonely tiffin.

In vain.   Let doubts assail the weak;
Unmoved and calm as 'Adam's Peak,'
Your 'blameless Arthur' hears them speak
      Of woes that wait him;
Naught can subdue his soul secure;
'Arthur will come again,' be sure,
Though matron shrewd and maid mature
      Conspire to mate him.

Vers de Société

But, Laura, on your side, forbear
To greet with too impressed an air
A certain youth with chestnut hair,—
　　　A youth unstable;
Albeit none more skilled can guide
The frail canoe on Thamis tide,
Or, trimmer-footed, lighter glide
　　　Through 'Guards' or 'Mabel.'

Be warned in time.　Without a trace
Of acquiescence on your face,
Hear, in the waltz's breathing-space,
　　　His airy patter;
Avoid the confidential nook;
If, when you sing, you find his look
Grow tender, close your music-book,
　　　And end the matter.

1870.

IN THE ROYAL ACADEMY

Hugh (*on furlough*).　　　Helen (*his cousin*).

Helen.

They have not come!　And ten is past,—
Unless, by chance, my watch is fast;
—Aunt Mabel surely told us 'ten.'

Hugh.

I doubt if she can do it, then.
In fact, their train. . .

Helen.

　　　　　That is,—you knew.
How could you be so treacherous, Hugh?

(280)

In the Royal Academy

HUGH.

Nay ;—it is scarcely mine, the crime,
One can't account for railway-time !
Where shall we sit ?   Not here, I vote ;—
At least, there 's nothing here of note.

HELEN.

Then *here* we'll stay, please.   Once for all,
I bar all artists,—great and small !
From now until we go in June
I shall hear nothing but this tune :—
Whether I like Long's ' Vashti,' or
Like Leslie's ' Naughty Kitty' more ;
With all that critics, right or wrong,
Have said of Leslie and of Long . . .
No.   If you value my esteem,
I beg you'll take another theme ;
Paint me some pictures, if you will,
But spare me these, for good and ill. . . .

HUGH.

' Paint you some pictures !'   Come, that 's kind !
You know I'm nearly colour-blind.

HELEN.

Paint, then, in words.   You did before ;
Scenes at—where was it ?   Dustypoor ?
You know . . .

HUGH (*with an inspiration*).

I'll try.

HELEN.

But mind they're pretty,
Not ' hog hunts.' . . .

HUGH.

You shall be Committee,
And say if they are ' out' or ' in.'

Vers de Société

HELEN.

I shall reject them all.   Begin.

HUGH.

Here is the first.   An antique Hall
(Like Chanticlere) with panelled wall.
A boy, or rather lad.   A girl,
Laughing with all her rows of pearl
Before a portrait in a ruff.
He meanwhile watches . . . .

HELEN.

That's enough,
It wants ' *verve*,' ' *brio*,' ' breadth,' ' design,' . . .
Besides, it's English.   I decline.

HUGH.

This is the next.   'Tis finer far :
A foaming torrent (say Braemar).
A pony grazing by a boulder,
Then the same pair, a little older,
Left by some lucky chance together.
He begs her for a sprig of heather. . . .

HELEN.

—' Which she accords with smile seraphic.'
I know it,—it was in the ' Graphic.'
Declined.

HUGH.

Once more, and I forego
All hopes of hanging, high or low :
Behold the hero of the scene,
In bungalow and palankeen . . . .

HELEN.

What !—all at once !   But that's absurd ;—
Unless he's Sir Boyle Roche's bird !

In the Royal Academy

HUGH.

Permit me—'Tis a Panorama,
In which the person of the drama,
Mid orientals dusk and tawny,
Mid warriors drinking brandy pawnee,
Mid scorpions, dowagers, and griffins,
In morning rides, at noonday tiffins,
In every kind of place and weather,
Is solaced . . . by a sprig of heather.

(*More seriously.*)

He puts that faded scrap before
The ' Rajah,' or the ' Koh-i-noor ' . . .
He would not barter it for all
Benares, or the Taj-Mahal . . .
It guides,—directs his every act,
And word, and thought—In short—in fact—
I mean . . . .

(*Opening his locket.*)

Look, Helen, that 's the heather !
(Too late ! Here come both Aunts together.)

HELEN.

What heather, Sir ?

(*After a pause.*)

And why . . . . ' too late ' ?
—Aunt Dora, how you've made us wait !
Don't you agree that it 's a pity
Portraits are hung by the Committee ?

1879.

(283)

Vers de Société

THE LAST DISPATCH

HURRAH! the Season's past at last;
    At length we've 'done' our pleasure.
Dear 'Pater,' if you *only* knew
How much I've *longed* for home and you,—
    Our own green lawn and leisure!

And then the pets! One half forgets
    The dear dumb friends—in Babel.
I hope my special fish is fed;—
I long to see poor Nigra's head
    Pushed at me from the stable!

I long to see the cob and 'Rob,'—
    Old Bevis and the Collie;
And *won't* we read in 'Traveller's Rest!'
Home readings after all are best;—
    None else seem half so 'jolly!'

One misses your dear kindly store
    Of fancies quaint and funny;
One misses, too, your kind *bon-mot*;—
The Mayfair wit I mostly know
    Has more of gall than honey!

How tired one grows of 'calls and balls!'
    This '*toujours perdrix*' wearies;
I'm longing, quite, for 'Notes on Knox';
(*Apropos*, I've the loveliest box
    For holding *Notes and Queries!*)

A change of place would suit my case.
    You'll take me?—on probation?
As 'Lady-help,' then, let it be;
I feel (as Lavender shall see),
    That Jams are *my* vocation!

The Last Dispatch

How's Lavender? My love to her.
    Does Briggs still flirt with Flowers?—
Has Hawthorn stubbed the common clear?—
You'll let me give *some* picnics, Dear,
    And ask the Vanes and Towers?

I met Belle Vane. 'HE's' still in Spain!
    Sir John won't let them marry.
Aunt drove the boys to Brompton Rink;
And Charley,—changing Charley,—think,
    Is now *au mieux* with Carry!

And NO. You know what '*No*' I mean—
    There's no one yet at present:
The Benedick I have in view
Must be a something wholly new,—
    One's father's *far* too pleasant.

So hey, I say, for home and you!
    Good-bye to Piccadilly;
Balls, beaux, and Bolton-row, adieu!
Expect me, Dear, at half-past two;
    Till then,—your Own Fond—MILLY.

1876.

'PREMIERS AMOURS'

Old Loves and old dreams,—
    ' Requiescant in pace.'
How strange now it seems,—
    ' Old' Loves and ' old' dreams!
Yet we once wrote you reams,
    Maude, Alice, and Gracie!
Old Loves and old dreams,—
    ' Requiescant in pace.'

WHEN I called at the 'Hollies' to-day,
  In the room with the cedar-wood presses,
Aunt Deb. was just folding away
    What she calls her 'memorial dresses.'

(285)

Vers de Sociéte

She'd the frock that she wore at fifteen,—
   Short-waisted, of course—my abhorrence;
She'd 'the loveliest'—something in 'een'
   That she wears in her portrait by Lawrence;

She'd the 'jelick' she used—'as a Greek,' (!)
   She'd the habit she got her bad fall in;
She had e'en the blue *moiré antique*
   That she opened Squire Grasshopper's ball in:—

New and old they were all of them there:—
   Sleek velvet and bombazine stately,—
She had hung them each over a chair—
   To the '*paniers*' she's taken to lately

(Which she showed me, I think, by mistake).
   And I conned o'er the forms and the fashions,
Till the faded old shapes seemed to wake
   All the ghosts of my passed-away 'passions';—

From the days of love's youthfullest dream,
   When the height of my shooting idea
Was to burn, like a young Polypheme,
   For a somewhat mature Galatea.

There was Lucy, who 'tiffed' with her first,
   And who threw me as soon as her third came;
There was Norah, whose cut was the worst,
   For she told me to wait till my 'berd' came;

Pale Blanche, who subsisted on salts;
   Blonde Bertha, who doted on Schiller;
Poor Amy, who taught me to waltz;
   Plain Ann, that I wooed for the 'siller';—

All danced round my head in a ring,
   Like 'The Zephyrs' that somebody painted,
All shapes of the feminine thing—
   Shy, scornful, seductive, and sainted,—

'Premiers Amours'

To my Wife, in the days she was young . . .
   'How, Sir,' says that lady, disgusted,
'Do you dare to include ME among
   Your loves that have faded and rusted?'

'Not at all!'—I benignly retort.
   (I was just the least bit in a temper!)
'Those, alas! were the fugitive sort,
   But you are my—*eadem semper!*'

Full stop,—and a Sermon. Yet think,—
   There was surely good ground for a quarrel,—
She had checked me when just on the brink
   Of—I feel—a remarkable MORAL.

1873.

THE SCREEN IN THE LUMBER ROOM

YES, here it is, behind the box,
   That puzzle wrought so neatly—
That paradise of paradox—
   We once knew so completely;
You see it? 'Tis the same, I swear,
   Which stood, that chill September,
Beside your Aunt Lavinia's chair
   The year when . . . You remember?

Look, Laura, look! You must recall
   This florid 'Fairy's Bower,'
This wonderful Swiss waterfall,
   And this old 'Leaning Tower';
And here's the 'Maiden of Cashmere,'
   And here is Bewick's 'Starling,'
And here the dandy cuirassier
   You thought was 'such a Darling!'

(287)

Vers de Société

Your poor dear Aunt ! you know her way
  She used to say this figure
Reminded her of Count D'Orsay
  ' In all his youthful vigour ' ;
And here 's the ' cot beside the hill '
  We chose for habitation,
The day that . . . But I doubt if still
  You'd like the situation !

Too damp—by far ! She little knew,
  Your guileless Aunt Lavinia,
Those evenings when she slumbered through
  ' The Prince of Abyssinia,'
That there were two beside her chair
  Who both had quite decided
To see things in a rosier air
  Than Rasselas provided !

Ah ! men wore stocks in Britain's land,
  And maids short waists and tippets,
When this old-fashioned screen was planned
  From hoarded scraps and snippets ;
But more—far more, I think—to me
  Than those who first designed it,
Is this—in Eighteen Seventy-Three
  I kissed you first behind it.
1886.

DAISY'S VALENTINES

ALL night through Daisy's sleep, it seems,
  Have ceaseless ' rat-tats ' thundered ;
All night through Daisy's rosy dreams
  Have devious Postmen blundered,
Delivering letters round her bed,—
Mysterious missives, sealed with red,
And franked of course with due Queen's-head,—
  While Daisy lay and wondered.

Daisy's Valentines

But now, when chirping birds begin,
    And Day puts off the Quaker,—
When Cook renews her morning din,
    And rates the cheerful baker,—
She dreams her dream no dream at all,
For, just as pigeons come at call,
Winged letters flutter down, and fall
    Around her head, and wake her.

Yes, there they are! With quirk and twist,
    And fraudful arts directed ;
(Save Grandpapa's dear stiff old 'fist,'
    Through all disguise detected ;)
But which is his,—her young Lothair's,—
Who wooed her on the school-room stairs
With three sweet cakes, and two ripe pears,
    In one neat pile collected?

'Tis there, be sure.   Though truth to speak
    (If truth may be permitted),
I doubt that young 'gift-bearing Greek'
    Is scarce for fealty fitted ;
For has he not (I grieve to say)
To two loves more, on this same day,
In just this same emblazoned way,
    His transient vows transmitted?

He *may* be true.   Yet, Daisy dear,
    That even youth grows colder
You'll find is no new thing, I fear ;
    And when you're somewhat older,
You'll read of one Dardanian boy
Who 'wooed with gifts' a maiden coy,—
Then took the morning train to Troy,
    In spite of all he'd told her.

L

But wait.   Your time will come.   And then,
   Obliging Fates, please send her
The bravest thing you have in men,
   Sound-hearted, strong, and tender;—
The kind of man, dear Fates, you know,
That feels how shyly Daisies grow,
And what soft things they are, and so
   Will spare to spoil or mend her.

1874

IN TOWN

   ' The blue fly sung in the pane.'—TENNYSON.

TOILING in Town now is 'horrid,'
   (There is that woman again!)—
June in the zenith is torrid,
   Thought gets dry in the brain.

There is that woman again:
   'Strawberries! fourpence a pottle!'
Thought gets dry in the brain;
   Ink gets dry in the bottle.

'Strawberries! fourpence a pottle!'
   Oh for the green of a lane!—
Ink gets dry in the bottle;
   'Buzz' goes a fly in the pane!

Oh for the green of a lane,
   Where one might lie and be lazy!
'Buzz' goes a fly in the pane;
   Bluebottles drive me crazy!

Where one might lie and be lazy,
   Careless of Town and all in it!—
Bluebottles drive me crazy:
   I shall go mad in a minute!

In Town

Careless of Town and all in it,
    With some one to soothe and to still you;—
I shall go mad in a minute;
    Bluebottle, then I shall kill you!

With some one to soothe and to still you,
    As only one's feminine kin do,—
Bluebottle, then I shall kill you:
    There now! I've broken the window!

As only one's feminine kin do,—
    Some muslin-clad Mabel or May!—
There now! I've broken the window!
    Bluebottle's off and away!

Some muslin-clad Mabel or May,
    To dash one with eau de Cologne;—
Bluebottle's off and away;
    And why should I stay here alone!

To dash one with eau de Cologne,
    All over one's eminent forehead;—
And why should I stay here alone!
    Toiling in Town now is 'horrid.'

1876.

A SONNET IN DIALOGUE

FRANK (*on the Lawn*).

COME to the Terrace, May,—the sun is low.

MAY (*in the House*).

Thanks, I prefer my Browning here instead.

FRANK.

There are two peaches by the strawberry bed.

Vers de Société

MAY.

They will be riper if we let them grow.

FRANK.

Then the Park-aloe is in bloom, you know.

MAY.

Also, her Majesty Queen Anne is dead.

FRANK.

But surely, May, your pony must be fed.

MAY.

And was, and is.   I fed him hours ago.
'Tis useless, Frank, you see I shall not stir.

FRANK.

Still, I had something you would like to hear.

MAY.

No doubt some new frivolity of men.

FRANK.

Nay,—'tis a thing the gentler sex deplores
Chiefly, I think . . .

MAY (*coming to the window*).

What is this secret, then?

FRANK (*mysteriously*).

There are no eyes more beautiful than yours !

1879.

GROWING GRAY

' On a l'âge de son cœur.'—A. D'HOUDETOT.

A LITTLE more toward the light;—
Me miserable! Here's one that's white,
    And one that's turning;
Adieu to song and 'salad days';
My Muse, let's go at once to Jay's,
    And order mourning.

We must reform our rhymes, my Dear,—
Renounce the gay for the severe,—
    Be grave, not witty;
We have no more the right to find
That Pyrrha's hair is neatly twined,—
    That Chloe's pretty.

Young Love's for us a farce that's played;
Light canzonet and serenade
    No more may tempt us;
Gray hairs but ill accord with dreams;
From aught but sour didactic themes
    Our years exempt us.

Indeed! you really fancy so?
You think for one white streak we grow
    At once satiric?
A fiddlestick! Each hair's a string
To which our ancient Muse shall sing
    A younger lyric.

The heart's still sound. Shall 'cakes and ale'
Grow rare to youth because *we* rail
    At schoolboy dishes?
Perish the thought! 'Tis ours to chant
When neither Time nor Tide can grant
    Belief with wishes.

1871.

VARIA

THE MALTWORM'S MADRIGAL

I DRINK of the Ale of Southwark, I drink of the Ale of
    Chepe ;
At noon I dream on the settle ; at night I cannot sleep ;
For my love, my love it groweth ; I waste me all the day ;
And when I see sweet Alison, I know not what to say.

The sparrow when he spieth his Dear upon the tree,
He beateth-to his little wing ; he chirketh lustily ;
But when I see sweet Alison, the words begin to fail ;
I wot that I shall die of Love—an I die not of Ale.

Her lips are like the muscadel ; her brows are black as ink ;
Her eyes are bright as beryl stones that in the tankard wink ;
But when she sees me coming, she shrilleth out—'Te-Hee !
Fye on thy ruddy nose, Cousin, what lackest thou of me ?'

'Fye on thy ruddy nose, Cousin ! Why be thine eyes so
    small ?
Why go thy legs tap-lappetty like men that fear to fall ?
Why is thy leathern doublet besmeared with stain and spot ?
Go to. Thou art no man (she saith)—thou art a Pottle-pot !'

'No man,' i'faith. 'No man !' she saith. And 'Pottle-pot'
    thereto !
'Thou sleepest like our dog all day ; thou drink'st as fishes
    do.'
I would that I were Tibb the dog ; he wags at her his tail ;
Or would that I were fish, in truth, and all the sea were Ale !

So I drink of the Ale of Southwark, I drink of the Ale of
    Chepe ;
All day I dream in the sunlight ; I dream and eke I weep,
But little lore of loving can any flagon teach,
For when my tongue is looséd most, then most I lose my
    speech.

1885.

Varia

AN APRIL PASTORAL

He.

	WHITHER away, fair Neat-herdess?
She.	Shepherd, I go to tend my kine.
He.	Stay thou, and watch this flock of mine.
She.	With thee? Nay, that were idleness.
He.	Thy kine will pasture none the less.
She.	Not so: they wait me and my sign.
He.	I'll pipe to thee beneath the pine.
She.	Thy pipe will soothe not their distress.
He.	Dost thou not hear beside the spring
	How the gay birds are carolling?
She.	I hear them. But it may not be.
He.	Farewell then, Sweetheart! Farewell now.
She.	Shepherd, farewell . . . Where goest thou?
He.	I go . . . to tend thy kine for thee!

1881.

A NEW SONG OF THE SPRING GARDENS

To the Burden of 'Rogues All.'

COME hither ye gallants, come hither ye maids,
To the trim gravelled walks, to the shady arcades;
Come hither, come hither, the nightingales call;—
Sing *Tantarara*,—Vauxhall!   Vauxhall!

Come hither, ye cits, from your Lothbury hives!
Come hither, ye husbands, and look to your wives!
For the sparks are as thick as the leaves in the Mall;—
Sing *Tantarara*,—Vauxhall!   Vauxhall!

Here the 'prentice from Aldgate may ogle a Toast!
Here his Worship must elbow the Knight of the Post!
For the wicket is free to the great and the small;—
Sing *Tantarara*,—Vauxhall!   Vauxhall!

(298)

A New Song of the Spring Gardens

Here Betty may flaunt in her mistress's sack !
Here Trip wear his master's brocade on his back !
Here a hussy may ride, and a rogue take the wall;
Sing *Tantarara*,—Vauxhall !   Vauxhall !

Here Beauty may grant, and here Valour may ask !
Here the plainest may pass for a Belle (in a mask) !
Here a domino covers the short and the tall ;—
Sing *Tantarara*,—Vauxhall !   Vauxhall !

'Tis a type of the world, with its drums and its din ;
'Tis a type of the world, for when once you come in
You are loth to go out ; like the world 'tis a ball ;—
Sing *Tantarara*,—Vauxhall !   Vauxhall !

　　1885.

A LOVE-SONG

(XVIII. CENT.)

WHEN first in CELIA's ear I poured
　　A yet unpractised pray'r,
My trembling tongue sincere ignored
　　The aids of 'sweet' and 'fair.'
I only said, as in me lay,
　　I'd strive her 'worth' to reach ;
She frowned, and turned her eyes away,—
　　So much for truth in speech.

Then DELIA came.   I changed my plan ;
　　I praised her to her face ;
I praised her features,—praised her fan,
　　Her lap-dog and her lace ;
I swore that not till Time were dead
　　My passion should decay ;
She, smiling, gave her hand, and said
　　'Twill last then—for a DAY.

　　1874.

Varia

OF HIS MISTRESS

(After Anthony Hamilton)

TO G. S.

She that I love is neither brown nor fair,
   And, in a word her worth to say,
   There is no maid that with her may
      Compare.

Yet of her charms the count is clear, I ween:
   There are five hundred things we see,
   And then five hundred too there be,
      Not seen.

Her wit, her wisdom are direct from Heaven:
   But the sweet Graces from their store
   A thousand finer touches more
      Have given.

Her cheek's warm dye what painter's brush could note?
   Beside her Flora would be wan,
   And white as whiteness of the swan
      Her throat.

Her supple waist, her arm from Venus came,
   Hebe her nose and lip confess,
   And, looking in her eyes, you guess
      Her name.

1885.

Varia

THE NAMELESS CHARM

(Expanded from an Epigram of Piron)

STELLA, 'tis not your dainty head,
   Your artless look, I own;
'Tis not your dear coquettish tread,
   Or this, or that, alone;

Nor is it all your gifts combined;
   'Tis something in your face,—
The untranslated, undefined,
   Uncertainty of grace,

That taught the Boy on Ida's hill
   To whom the meed was due;
All three have equal charms—but still
   This one I give it to!

1885.

TO PHIDYLE

(HORACE, III. 23)

INCENSE, and flesh of swine, and this year's grain,
At the new moon, with suppliant hands, bestow,
O rustic Phidyle!   So naught shall know
Thy crops of blight, thy vine of Afric bane,
And hale the nurslings of thy flock remain
Through the sick apple-tide.   Fit victims grow
'Twixt holm and oak upon the Algid snow,
Or Alban grass, that with their necks must stain
The Pontiff's axe: to thee can scarce avail
Thy modest gods with much slain to assail,
Whom myrtle crowns and rosemary can please.
Lay on the altar a hand pure of fault;
More than rich gifts the Powers it shall appease,
Though pious but with meal and crackling salt.
1878.

Varia

TO HIS BOOK

(HOR., EP. I. 20)

FOR mart and street you seem to pine
With restless glances, Book of mine !
Still craving on some stall to stand,
Fresh pumiced from the binder's hand.
You chafe at locks, and burn to quit
Your modest haunt and audience fit
For hearers less discriminate.
I reared you up for no such fate.
Still, if you *must* be published, go ;
But mind, you can't come back, you know !

' What have I done ? ' I hear you cry,
And writhe beneath some critic's eye ;
' What did I want ? '—when, scarce polite,
They do but yawn, and roll you tight.
And yet methinks, if I may guess
(Putting aside your heartlessness
In leaving me and this your home),
You should find favour, too, at Rome.
That is, they'll like you while you're young,
When you are old, you'll pass among

The Great Unwashed,—then thumbed and sped,
Be fretted of slow moths, unread,
Or to Ilerda you'll be sent,
Or Utica, for banishment !
And I, whose counsel you disdain,
At that your lot shall laugh amain,
Wryly, as he who, like a fool,
Thrust o'er the cliff his restive mule.

To his Book

Nay ! there is worse behind.   In age
They e'en may take your babbling page
In some remotest ' slum ' to teach
Mere boys their rudiments of speech !

But go.   When on warm days you see
A chance of listeners, speak of me.
Tell them I soared from low estate,
A freedman's son, to higher fate
(That is, make up to me in worth
What you must take in point of birth);
Then tell them that I won renown
In peace and war, and pleased the town,
Paint me as early gray, and one
Little of stature, fond of sun,
Quick-tempered, too,—but nothing more.
Add (if they ask) I'm forty-four,
Or was, the year that over us
Both Lollius ruled and Lepidus.

1887.

FOR A COPY OF HERRICK

MANY days have come and gone,
Many suns have set and shone,
HERRICK, since thou sang'st of Wake,
Morris-dance and Barley-break ;—
Many men have ceased from care,
Many maidens have been fair,
Since thou sang'st of JULIA's eyes,
JULIA's lawns and tiffanies ;—
Many things are past : but thou,
GOLDEN-MOUTH, art singing now,
Singing clearly as of old,
And thy numbers are of gold !

1887.

Varia

WITH A VOLUME OF VERSE

About the ending of the Ramadán,
When leanest grows the famished Mussulman,
A haggard ne'er-do-well, Mahmoud by name,
At the tenth hour to Caliph OMAR came.
'Lord of the Faithful (quoth he), at the last
The long moon waneth, and men cease to fast;
Hard then, O hard! the lot of him must be,
Who spares to eat . . . but not for piety!'
'Hast thou no calling, Friend?'—the Caliph said.
'Sir, I make verses for my daily bread.'
'Verse!'—answered OMAR. ''Tis a dish, indeed,
Whereof but scantily a man may feed.
Go. Learn the Tenter's or the Potter's Art,—
Verse is a drug not sold in any mart.'

I know not if that hungry Mahmoud died;
But this I know—he must have versified,
For, with his race, from better still to worse,
The plague of writing follows like a curse;
And men will scribble though they fail to dine,
Which is the Moral of more Books than mine.

1885.

Varia

FOR THE AVERY 'KNICKERBOCKER'

(WITH ORIGINAL DRAWINGS BY G. H. BOUGHTON)

SHADE of Herrick, Muse of Locker,
Help me sing of Knickerbocker!

BOUGHTON, had you bid me chant
Hymns to Peter Stuyvesant!
Had you bid me sing of Wouter,
(He! the Onion-head! the Doubter!)
But to rhyme of this one,—Mocker!
Who shall rhyme to Knickerbocker?

Nay, but where my hand must fail
There the more shall yours avail;
You shall take your brush and paint
All that ring of figures quaint,—
All those Rip-van-Winkle jokers,—
All those solid-looking smokers,
Pulling at their pipes of amber
In the dark-beamed Council-Chamber.

Only art like yours can touch
Shapes so dignified . . . and Dutch;
Only art like yours can show
How the pine-logs gleam and glow,
Till the fire-light laughs and passes
'Twixt the tankards and the glasses,
Touching with responsive graces
All those grave Batavian faces,—
Making bland and beatific
All that session soporific.

Then I come and write beneath,
BOUGHTON, he deserves the wreath;
He can give us form and hue—
This the Muse can never do!

1892.

Varia

TO A PASTORAL POET

(H. C. B.)

AMONG my best I put your Book,
O Poet of the breeze and brook!
(That breeze and brook which blows and falls
More soft to those in city walls)
Among my best: and keep it still
Till down the fair grass-girdled hill,
Where slopes my garden-slip, there goes
The wandering wind that wakes the rose,
And scares the cohort that explore
The broad-faced sun-flower o'er and o'er
Or starts the restless bees that fret
The bindweed and the mignonette.

Then I shall take your Book, and dream
I lie beside some haunted stream;
And watch the crisping waves that pass,
And watch the flicker in the grass;
And wait—and wait—and wait to see
The Nymph . . . that never comes to me!

1887.

TO ONE WHO BIDS ME SING

'The straw is too old to make pipes of.'—DON QUIXOTE.

YOU ask a 'many-winter'd' Bard
    Where hides his old vocation?
I'll give—the answer is not hard—
    A classic explanation.

'Immortal' though he be, he still,
    Tithonus-like, grows older,
While she, his Muse of Pindus Hill,
    Still bares a youthful shoulder.

(306)

To one who bids me Sing

Could that too-sprightly Nymph but leave
    Her ageless grace and beauty,
They might, betwixt them both, achieve
    A hymn *de Senectute;*

But She—She can't grow gray; and so,
    Her slave, whose hairs are falling,
Must e'en his Doric flute forgo,
    And seek some graver calling,—

Not ill-content to stand aside,
    To yield to minstrels fitter
His singing-robes, his singing-pride,
    His fancies sweet—and bitter !

1895.

'SAT EST SCRIPSISSE'

(TO E. G., WITH A COLLECTION OF ESSAYS)

WHEN You and I have wandered beyond the reach of call,
And all our Works immortal lie scattered on the Stall,
It may be some new Reader, in that remoter age,
Will find the present Volume and listless turn the page.

For him I speak these verses.   And, Sir (I say to him),
This Book you see before you,—this masterpiece of Whim,
Of Wisdom, Learning, Fancy (if you will, please, attend),—
Was written by its Author, who gave it to his Friend.

For they had worked together,—been Comrades of the Pen ;
They had their points at issue, they differed now and then ;
But both loved Song and Letters, and each had close at
    heart
The hopes, the aspirations, the ' dear delays' of Art.

Varia

And much they talked of Measures, and more they talked
    of Style,
Of Form and 'lucid Order,' of 'labour of the File';
And he who wrote the writing, as sheet by sheet was penned
(This all was long ago, Sir!), would read it to his Friend.

They knew not, nor cared greatly, if they were spark or star;
They knew to move is somewhat, although the goal be far;
And larger light or lesser, this thing at least is clear,
They served the Muses truly,—their service was sincere.

This tattered page you see, Sir, this page alone remains
(Yes,—fourpence is the lowest!) of all those pleasant pains;
And as for him that read it, and as for him that wrote,
No Golden Book enrolls them among its 'Names of Note.'

And yet they had their office. Though they to-day are
    passed,
They marched in that procession where is no first or last;
Though cold is now their hoping, though they no more
    aspire,
They too had once their ardour—they handed on the fire.

    1893 [1892].

PROLOGUES AND EPILOGUES

PROLOGUE TO ABBEY'S EDITION OF
'SHE STOOPS TO CONQUER'

In the year Seventeen Hundred and Seventy and Three,
When the GEORGES were ruling o'er Britain the free,
There was played a new play, on a new-fashioned plan,
By the GOLDSMITH who brought out the *Good-Natur'd Man*.
New-fashioned, in truth—for this play, it appears,
Dealt largely in laughter, and nothing in tears,
While the type of those days, as the learnèd will tell ye,
Was the CUMBERLAND whine or the whimper of KELLY.
So the Critics pooh-poohed, and the Actresses pouted,
And the Public were cold, and the Manager doubted ;
But the Author had friends, and they all went to see it.
Shall we join them in fancy? You answer, So be it !

Imagine yourself then, good Sir, in a wig,
Either grizzle or bob—never mind, you look big.
You've a sword at your side, in your shoes there are buckles,
And the folds of fine linen flap over your knuckles.
You have come with light heart, and with eyes that are
    brighter,
From a pint of red Port, and a steak at the Mitre ;
You have strolled from the Bar and the purlieus of Fleet,
And you turn from the Strand into Catherine Street ;
Thence climb to the law-loving summits of Bow,
Till you stand at the Portal all play-goers know.
See, here are the 'prentice lads laughing and pushing,
And here are the seamstresses shrinking and blushing,
And here are the urchins who, just as to-day, Sir,
Buzz at you like flies with their ' Bill o' the Play, Sir?'

Yet you take one, no less, and you squeeze by the Chairs,
With their freights of fine ladies, and mount up the stairs;
So issue at last on the House in its pride,
And pack yourself snug in a box at the side.

Here awhile let us pause to take breath as we sit,
Surveying the humours and pranks of the Pit,—
With its Babel of chatterers buzzing and humming,
With its impudent orange-girls going and coming,
With its endless surprises of face and of feature,
All grinning as one in a gust of good-nature.
Then we turn to the Boxes where TRIP in his lace
Is aping his master, and keeping his place.
Do but note how the Puppy flings back with a yawn,
Like a Duke at the least, or a Bishop in lawn!

Then sniffs at his bouquet, whips round with a smirk,
And ogles the ladies at large—like a Turk.
But the music comes in, and the blanks are all filling,
And TRIP must trip up to the seats at a shilling;
And spite of the mourning that most of us wear
The House takes a gay and a holiday air;
For the fair sex are clever at turning the tables,
And seem to catch coquetry even in sables.
Moreover, your mourning has ribbons and stars,
And is sprinkled about with the red coats of Mars.

Look, look, there is WILKES! You may tell by the squint;
But he grows every day more and more like the print
(Ah! HOGARTH *could* draw!); and behind at the back
HUGH KELLY, who looks all the blacker in black.
That is CUMBERLAND next, and the prim-looking person
In the corner, I take it, is *Ossian* MACPHERSON.
And rolling and blinking, here, too, with the rest,
Comes sturdy old JOHNSON, dressed out in his best;

'She Stoops to Conquer'

How he shakes his old noddle! I'll wager a crown,
Whatever the law is, *he's* laying it down!
Beside him is REYNOLDS, who's deaf; and the hale
Fresh, farmer-like fellow, I fancy, is THRALE.
There is BURKE with GEORGE STEEVENS. And somewhere,
    no doubt,
Is the AUTHOR—too nervous just now to come out;
He's a queer little fellow, grave-featured, pock-pitten,
Tho' they say, in his cups, he's as gay as a kitten.

But where is our play-bill? *Mistakes of a Night!*
If the title's prophetic, I pity his plight!
She Stoops. Let us hope she won't fall at full length,
For the piece—so 'tis whispered—is wanting in strength.
And the humour is 'low!'—you are doubtless aware
There's a character, even, that 'dances a bear!'
Then the cast is so poor,—neither marrow nor pith!
Why can't they get WOODWARD or Gentleman SMITH!
'LEE LEWES!' Who's LEWES? The fellow has played
Nothing better, they tell me, than harlequinade!
'DUBELLAMY'—'QUICK,'—these are nobodies. Stay, I
Believe I saw QUICK once in *Beau Mordecai.*
Yes, QUICK is not bad. Mrs. GREEN, too, is funny;
But SHUTER, ah! SHUTER's the man for my money!
He's the quaintest, the oddest of mortals, is SHUTER,
And he has but one fault—he's too fond of the pewter.
Then there's little BULKELY . . .

                But here in the middle,
From the orchestra comes the first squeak of a fiddle.
Then the bass gives a growl, and the horn makes a dash,
And the music begins with a flourish and crash,
And away to the zenith goes swelling and swaying,
While we tap on the box to keep time to the playing.
And we hear the old tunes as they follow and mingle,
Till at last from the stage comes a ting-a-ting tingle;

And the fans cease to whirr, and the House for a minute
Grows still as if naught but wax figures were in it.
Then an actor steps out, and the eyes of all glisten.
Who is it? *The Prologue.* He's sobbing. Hush! listen.

> [*Thereupon enters Mr. Woodward in black, with a
> handkerchief to his eyes, to speak Garrick's Prologue,
> after which comes the play. In the volume for
> which the foregoing additional Prologue was written
> the following Envoi was added.*]

1888.

L'ENVOI

GOOD-BYE to you, KELLY, your fetters are broken!
Good-bye to you, CUMBERLAND, GOLDSMITH has spoken!
Good-bye to sham Sentiment, moping and mumming,
For GOLDSMITH has spoken and SHERIDAN'S coming;
And the frank Muse of Comedy laughs in free air
As she laughed with the Great Ones, with SHAKESPEARE,
    MOLIÈRE!

1888.

PROLOGUE TO ABBEY'S 'QUIET LIFE'

EVEN as one in city pent,
   Dazed with the stir and din of town,
Drums on the pane in discontent,
   And sees the dreary rain come down,
Yet, through the dimmed and dripping glass,
Beholds, in fancy, visions pass
Of Spring that breaks with all her leaves,
Of birds that build in thatch and eaves,
Of woodlands where the throstle calls,
Of girls that gather cowslip balls,
Of kine that low, and lambs that cry,
Of wains that jolt and rumble by,

(314)

Of brooks that sing by brambly ways,
Of sunburned folk that stand at gaze,
Of all the dreams with which men cheat
The stony sermons of the street,
So, in its hour, the artist brain
   Weary of human ills and woes,
Weary of passion and of pain,
   And vaguely craving for repose,
Deserts awhile the stage of strife
To draw the even, ordered life,
The easeful days, the dreamless nights,
The homely round of plain delights,
The calm, the unambitioned mind,
Which all men seek, and few men find.

EPILOGUE.

LET the dream pass, the fancy fade !
We clutch a shape, and hold a shade.
Is Peace *so* peaceful ?—Nay,—who knows ?
There are volcanoes under snows.

1889.

DEDICATION OF 'THE STORY OF ROSINA'

(TO AN IDEAL READER)

WHAT would our modern maids to-day ?
   I watch, and can't conjecture :
A dubious tale ?—an Ibsen play ?—
   A pessimistic lecture ?

I know not.   But this, Child, I know
   You like things sweet and seemly,
Old-fashioned flowers, old shapes in Bow,
   'Auld Robin Gray' (extremely) ;

(315)

You—with my ' Dorothy '[1]—delight
  In fragrant cedar-presses ;
In window corners warm and bright,
  In lawn, and lilac dresses ;

You still can read, at any rate,
  Charles Lamb and ' Evelina ' ;
To you, My Dear, I dedicate
  This ' STORY OF ROSINA.'

1895.

PROLOGUE TO 'EIGHTEENTH CENTURY VIGNETTES'

(THIRD SERIES)

'*Versate* . . .
Quid valeant humeri.'—HOR. *Ars Poetica.*

How shall a Writer change his ways ?
Read his Reviewers' blame, not praise.
In blame, as Boileau said of old,
The truth is shadowed, if not told.

* * * * * *

There ! Let that row of stars extend
To hide the faults I mean to mend.
Why should the Public need to know
The standard that I fall below ?
Or learn to search for that defect
My Critic bids me to correct ?
No : in this case the Worldly-Wise
Keep their own counsel—and revise.

[1] See *ante*, p. 76.

Prologue to '18th Century Vignettes'

Yet something of my Point of View
I may confide, my Friend, to You.
I don't pretend to paint the vast
And complex picture of the Past:
Not mine the wars of humankind,
'The furious troops in battle joined';
Not mine the march, the counter-march,
The trumpets, the triumphal arch.
For detail, detail, most I care
(*Ce superflu, si nécessaire !*) ;
I cultivate a private bent
For episode, for incident ;
I take a page of Some One's life,
His quarrel with his friend, his wife,
His good or evil hap at Court,
'His habit as he lived,' his sport,
The books he read, the trees he planted,
The dinners that he ate—or wanted :
As much, in short, as one may hope
To cover with a microscope.

I don't taboo a touch of scandal,
If Gray or Walpole hold the candle ;
Nor do I use a lofty tone
Where faults are weaknesses alone.

In studies of Life's seamy side
I own I feel no special pride ;
The Fleet, the round-house, and the gibbets
Are not among my prize exhibits ;
Nor could I, if I would, outdo
What Fielding wrote, or Hogarth drew.

Yet much I love to arabesque
What Gautier christened a 'Grotesque' ;

To take his oddities and ' lunes,'
And drape them neatly with festoons,
Until, at length, I chance to get
The thing I designate ' Vignette.'

To sum the matter then :—My aim
Is modest.   This is all I claim :
To paint a part and not the whole,
The trappings rather than the soul.

The Evolution of the Time,
The silent Forces fighting Crime,
The Fetishes that fail, and pass,
The struggle between Class and Class,
The Wealth still adding land to lands,
The Crown that falls, the Faith that stands . . .
All this I leave to abler hands.

1896.

EPILOGUE TO 'EIGHTEENTH CENTURY VIGNETTES'

(SECOND SERIES)

' WHAT is it then,'—some Reader asks,—
    ' What is it that attaches
Your fancy so to fans and masks,—
    To periwigs and patches ?

' Is Human Life to-day so poor,—
    So bloodless,—you disdain it,
To ' galvanize ' the Past once more ? '
    —Permit me.   I'll explain it.

This Age I grant (and grant with pride),
    Is varied, rich, eventful ;
But, if you touch its weaker side,
    Deplorably resentful :

(318)

Epilogue to ' 18th Century Vignettes'

Belaud it, and it takes your praise
    With air of calm conviction;
Condemn it, and at once you raise
    A storm of contradiction.

Whereas with these old Shades of mine,
    Their ways and dress delight me;
And should I trip by word or line,
    They cannot well indict me.

Not that I think to err.   I seek
    To steer 'twixt blame and blindness;
I strive (as some one said in Greek)
    To speak the truth with kindness:

But—should I fail to render clear
    Their title, rank, or station—
I still may sleep secure, nor fear
    A suit for defamation.

1894.

ESSAYS IN OLD FRENCH
FORMS

'They are a school to win
The fair French daughter to learn English in ;
And, gracèd with her song,
To make the language sweet upon her tongue.'
BEN JONSON, *Underwoods.*

As, to the pipe, with rhythmic feet
In windings of some old-world dance,
The smiling couples cross and meet,
Join hands, and then in line advance,
So, to these fair old tunes of France,
Through all their maze of to and fro,
The light-heeled numbers laughing go,
Retreat, return, and ere they flee,
One moment pause in panting row,
And seem to say—Vos plaudite !

1880.

ROSE-LEAVES

' Sans peser.—Sans rester.'

A KISS.

ROSE kissed me to-day.
    Will she kiss me to-morrow?
Let it be as it may,
Rose kissed me to-day,
But the pleasure gives way
    To a savour of sorrow ;—
Rose kissed me to-day,—
    Will she kiss me to-morrow?

CIRCE.

IN the School of Coquettes
    Madam Rose is a scholar :—
O, they fish with all nets
In the School of Coquettes !
When her brooch she forgets
    'Tis to show her new collar ;
In the School of Coquettes
    Madam Rose is a scholar !

A TEAR.

THERE 's a tear in her eye,—
    Such a clear little jewel !
What *can* make her cry ?
There 's a tear in her eye.
' Puck has killed a big fly,—
    And it 's *horribly* cruel ' ;
There 's a tear in her eye,—
    Such a clear little jewel !

M 2

A GREEK GIFT.

HERE's a present for Rose,
 How pleased she is looking !
Is it verse ?—is it prose ?
Here's a present for Rose !
'*Plats*,' '*Entrées*,' and '*Rôts*,'—
 Why, it's 'Gouffé on Cooking.'
Here's a present for Rose,
 How *pleased* she is looking !

' URCEUS EXIT.'

I INTENDED an Ode,
 And it turned to a Sonnet.
It began *à la mode*,
I intended an Ode ;
But Rose crossed the road
 In her latest new bonnet ;
I intended an Ode ;
 And it turned to a Sonnet.

1874.

'PERSICOS ODI'

DAVUS, I detest
 Orient display ;
Wreaths on linden drest,
Davus, I detest.
Let the late rose rest
 Where it fades away :—
Davus, I detest
 Orient display.

Naught but myrtle twine
 Therefore, Boy, for me,
Sitting 'neath the vine,—
Naught but myrtle twine ;

(324)

Fitting to the wine,
    Not unfitting thee ;
Naught but myrtle twine
    Therefore, Boy, for me.

1878.

'PERSICOS ODI'

(POCKET VERSION)

'DAVUS, I detest
    Persian decoration ;
Roses and the rest,
Davus, I detest.
Simple myrtle best
    Suits *our* modest station :—
Davus, I detest
    Persian decoration.'

1877.

THE WANDERER

LOVE comes back to his vacant dwelling,—
    The old, old Love that we knew of yore !
    We see him stand by the open door,
With his great eyes sad, and his bosom swelling.

He makes as though in our arms repelling,
    He fain would lie as he lay before ;—
Love comes back to his vacant dwelling,—
    The old, old Love that we knew of yore !

Ah, who shall help us from over-spelling
    That sweet forgotten, forbidden lore !
    E'en as we doubt in our heart once more,
With a rush of tears to our eyelids welling,
Love comes back to his vacant dwelling.

1880.

'VITAS HINNULEO'

You shun me, Chloe, wild and shy
   As some stray fawn that seeks its mother
Through trackless woods.   If spring-winds sigh,
   It vainly strives its fears to smother ;—

Its trembling knees assail each other
   When lizards stir the bramble dry ;—
   You shun me, Chloe, wild and shy
As some stray fawn that seeks its mother.

And yet no Libyan lion I,—
   No ravening thing to rend another ;
Lay by your tears, your tremors by—
   A Husband's better than a brother ;
Nor shun me, Chloe, wild and shy
   As some stray fawn that seeks its mother.

1877.

'ON LONDON STONES'

On London stones I sometimes sigh
For wider green and bluer sky ;—
   Too oft the trembling note is drowned
   In this huge city's varied sound ;—
'Pure song is country born'—I cry.

Then comes the spring,—the months go by,
The last stray swallows seaward fly ;
   And I—I too !—no more am found
       On London stones !

In vain !—the woods, the fields deny
That clearer strain I fain would try ;
   Mine is an urban Muse, and bound
   By some strange law to paven ground ;
Abroad she pouts ;—she is not shy
       On London stones !

1876.

'YOU BID ME TRY'

You bid me try, BLUE-EYES, to write
A Rondeau.   What !—forthwith ?—to-night ?
   Reflect.   Some skill I have, 'tis true ;—
   But thirteen lines !—and rhymed on two !
'Refrain,' as well.   Ah, hapless plight !

Still, there are five lines,—ranged aright.
These Gallic bonds, I feared, would fright
   My easy Muse.   They did, till you—
      You bid me try !

That makes them eight.   The port's in sight ;—
'Tis all because your eyes are bright !
   Now just a pair to end in ' oo '—
   When maids command, what can't we do
Behold !—the RONDEAU, tasteful, light,
      You bid me try !

1876.

'FAREWELL, RENOWN !'

FAREWELL, Renown !   Too fleeting flower,
That grows a year to last an hour ;—
   Prize of the race's dust and heat,
   Too often trodden under feet,—
Why should I court your ' barren dower ? '

Nay ;—had I Dryden's angry power,—
The thews of Ben,—the wind of Gower,—
   Not less my voice should still repeat,
      ' Farewell, Renown !'

(327)

Farewell !—Because the Muses' bower
Is filled with rival brows that lower ;—
   Because, howe'er his pipe be sweet,
   The Bard, that 'pays,' must please the street ;—
But most . . . because the grapes are sour,—
         Farewell, Renown !

1876.

'MORE POETS YET!'

(TO J. L. W.)

'MORE Poets yet !'—I hear him say,
Arming his heavy hand to slay ;—
   'Despite my skill and "swashing blow,"
   They seem to sprout where'er I go ;—
I killed a host but yesterday !'

Slash on, O Hercules ! You may.
Your task 's, at best, a Hydra-fray ;
   And though *you* cut, not less will grow
         More Poets yet !

Too arrogant ! For who shall stay
The first blind motions of the May ?
   Who shall out-blot the morning glow ?—
   Or stem the full heart's overflow ?
Who ? There will rise, till Time decay,
         More Poets yet !

1876.

'WITH PIPE AND FLUTE'

(TO E. G.)

WITH pipe and flute the rustic Pan
Of old made music sweet for man;
    And wonder hushed the warbling bird,
    And closer drew the calm-eyed herd,—
The rolling river slowlier ran.

Ah! would,—ah! would, a little span,
Some air of Arcady could fan
    This age of ours, too seldom stirred
             With pipe and flute!

But now for gold we plot and plan;
And from Beersheba unto Dan,
    Apollo's self might pass unheard,
    Or find the night-jar's note preferred;—
Not so it fared, when time began,
             With pipe and flute!

1877.

TO A JUNE ROSE

(TO A. P.)

O ROYAL Rose! the Roman dress'd
His feast with thee; thy petals press'd
    Augustan brows; thine odour fine,
    Mix'd with the three-times-mingled wine,
Lent the long Thracian draught its zest.

What marvel then, if host and guest,
By Song, by Joy, by Thee caress'd,
    Half-trembled on the half-divine,
        O royal Rose!

And yet—and yet—I love thee best
In our old gardens of the West,
  Whether about my thatch thou twine,
  Or Hers, that brown-eyed maid of mine,
Who lulls thee on her lawny breast,
        O royal Rose !

1885.

TO DAFFODILS

(TO A. J. M.)

O YELLOW flowers by HERRICK sung !
O yellow flowers that danced and swung
  In WORDSWORTH'S verse, and now to me,
  Unworthy, from this 'pleasant lea,'
Laugh back, unchanged and ever young;—

Ah, what a text to us o'erstrung,
O'erwrought, o'erreaching, hoarse of lung,
  You teach by that immortal glee,
        O yellow flowers !

We, by the Age's oestrus stung,
Still hunt the New with eager tongue,
  Vexed ever with the Old, but ye,
  What ye have been ye still shall be,
When we are dust the dust among,
        O yellow flowers !

1885.

Essays in Old French Forms

ON THE HURRY OF THIS TIME

(TO F. G.)

WITH slower pen men used to write,
Of old, when ' letters ' were ' polite ' ;
   In ANNA'S, or in GEORGE'S days,
   They could afford to turn a phrase,
Or trim a straggling theme aright.

They knew not steam ; electric light
Not yet had dazed their calmer sight ;—
   They meted out both blame and praise
      With slower pen.

Too swiftly now the Hours take flight !
What 's read at morn is dead at night :
   Scant space have we for Art's delays,
   Whose breathless thought so briefly stays,
We may not work—ah ! would we might !—
      With slower pen.

1882.

'WHEN BURBADGE PLAYED'

(TO L. B.)

WHEN Burbadge played, the stage was bare
Of fount and temple, tower and stair ;
   Two backswords eked a battle out ;
   Two supers made a rabble rout ;
The Throne of Denmark was a chair !

And yet, no less, the audience there
Thrilled through all changes of Despair,
   Hope, Anger, Fear, Delight, and Doubt
      When Burbadge played !

This is the Actor's gift ; to share
All moods, all passions, nor to care
    One whit for scene, so he without
    Can lead men's minds the roundabout,
Stirred as of old those hearers were
        When Burbadge played !

1885.

A GREETING

(TO W. C.)

BUT once or twice we met, touched hands.
To-day between us both expands
    A waste of tumbling waters wide,—
    A waste by me as yet untried,
Vague with the doubt of unknown lands.

Time like a despot speeds his sands :
A year he blots, a day he brands ;
    We wa ed, we talked by Thamis' side
        But once or twice.

What makes a friend ?   What filmy strands
Are these that turn to iron bands ?
    What knot is this so firmly tied
    That naught but Fate can now divide ?—
Ah, these are things one understands
        But once or twice !

1890

Essays in Old French Forms

LÉAL SOUVENIR

(E. F. B.)

'For old sake's sake!' 'Twere hard to choose
Words fitter for an old-world Muse
　　Than these, that in their cadence bring
　　Faint fragrance of the posy-ring,
And charms that rustic lovers use.

The long day lengthens, and we lose
The first pale flush, the morning hues,—
　　Ah! but the back-look, lingering,
　　　　For old sake's sake!

That we retain. Though Time refuse
To lift the veil on forward views,
　　Despot in most, he is not king
　　Of those kind memories that cling
Around his travelled avenues
　　　　For old sake's sake!

1892.

AFTER WATTEAU

(TO F. W.)

'*Embarquons-nous!*' I seem to go
Against my will. 'Neath alleys low
　　I bend, and hear across the air—
　　Across the stream—faint music rare,—
Whose '*cornemuse,*' whose '*chalumeau*'?

Hark! was not that a laugh I know?
Who was it, hurrying, turned to show
　　The galley swinging by the stair?—
　　　　'*Embarquons-nous!*'

The silk sail flaps, light breezes blow;
Frail laces flutter, satins flow;
   You, with the love-knot in your hair,
   ' *Allons, embarquons pour Cythère* ';
 . .You will not? Press her, then, PIERROT,—
           ' *Embarquons-nous !* '

1893.

TO ETHEL

               (Who wishes she had lived—

     ' *In teacup-times of hood and hoop,*
      Or while the patch was worn. ')

' IN teacup-times ! ' The style of dress
Would suit your beauty, I confess;
   BELINDA-like, the patch you'd wear;
   I picture you with powdered hair,—
You'd make a charming Shepherdess !

And I—no doubt—could well express
SIR PLUME's complete conceitedness,—
   Could poise a clouded cane with care
          ' In teacup-times ! '

The parts would fit precisely—yes:
We should achieve a huge success !
   You should disdain, and I despair,
   With quite the true Augustan air;
But . . . could I love you more, or less,—
          ' In teacup-times ' ?

1878.

'WHEN *FINIS* COMES'

WHEN *Finis* comes, the BOOK we close,
And somewhat sadly, Fancy goes,
   With backward step, from stage to stage
   Of that accomplished pilgrimage . . .
The thorn lies thicker than the rose !

There is so much that no one knows,—
So much un-reached that none suppose ;
   What flaws ! what faults !—on every page,
         When *Finis* comes.

Still,—they must pass !   The swift Tide flows.
Though not for all the laurel grows,
   Perchance, in this be-slandered age,
   The worker, mainly, wins his wage ;—
And Time will sweep both friends and foes
        When FINIS comes !

1877.

'O FONS BANDUSIAE'

O BABBLING Spring, than glass more clear,
Worthy of wreath and cup sincere,
   To-morrow shall a kid be thine
   With swelled and sprouting brows for sign,—
Sure sign !— of loves and battles near.

Child of the race that butt and rear !
Not less, alas ! his life-blood dear
   Must tinge thy cold wave crystalline,
        O babbling Spring !

Thee Sirius knows not.   Thou dost cheer
With pleasant cool the plough-worn steer,—
 The wandering flock.   This verse of mine
 Will rank thee one with founts divine ;
Men shall thy rock and tree revere,
   O babbling Spring !

1877.

'EXTREMUM TANAIN'

(TO J. K.)

BEFORE thy doors too long of late,
O Lyce, I bewail my fate ;
 Not Don's barbarian maids, I trow,
 Would treat their luckless lovers so ;
Thou,—thou alone art obstinate.

Hast thou nor eyes nor ears, Ingrate !
Hark ! how the NORTH WIND shakes thy gate !
 Look ! how the laurels bend with snow
   Before thy doors !

Lay by thy pride,—nor hesitate,
Lest Love and I grow desperate ;
 If prayers, if gifts for naught must go,
 If naught my frozen pallor show,—
Beware ! . . . I shall not always wait
   Before thy doors !

1877.

'VIXI PUELLIS'

We loved of yore, in warfare bold,
　　Nor laurelless.　Now all must go ;
　　Let this left wall of Venus show
The arms, the tuneless lyre of old.

Here let them hang, the torches cold,
　　The portal-bursting bar, the bow,
　　　　　　We loved of yore.

But thou, who Cyprus sweet dost hold,
　　And Memphis free from Thracian snow,
　　Goddess and queen, with vengeful blow,
Smite,—smite but once that pretty scold
　　　　　　We loved of yore !

1877.

'WHEN I SAW YOU LAST, ROSE'

When I saw you last, Rose,
You were only so high ;—
How fast the time goes !

Like a bud ere it blows,
You just peeped at the sky,
When I saw you last, Rose !

Now your petals unclose,
Now your May-time is nigh ;—
How fast the time goes !

And a life,—how it grows !
You were scarcely so shy,
When I saw you last, Rose !

(337)

In your bosom it shows
There's a guest on the sly;
(How fast the time goes!)

Is it Cupid? Who knows!
Yet you used not to sigh,
When I saw you last, Rose;—
How fast the time goes!

1877.

ON A NANKIN PLATE

'AH me, but it might have been!
Was there ever so dismal a fate?'—
Quoth the little blue mandarin.

'Such a maid as was never seen!
She passed, tho' I cried to her "Wait,"—
Ah me, but it might have been!

'I cried, "O my Flower, my Queen,
Be mine!" 'Twas precipitate,'—
Quoth the little blue mandarin,—

'But then . . . she was just sixteen,—
Long-eyed,—as a lily straight,—
Ah me, but it might have been!

'As it was, from her palankeen,
She laughed—"You're a week too late!"'
(Quoth the little blue mandarin.)

'That is why, in a mist of spleen,
I mourn on this Nankin Plate.
Ah me, but it might have been!'—
Quoth the little blue mandarin.

1883.

Essays in Old French Forms

FOR A COPY OF THEOCRITUS

O SINGER of the field and fold,
THEOCRITUS! Pan's pipe was thine,—
Thine was the happier Age of Gold.

For thee the scent of new-turned mould,
The bee-hives, and the murmuring pine,
O Singer of the field and fold!

Thou sang'st the simple feasts of old,—
The beechen bowl made glad with wine . . .
Thine was the happier Age of Gold.

Thou bad'st the rustic loves be told,—
Thou bad'st the tuneful reeds combine,
O Singer of the field and fold!

And round thee, ever-laughing, rolled
The blithe and blue Sicilian brine :
Thine was the happier Age of Gold.

Alas for us! Our songs are cold ;
Our Northern suns too sadly shine :—
O Singer of the field and fold,
Thine was the happier Age of Gold

1879.

'TU NE QUAESIERIS'

SEEK not, O Maid, to know
(Alas! unblest the trying!)
When thou and I must go.

No lore of stars can show.
What shall be, vainly prying,
Seek not, O Maid, to know.

(339)

Will Jove long years bestow?—
Or is't with this one dying,
That thou and I must go,

Now,—when the great winds blow,
And waves the reef are plying?
Seek not, O Maid, to know.

Rather let clear wine flow,
On no vain hope relying;
When thou and I must go

Lies dark;—then be it so.
Now,—*now*, churl Time is flying;
Seek not, O Maid, to know
When thou and I must go.

1877.

THE PRODIGALS

'PRINCES!—and you, most valorous,
    Nobles and Barons of all degrees!
Hearken awhile to the prayer of us,—
    Beggars that come from the over-seas!
    Nothing we ask or of gold or fees;
Harry us not with the hounds we pray;
    Lo,—for the surcote's hem we seize,—
Give us—ah! give us—but Yesterday!'

'Dames most delicate, amorous!
    Damosels blithe as the belted bees!
Hearken awhile to the prayer of us,—
    Beggars that come from the over-seas!
    Nothing we ask of the things that please;
Weary are we, and worn, and gray;
    Lo,—for we clutch and we clasp your knees,—
Give us—ah! give us—but Yesterday!'

The Prodigals

'Damosels—Dames, be piteous!'
  (But the dames rode fast by the roadway trees.)
'Hear us, O Knights magnanimous!'
  (But the knights pricked on in their panoplies.)
  Nothing they gat or of hope or ease,
But only to beat on the breast and say :—
  'Life we drank to the dregs and lees;
Give us—ah! give us—but Yesterday!'

ENVOY.

Youth, take heed to the prayer of these!
Many there be by the dusty way,—
  Many that cry to the rocks and seas
'Give us—ah! give us—but Yesterday!

1876.

ON A FAN THAT BELONGED TO THE MARQUISE DE POMPADOUR

Chicken-skin, delicate, white,
  Painted by Carlo Vanloo,
Loves in a riot of light,
  Roses and vaporous blue;
  Hark to the dainty *frou-frou!*
Picture above, if you can,
  Eyes that could melt as the dew,—
This was the Pompadour's fan!

See how they rise at the sight,
  Thronging the *Œil de Bœuf* through,
Courtiers as butterflies bright,
  Beauties that Fragonard drew,
  Talon-rouge, falbala, queue,
Cardinal, Duke,—to a man,
  Eager to sigh or to sue,—
This was the Pompadour's fan!

(341)

Ah, but things more than polite
　　Hung on this toy, *voyez-vous !*
Matters of state and of might,
　　Things that great ministers do ;
　　Things that, maybe, overthrew
Those in whose brains they began ;
　　Here was the sign and the cue,—
This was the Pompadour's fan !—

ENVOY.

　　WHERE are the secrets it knew ?
　　　　Weavings of plot and of plan ?
　　　　—But where is the Pompadour, too ?
　　This was the Pompadour's *Fan !*
1878.

A BALLAD TO QUEEN ELIZABETH
of the Spanish Armada

KING PHILIP had vaunted his claims ;
　　He had sworn for a year he would sack us ;
With an army of heathenish names
　　He was coming to fagot and stack us ;
　　Like the thieves of the sea he would track us,
And shatter our ships on the main ;
　　But we had bold Neptune to back us,—
And where are the galleons of Spain ?

His carackes were christened of dames
　　To the kirtles whereof he would tack us ;
With his saints and his gilded stern-frames,
　　He had thought like an egg-shell to crack us :
　　Now Howard may get to his Flaccus,
And Drake to his Devon again,
　　And Hawkins bowl rubbers to Bacchus,—
For where are the galleons of Spain ?

(342)

A Ballad to Queen Elizabeth

Let his Majesty hang to St. James
    The axe that he whetted to hack us ;
He must play at some lustier games
    Or at sea he can hope to out-thwack us ;
    To his mines of Peru he would pack us
To tug at his bullet and chain ;
    Alas ! that his Greatness should lack us !—
But where are the galleons of Spain ?

ENVOY.

GLORIANA ! the Don may attack us
Whenever his stomach be fain ;
    He must reach us before he can rack us
And where are the galleons of Spain ?

1877.

A BALLAD OF HEROES

'*Now all your victories are in vain.*'—MARY F. ROBINSON.

BECAUSE you passed, and now are not,—
    Because, in some remoter day,
Your sacred dust from doubtful spot
    Was blown of ancient airs away,—
    Because you perished,—must men say
Your deeds were naught, and so profane
    Your lives with that cold burden ?   Nay
The deeds you wrought are not in vain !

Though, it may be, above the plot
    That hid your once imperial clay,
No greener than o'er men forgot
    The unregarding grasses sway ;—
    Though there no sweeter is the lay
From careless bird,—though you remain
    Without distinction of decay,—
The deeds you wrought are not in vain !

No.   For while yet in tower or cot
   Your story stirs the pulses' play ;
And men forget the sordid lot—
   The sordid care, of cities gray ;—
   While yet, beset in homelier fray,
They learn from you the lesson plain
   That Life may go, so Honour stay,—
The deeds you wrought are not in vain !

ENVOY.

HEROES of old !   I humbly lay
   The laurel on your graves again ;
Whatever men have done, men may,—
   The deeds you wrought are not in vain.

1878.

THE BALLAD OF THE THRUSH

ACROSS the noisy street
   I hear him careless throw
One warning utterance sweet ;
   Then faint at first, and low,
   The full notes closer grow ;
Hark ! what a torrent gush !
   They pour, they overflow—
Sing on, sing on, O Thrush !

What trick, what dream's deceit
   Has fooled his fancy so
To scorn of dust and heat ?
   I, prisoned here below,
   Feel the fresh breezes blow ;
And see, thro' flag and rush,
   Cool water sliding slow—
Sing on, sing on, O Thrush !

(344)

The Ballad of the Thrush

Sing on.   What though thou beat
   On that dull bar, thy foe !
Somewhere the green boughs meet
   Beyond the roofs a-row ;
   Somewhere the blue skies show,
Somewhere no black walls crush
   Poor hearts with hopeless woe—
Sing on, sing on, O Thrush !

ENVOY.

BIRD, though they come, we know,
   The empty cage, the hush ;
Still, ere the brief day go,
   Sing on, sing on, O Thrush !

1883.

THE BALLAD OF THE BARMECIDE

To one in Eastern clime,—'tis said,—
   There came a man at eve with ' Lo !
Friend, ere the day be dimmed and dead,
   Hast thou a mind to feast, and know
   Fair cates, and sweet wine's overflow ? '
To whom that other fain replied—
   ' Lead on.   Not backward I nor slow ;—
Where is thy feast, O Barmecide ? '

Thereon the bidder passed and led
   To where, apart from dust and glow,
They found a board with napery spread,
   And gold, and glistering cups a-row.
   ' Eat,' quoth the host, yet naught did show.
To whom his guest—' Thy board is wide ;
   But barren is the cheer, I trow ;
Where is thy feast, O Barmecide ? '

(345)

'Eat,' quoth the man not less, and fed
  From meats unseen, and made as though
He drank of wine both white and red.
  'Eat,—ere the day to darkness grow.
  Short space and scant the Fates bestow!'
What time his guest him wondering eyed,
  Muttering in wrath his beard below—
'Where is thy feast, O Barmecide?'

ENVOY.

LIFE,—'tis of thee they fable so.
  Thou bidd'st us eat, and still denied,
Still fasting, from thy board we go:—
  'Where is *thy* feast, O Barmecide?'

1879.

THE BALLAD OF IMITATION

' C'est imiter quelqu'un que de planter des choux.'—ALFRED DE MUSSET.

IF they hint, O Musician, the piece that you played
  Is nought but a copy of Chopin or Spohr;
That the ballad you sing is but merely 'conveyed'
  From the stock of the Arnes and the Purcells of yore;
  That there's nothing, in short, in the words or the score
That is not as out-worn as the 'Wandering Jew,'
  Make answer—Beethoven could scarcely do more—
That the man who plants cabbages imitates, too!

If they tell you, Sir Artist, your light and your shade
  Are simply 'adapted' from other men's lore;
That—plainly to speak of a 'spade' as a 'spade'—
  You've 'stolen' your grouping from three or from four;

(346)

The Ballad of Imitation

That (however the writer the truth may deplore),
'Twas Gainsborough painted *your* ' Little Boy Blue ' ;
  Smile only serenely—though cut to the core—
For the man who plants cabbages imitates, too !

And you too, my Poet, be never dismayed
  If they whisper your Epic—' Sir Éperon d'Or '—
Is nothing but Tennyson thinly arrayed
  In a tissue that 's taken from Morris's store ;
    That no one, in fact, but a child could ignore
That you ' lift ' or ' accommodate ' all that you do ;
  Take heart—though your Pegasus' withers be sore—
For the man who plants cabbages imitates, too !

———

Postscriptum—And you, whom we all so adore,
  Dear Critics, whose verdicts are always so new !—
One word in your ear.   There were Critics before . . .
  And the man who plants cabbages imitates, too !

    1878.

THE BALLAD OF PROSE AND RHYME

When the ways are heavy with mire and rut,
  In November fogs, in December snows,
When the North Wind howls, and the doors are shut,—
  There is place and enough for the pains of prose ;
    But whenever a scent from the whitethorn blows,
And the jasmine-stars at the casement climb,
  And a Rosalind-face at the lattice shows,
Then hey !—for the ripple of laughing rhyme !

When the brain gets dry as an empty nut,
  When the reason stands on its squarest toes,
When the mind (like a beard) has a ' formal cut,'—
  There is place and enough for the pains of prose ;

But whenever the May-blood stirs and glows,
And the young year draws to the 'golden prime,'
   And Sir Romeo sticks in his ear a rose,—
Then hey!—for the ripple of laughing rhyme!

In a theme where the thoughts have a pedant-strut,
   In a changing quarrel of 'Ayes' and 'Noes,'
In a starched procession of 'If' and 'But,' —
   There is place and enough for the pains of prose;
   But whenever a soft glance softer grows
And the light hours dance to the trysting-time,
   And the secret is told 'that no one knows,'—
Then hey!—for the ripple of laughing rhyme!

ENVOY.

In the work-a-day world,—or its needs and woes,
There is place and enough for the pains of prose;
But whenever the May-bells clash and chime,
Then hey!—for the ripple of laughing rhyme!

1878.

'O NAVIS'

Ship, to the roadstead rolled,
   What dost thou?—O, once more
Regain the port. Behold!
   Thy sides are bare of oar,
   Thy tall mast wounded sore
Of Africus, and see,
   What shall thy spars restore!—
Tempt not the tyrant sea!

What cable now will hold
   When all drag out from shore!
What god canst thou, too bold,
   In time of need implore!

(348)

'O Navis'

Look! for thy sails flap o'er,
Thy stiff shrouds part and flee,
    Fast—fast thy seams outpour,—
Tempt not the tyrant sea!

What though thy ribs of old
    The pines of Pontus bore!
Not now to stern of gold
    Men trust, or painted prore!
    Thou, or thou count'st it store
A toy of winds to be,
    Shun thou the Cyclads' roar,—
Tempt not the tyrant sea!

ENVOY.

SHIP OF THE STATE, before
    A care, and now to me
A hope in my heart's core,—
    Tempt not the tyrant sea!

1883.

THE DANCE OF DEATH

(AFTER HOLBEIN)

'Contra vim MORTIS
Non est medicamen in hortis.'

HE is the despots' Despot.   All must bide,
Later or soon, the message of his might;
Princes and potentates their heads must hide,
Touched by the awful sigil of his right;
Beside the Kaiser he at eve doth wait
And pours a potion in his cup of state;
The crownèd Queen his bidding must obey;
No keen-eyed Cardinal shall him affray;
And to the Dame that wantoneth he saith—
'Let be, Sweet-heart, to junket and to play.'
There is no King more terrible than Death.

The Churl of Rank, rejoicing in his pride,
He draweth down ; before the armèd Knight
With jingling bridle-rein he still doth ride ;
He crosseth the strong Captain in the fight ;
The Burgher grave he beckons from debate ;
He hales the Abbot by his shaven pate,
Nor for the Abbess' wailing will delay ;
No bawling Mendicant shall say him nay ;
E'en to the pyx the Priest he followeth,
Nor can the Leech his chilling finger stay . . .
There is no King more terrible than Death.

All things must bow to him.   And woe betide
The Wine-bibber,—the Roisterer by night ;
Him the feast-master, many bouts defied,
Him 'twixt the pledging and the cup shall smite ;
Woe to the Lender at usurious rate,
The hard Rich Man, the hireling Advocate :
Woe to the Judge that selleth Law for pay ;
Woe to the Thief that like a beast of prey
With creeping tread the traveller harryeth :—
These, in their sin, the sudden sword shall slay . . .
There is no King more terrible than Death.

He hath no pity,—nor will be denied.
When the low hearth is garnishèd and bright,
Grimly he flingeth the dim portal wide,
And steals the Infant in the Mother's sight ;
He hath no pity for the scorned of fate :—
He spares not Lazarus lying at the gate,
Nay, nor the Blind that stumbleth as he may ;
Nay, the tired Ploughman,—at the sinking ray,—
In the last furrow,—feels an icy breath,
And knows a hand hath turned the team astray . . .
There is no King more terrible than Death.

The Dance of Death

He hath no pity.   For the new-made Bride,
Blithe with the promise of her life's delight,
That wanders gladly by her Husband's side,
He with the clatter of his drum doth fright,
He scares the Virgin at the convent grate ;
The Maid half-won, the Lover passionate ;
He hath no grace for weakness and decay :
The tender Wife, the Widow bent and gray,
The feeble Sire whose footstep faltereth,—
All these he leadeth by the lonely way . . .
There is no King more terrible than Death.

ENVOY.

YOUTH, for whose ear and monishing of late,
I sang of Prodigals and lost estate,
Have thou thy joy of living and be gay ;
But know not less that there must come a day,—
Aye, and perchance e'en now it hasteneth,—
When thine own heart shall speak to thee and say,—
There is no King more terrible than Death.

1877.

CARMINA VOTIVA

AND OTHER OCCASIONAL VERSES

(Too hard it is to sing
In these untuneful times,
When only coin can ring,
And no one cares for rhymes !

Alas ! for him who climbs
To Aganippe's spring:
Too hard it is to sing
In these untuneful times !

His kindred clip his wing;
His feet the critic limes ;
If Fame her laurel bring,
Old age his forehead rimes :
Too hard it is to sing
In these untuneful times !)

1876 [1875].

A BALLAD OF THE QUEEN'S MAJESTY

(JUNE 22, 1897)

NAME that has been thy nation's shield
  On many an alien shore and sea;
Name that in many a fateful field
  Has taught the stubborn foe to flee;
  Promise and proof of virtues three,
Valour unvaunting, vigour, verve,
  We hail thy white-winged Sovereignty,
VICTORIA! WHOM GOD PRESERVE!

Monarchs there are to whom men yield
  Obeisance—in a bondman's key;
Monarchs whose sceptred might doth wield
  Only the rod of Tyranny;
  We, in free homage, being free,—
We joy that naught can shake or curve
  Thy rectitude of Royalty,
VICTORIA! WHOM GOD PRESERVE!

Therefore from all our towers be pealed
  The note of greeting; therefore be,
As from a thousand springs unsealed,
  Outpoured the tide of mirth and glee;
  For surely not to-day shall we
From sixty years' allegiance swerve,
  Or shame thy twice-told Jubilee,
VICTORIA! WHOM GOD PRESERVE!

ENVOY.

QUEEN!—to whom true men bend the knee,
  Our island heart and brain and nerve
Are loyal—loyal unto thee,
  VICTORIA! WHOM GOD PRESERVE!

1897.

Carmina Votiva

A MADRIGAL

[*Written for* Choral Songs in Honour of Queen Victoria, 1899, *and
set to music by* Sir HUBERT PARRY.]

WHO can dwell with greatness! Greatness is too high;
Flowers are for the meadow, suns are for the sky :—
Ah! but there is greatness in this land of ours,
High as is the sunlight, humble as the flowers!

QUEEN, of thee the fable! LADY, thine the fate!
Royal, and yet lowly, lowly, and yet great ;—
Great in far dominion, great in bannered years,
Greater still as woman, greatest in thy tears!

1899.

RANK AND FILE

(SOUTH AFRICA, 1900)

O UNDISTINGUISHED Dead!
Whom the bent covers, or the rock-strewn steep
Shows to the stars, for you I mourn,— I weep,
O undistinguished Dead!

None knows your name.
Blacken'd and blurr'd in the wild battle's brunt,
Hotly you fell . . . with all your wounds in front :
This is your fame!

1900.

Carmina Votiva

VERSES READ AT THE DINNER OF THE OMAR KHAYYÁM CLUB

MARCH 25, 1897

'—*Medio de fonte leporum*
surgit OMARI *aliquid.*'—LUCRETIUS (*adapted*).

While we the Feast by Fruit and Wine prolong,
A Bard bobs up, and bores us with a Song.—THE APICIAD.

'TWAS Swift who said that people 'view
In HOMER more than HOMER knew.'
I can't pretend to claim the gift
Of playing BENTLEY upon SWIFT;
But I suspect the reading true
Is 'OMAR more than OMAR knew,'—
Or why this large assembly met
Lest we this OMAR should forget?
(In a parenthesis I note
Our RUSTUM here, without red coat;
Where SOHRAB sits I'm not aware,
But that's FIRDAUSI in the Chair!)—
I say then that we now are met
Lest we this OMAR should forget,
Who, ages back, remote, obscure,
Wrote verses once at Naishápúr,—
Verses which, as I understand,
Were merely copied out by hand,
And now, without etched plates, or aid
Of India paper, or hand-made,
Bid fair Parnassus' top to climb,
And knock the Classics out of time.

Persicos odi—Horace said,
And therefore is no longer read.
Time, who could simply not endure
Slight to the Bard of Naishápúr,

(357)

Carmina Votiva

(Time, by the way, was rather late
For one so often up-to-date !)
Went swiftly to the Roll of Fame
And blotted Q. H. F. his name,
Since when, for every Youth or Miss
That knows *Quis multa gracilis*,
There are a hundred who can tell
What OMAR thought of Heav'n and Hell;
Who BAHRÁM was; and where (at need)
Lies hid the Beaker of JAMSHYD ;—
In short, without a break can quote
Most of what OMAR ever wrote.

Well, OMAR KHAYYÁM wrote of Wine,
And all of us, sometimes, must dine ;
And OMAR KHAYYÁM wrote of Roses,
And all of us, no doubt, have noses ;
And OMAR KHAYYÁM wrote of Love,
Which some of us are not above.
Also, he charms to this extent,
We don't know, always, what he meant.
Lastly, the man's so plainly dead
We can heap honours on his head.

Then, too, he scores in other wise
By his 'deplorable demise.'
There is so much that we could say
Were he a Bard of yesterday !
We should discuss his draughts and pills,
His baker's and his vintner's bills ;
Rake up—perhaps 'tis well we can't—
Gossip about his maiden aunt ;
And all that marketable matter
Which FREEMAN nicknamed 'Harriet-chatter !'

But here not even Persian candles
Can light us to the smallest scandals;—
Thus far your OMAR gains at least
By having been so long deceased.

Failing of this, we needs must fall
Back on his *opus* after all:—
Those quatrains so compact, complete,
So suited to FITZGERALD'S feet,
(And, let us add, so subtly planned
To tempt the imitative band !)—
Those censers of Omari ware
That breathe into the perfumed air
His doubt, his unrest, his despair;—
Those jewels-four-lines-long that show,
Eight hundred years and more ago,
An old thing underneath the sun
In Babylonish Babylon:—
A Body and a Soul at strife
To solve the Mystery of Life !

So then all hail to OMAR K. !
(To take our more familiar way)
Though much of what he wrote and did
In darkest mystery is hid ;
And though (unlike our bards) his task
Was less to answer than to ask ;
For all his endless Why and Whether,
He brings us here to-night together ;
And therefore (as I said before),
Hail ! OMAR KHAYYÁM, hail ! once more !

1897.

Carmina Votiva

'UNDER WHICH KING?'

(Verses read at the Dinner of the
Omar Khayyám Club.   March, 1903)

'Under which king, Bezonian? Speak, or die.'
        —2 Henry IV. Act v., Scene 3.

'Under which king?' you ask, my friend.
        'The Hermit of the Suffolk shore?—
    The Tent-maker of Naishápúr?—
Omar, FitzGerald—which?'   Perpend.

The great Corneille, when pressed of yore,
        To judge two sonnets, answered thus:—
        'One, in its way, is marvellous;
And yet—I like the other more.'

This is my case betwixt your twain.
        But if you further question why
        I sit in this brave company,
I will—with your good leave—explain.

Life is a toilsome thing at best:
        We all too-heavy burdens bear,
        And groaning 'neath our load of care,
Run to and fro in search of rest.

We find it where this board is set:
        Kind looks across the napery gleam;
        The Past, the Future, grow a dream;
And— for the moment—we forget.

Omar, FitzGerald—these are all
        But phantasies.   We snuff the air;
        The green spot in the desert bare;
The Opiate of the Interval!

1903.

Carmina Votiva.

FOR A COPY OF 'THE COMPLEAT ANGLER'

'Le rêve de la vie champêtre a été de tout temps l'idéal des villes.'—GEORGE SAND.

I CARE not much how folks prefer
To dress your *Chubb* or *Chavender;*
I care no whit for line or hook,
But still I love old IZAAK's book,
Wherein a man may read at ease
Of 'gandergrass' and 'culverkeys,'
Or with half-pitying wonder, note
What *Topsell*, what *Du Bartas* wrote,
Or list the song, by *Maudlin* sung,
That *Marlowe* made when he was young :—
These things, in truth, delight me more
Than all old IZAAK's angling lore.

These were his SECRET.   What care I
How men concoct the Hawthorn-fly,
Who could as soon 'stroke Syllabub'
As catch your *Chavender* or *Chubb;*
And might not, in ten years, arrive
At baiting hooks with frogs, alive !—
But still I love old IZAAK's page,
Old IZAAK's simple *Golden Age,*
Where blackbirds flute from ev'ry bough,
Where lasses 'milk the sand-red cow,'
Where lads are 'sturdy foot-ball swains,'
And nought but soft ' May-butter' rains ;
Where you may breathe untainted air
Either at *Hodsden* or at *Ware ;*
And sing, or slumber, or look wise
Till *Phoebus* sink adown the skies ;

Then, laying rod and tackle by,
Choose out some 'cleanly Alehouse' nigh,
With ballads 'stuck about the wall,'
Of *Joan of France* or *English Mall*—
With sheets that smell of lavender—
There eat your *Chubb* (or *Chavender*).
And keep old IZAAK's honest laws
For 'mirth that no repenting draws'—
To wit, a friendly stave or so,
That goes to *Heigh-trolollie-loe*,
Or, more to make the ale-can pass,
A hunting song of *William Basse*—
Then talk of fish and fishy diet,
And dream you—'Study to be quiet.'

1899.

FOR 'AN APPENDIX TO THE ROWFANT LIBRARY'

(F. L. L.: IN MEMORIAM)

'HIS Books.' Oh yes, his Books I know,—
  Each worth a monarch's ransom;
But now, beside their row on row,
  I see, erect and handsome,

The courtly Owner, glass in eye,
  With half-sad smile, forerunning
Some triumph of an apt reply,—
  Some master-stroke of punning.

Where shall we meet his like again?
  Where hear, in such perfection,
Such genial talk of gods and men,—
  Such store of recollection;

Or where discern a verse so neat,
  So well-bred and so witty,—
So finished in its least conceit,
  So mixed of mirth and pity?

POPE taught him rhythm, PRIOR ease,
  PRAED buoyancy and banter;
What modern bard would learn from these?
  Ah, *tempora mutantur !*

The old *régime* departs,—departs;
  Our days of mime and mocker,
For all their imitative arts,
  Produce no FREDERICK LOCKER.
1900 [1899].

'GOOD LUCK TO YOUR FISHING!'

[*For a Picture by* G. F. WATTS, R. A.]

GOOD luck to your fishing !
  And what have you caught ?
Ah, would that my wishing
  Were more than a thought !
Ah, would you had caught her,
  Young Chloe, for me,—
Young Chloe, the daughter
  Of Proteus, the sea !

She irks me, she irks me,
  With blue of her eyes ;
She irks me, she irks me,
  With little drawn sighs ;
She lures me with laughter,
  She tempts me with tears ;
And hope follows after,—
  Hope only,—and fears !

Good luck to your fishing !
  But would you had caught
That maid beyond wishing,
  That maid beyond thought !
O cast the line deeper,
  Deep—deep in the sea ;
And catch her, and keep her,
  Dan Cupid, for me !

1901 [1900].

'WHEN THIS OLD WORLD WAS NEW'

WHEN this old world was new,
Before the towns were made,
Love was a shepherd too.

Clear-eyed as flowers men grew,
Of evil unafraid,
When this old world was new.

No skill had they to woo,
Who but their hearts obey'd—
Love was a shepherd too.

What need to feign or sue ?
Not thus was life delay'd
When this old world was new.

Under the cloudless blue
They kiss'd their shepherd-maid—
Love was a shepherd too.

They knew but joy ; they knew
No pang of Love decay'd :
When this old world was new,
Love was a shepherd too.

1901.

Carmina Votiva

FOR A COPY OF 'THE VICAR OF WAKEFIELD'

By GOLDSMITH's tomb the City's cry
   Grows faint and distant ; now no more,
   From that famed street he trod of yore,
Men.turn where those old Templars lie !

Only some dreamer such as I
   Pauses awhile from dust and roar
               By GOLDSMITH's tomb !

And then—ah, then !—when none is nigh,
   What shadowy shapes, unseen before,
   Troop back again from Lethe's shore !—
How the ghosts gather then, and sigh
               By GOLDSMITH's tomb !

1883.

AFTER A HOLIDAY

THREE little ducks by a door,
   Snuggling aside in the sun ;
The sweep of a threshing-floor,
   A flail with its One-two, One ;

A shaggy-haired, loose-limbed mare,
   Grave as a master at class ;
A foal with its heels in the air,
   Rolling, for joy, in the grass ;

A sunny-eyed, golden-haired lad,
   Laughing, astride on a wall ;
A collie-dog, lazily glad . . .
   Why do I think of it all ?

Why? From my window I see
  Once more, through the dust-dry pane,
The sky like a great Dead Sea,
  And the lash of the London rain;

And I read—here in London town,
  Of a murder done at my gate,
And a goodly ship gone down,
  And of homes made desolate;

And I know, with the old sick heart,
  That but for a moment's space
We may shut our sense, and part
  From the pain of this tarrying-place.

1901.

FOR A CHARITY ANNUAL

In Angel-Court the sunless air
  Grows faint and sick; to left and right
  The cowering houses shrink from sight,
Huddled and hopeless, eyeless, bare.

Misnamed, you say? For surely rare
  Must be the angel-shapes that light
              In Angel-Court!

Nay! the Eternities are there.
  Death at the doorway stands to smite;
  Life in its garrets leaps to flight;
And Love has climbed that crumbling stair
              In Angel-Court.

1901.

Carmina Votiva

THE PHILOSOPHY OF THE PORCH

BY A SUMMER-DAY STOIC

(TO ARTHUR MUNBY)

' *Cultivons notre jardin.*'—VOLTAIRE.

ACROSS my Neighbour's waste of whins
 For roods the rabbit burrows;
You scarce can see where first begins
 His range of steaming furrows;
I am not sad that he is great,
 He does not ask my pardon;
Beside his wall I cultivate
 My modest patch of garden.

I envy not my Neighbour's trees;
 To me it nowise matters
Whether in east or western breeze
 His 'dry-tongued laurel patters.'
Me too the bays become; but still,
 I sleep without narcotics,
Though he should bind his brows at will
 With odorous exotics.

Let Goodman Greenfat, glad to dine,
 With true *bon-vivant's* benison,
Extol my Neighbour's wit and wine—
 His virtue and his venison:
I care not! Still for me the gorse
 Will blaze about the thicket;
The Common's purblind pauper horse
 Will peer across my wicket;

For me the geese will thread the furze,
 In hissing file, to follow
The tinker's sputtering wheel that whirs
 Across the breezy hollow;

And look, where smoke of gipsy huts
   Curls blue against the bushes—
That little copse is famed for nuts,
   For nightingales and thrushes!

But hark! I hear my Neighbour's drums!
   Some dreary deputation
Of Malice or of Wonder comes
   In guise of Adulation.
Poor Neighbour! Though you 'call the tune,'
   One little pinch of care is
Enough to clog a whole balloon
   Of *aura popularis;*

Not amulets, nor epiderm
   As tough as armadillo's,
Can shield you if Suspicion worm
   Between your poppied pillows;
And though on ortolans you sup,
   Beside you shadowy sitters
Can pour in your ungenial cup
   Unstimulating bitters.

Let Envy crave, and Avarice save;
   Let Folly ride her circuit;
I hold that—on this side the grave—
   To find one's vein and work it,
To keep one's wants both fit and few,
   To cringe to no condition,
To count a truthful friend or two—
   May bound a man's ambition.

Swell, South-wind, swell my Neighbour's sails;
   Fill, Fortune, fill his coffers;
If Fate has made his rôle the whale's,
   And me the minnow's offers,

The Philosophy of the Porch

I am not sad that he is great ;
    He need not ask my pardon ;
Beside his wall I cultivate
    My modest patch of garden.

1871.

THE HOLOCAUST

' Heart-free, with the least little touch of spleen.'—MAUD.

ABOVE my mantelshelf there stands
    A little bronze sarcophagus,
Carved by its unknown artist's hands,
    With this one word—AMORIBUS !

Along the lid a Love lies dead—
    Across his breast his broken bow ;
Elsewhere they dig his tiny bed,
    And round it women wailing go :

A trick, a toy—mere ' Paris ware,'
    Some Quartier-Latin sculptor's whim,
Wrought in a fit of mock despair,
    With sight, it may be, something dim,

Because the love of yesterday
    Had left the *grenier*, light MUSETTE,
And she who made the morrow gay,
    LUTINE or MIMI, was not yet—

A toy.   But ah ! what hopes deferred
    (O friend, with sympathetic eye !),
What vows (now decently interred)
    Within that ' narrow compass ' lie !

For there, last night, not sadly, too,
    With one live ember I cremated
A nest of cooing *billets-doux*,
    That just two decades back were dated.

1889.

THE BALLAD OF THE BORE

'*Garrulus hunc quando consumet cunque.*'—Hor. Sat. I. ix. 33.

I SEE him come from far,
    And, sick with hopelessness,
Invoke some kindly star,—
    I see him come, no less.
    Is there no sure recess
Where hunted men may lie?
    Ye gods, it is too hard!
I feel his glittering eye,—
    Defend us from The Bard!

He knows nor let nor bar:
    With ever-nearing stress,
Like Juggernaut his car,
    I see him onward press;
    He waves a huge MS.;
He puts evasion by,
    He stands—as one on guard,
And reads—how volubly!—
    Defend us from The Bard!

He reads—of Fates that mar,
    Of Woes beyond redress,
Of all the Moons that are,
    Of Maids that never bless
    (As one, indeed, might guess);
Of Vows, of Hopes too high,
    Of Dolours by the yard
That none believe (nor buy),—
    Defend us from The Bard!

(370)

The Ballad of the Bore

ENVOY.

PRINCE PHOEBUS, all must die,
  Or well- or evil-starred,
  Or whole of heart or scarred ;
But why in this way—why?
  Defend us from The Bard !

1887.

JULY

(Virelai nouveau)

GOOD-BYE to the Town !—good-bye !
Hurrah ! for the sea and the sky !

In the street the flower-girls cry ;
In the street the water-carts ply ;
And a fluter, with features awry,
Plays fitfully ' Scots wha hae '—
And the throat of that fluter is dry ;
Good-bye to the Town !—good-bye !

And over the roof-tops high
Comes a waft like a dream of the May ;
And a lady-bird lit on my tie,
And a cock-chafer came with the tray ;
And a butterfly (no one knows why)
Mistook my Aunt's cap for a spray ;
And ' next door ' and ' over the way '
The neighbours take wing and fly ;
Hurrah ! for the sea and the sky !

To Buxton, the waters to try,
To Buxton goes old Mrs. Bligh ;
And the Captain to Homburg and play
Will carry his cane and his eye ;

And even Miss Morgan Lefay
Is flitting—to far Peckham Rye;
And my Grocer has gone—in a 'Shay,'
And my Tailor has gone—in a 'Fly':
Good-bye to the Town!—good-bye!

And it 's O for the sea and the sky!
And it 's O for the boat and the bay!
For the white foam whirling by,
And the sharp salt edge of the spray!
For the wharf where the black nets fry,
And the wrack and the oar-weed sway!
For the stroll when the moon is high
To the nook by the Flag-house gray!
For the *risus ab angulo* shy
From the Someone we designate 'Di!'
For the moment of silence, the sigh!
'How I dote on a Moon!' 'So do I!'
For the token we snatch on the sly!
(With nobody there to say Fie!)
Hurrah! for the sea and the sky!

*So Phyllis, the fawn-footed, hie
For a Hansom!   Ere close of the day
Between us a 'world' must lie:
Good-bye to the Town!   GOOD-BYE!
Hurrah! for the sea and the sky!*

1876.

Carmina Votiva

NOTES OF A HONEYMOON

' Dans ce ravissant opéra qu'on appelle l'amour, le libretto n'est presque rien.'—Victor Hugo.

In the Train.

At last we are free,—
  All hail, Hymenaeus !
From C., and from D.,—
At last !—we are free.
What a comfort 'twill be
  ' Mrs. Grundy' can't see us !
At last we are free,—
  All hail, Hymenaeus !

From the Hotel Window.

'What a mountain !' 'What ferns !'
  'And a pond, too, for Rover !'
Da capo—in turns.
'What a mountain !' 'What ferns !'
Meanwhile the toast burns,
  And the kettle boils over ;—
'What a mountain !' 'What ferns !'
  'And a pond, too, for Rover.'

The First Walk.

'Join hands for a peep.
  You must keep yourself steady.
See the cliff goes down steep,—
Join hands for a peep.
This they call "Lovers' Leap,"—
  We have leaped it already !
Join hands for a peep.
  You must keep yourself steady !'

(373)

Carmina Votiva

Arcadia.

'I can hear a sheep-bell.'
   'There are doves cooing yonder.'
'It sounds like a spell,—
I can hear a sheep-bell.'
'Shall we like this as well—
   In a twelvemonth?' '*I wonder!*'
'I can hear a sheep-bell.'
   'There are doves cooing yonder.'

At a Bookstall.

'Here it is in the "Times",'—
   'Dear Charlie,—how funny!'
'Twixt a "Smith" and a "Symes",—
Here it is!—in the "Times."
And it's *not* with the "crimes"!'
   'You must pay. *I've* no money!
Here it is in the "Times",—
   Dear Charlie,—how funny!'

Misgivings (No. 1).

'Poor Papa,—he's alone!'
   She is sure he must miss her.
There's a tear in the tone,—
'*Poor* Papa! *He's* alone!'
At this point, I own,
   There is naught but to kiss her.
'Poor Papa,—he's alone!'
   She is sure he must miss her.

Misgivings (No. 2).

By-play as before.
   'Then you'll love me for ever?'
'For ever—and more!'
   (By-play as before.)

(374)

'Never think me a "bore"?—
    Never laugh at me?' 'NEVER!!'
By-play as before.
    'Then you'll love me for ever?'

THE SUM TOTAL.

She is all that is sweet!
    I must learn to deserve her.
Bright, kind . . . I repeat—
She is all that is sweet!
(Here a noise in the street
    Puts an end to my fervour.)
She is all that is sweet!
    I must learn to deserve her.

1878.

'CHANGE'

FREEZE, freeze, O icy wind!
    LUCILLA'S cap's awry;
No signal undesigned
    To those that read the sky.

Dull drags the breakfast by:
    She's something on her mind;—
    Freeze, freeze, O icy wind!
LUCILLA'S cap's awry!

'You're tired—' 'And you're unkind!'
    'You're cross—' 'That I deny!'
'Perhaps you're both combined.'
    'I'm tired of You.—Good-bye!'—
Freeze, freeze, O icy wind!
    LUCILLA'S cap's awry!

1877.

'FAIR'

BLOW, blow, Etesian gale !
    LUCILLA'S cap is straight ;
Fill fast the flowing sail
    Of happy man and mate.

'What is it, Dear?—A plate?
    Do taste this potted quail !'
    Blow, blow, Etesian gale !
LUCILLA'S cap is straight.

' More sugar ?—No ? You're pale.
    My Own, you work too late !
Ah me, if *you* should fail !
    I'll see you to the gate.'—
Blow, blow, Etesian gale !
    LUCILLA'S cap is straight.

1877.

THE SONG OF THE SEA WIND

How it sings, sings, sings,
    Blowing sharply from the sea-line,
With an edge of salt that stings ;
    How it laughs aloud, and passes,
    As it cuts the close cliff-grasses ;
    How it sings again, and whistles
    As it shakes the stout sea-thistles—
    How it sings !

The Song of the Sea Wind

How it shrieks, shrieks, shrieks,
  In the crannies of the headland,
In the gashes of the creeks;
   How it shrieks once more, and catches
   Up the yellow foam in patches;
    How it whirls it out and over
    To the corn-field and the clover—
     How it shrieks!

How it roars, roars, roars,
  In the iron under-caverns,
In the hollows of the shores;
   How it roars anew, and thunders,
   As the strong hull splits and sunders:
    And the spent ship, tempest-driven,
    On the reef lies rent and riven—
     How it roars!

How it wails, wails, wails,
  In the tangle of the wreckage,
In the flapping of the sails;
   How it sobs away, subsiding,
   Like a tired child after chiding;
    And across the ground-swell rolling,
    You can hear the bell-buoy tolling—
     How it wails!

1901 [1885].

Carmina Votiva

TO F. M. D.

(With a volume of Herbert)

I

When I go
　From my place
　At your feet,
　　Sweet,
All I know
　Of your face
I recall,—
　　All;
Being by
　(In the net)
　I forget.
　　Why?

1885 [1868].

II

Being by,
　I but hear
What you say,—
　　Yea,
Naught am I
　But an ear
To the word
　　Heard;
Then I go
　And the grace
Of your face
　　Know.

TO LORD DE TABLEY

STILL may the muses foster thee, O Friend,
　Who, while the vacant quidnuncs stand at gaze,
Wond'ring what Prophet next the Fates may send,
　　Still tread'st the ancient ways;

Still climb'st the clear-cold altitudes of Song,
　Or ling'ring 'by the shore of old Romance,'
Heed'st not the vogue, how little or how long,
　　Of marvels made in France.

Still to the summits may thy face be set,
　And long may we, that heard thy morning rhyme,
Hang on thy noon-day music, nor forget
　　In the hushed even-time!

1896 [1894].

Carmina Votiva

A 'DEPARTMENTAL DITTY'

TO THE HON. T. H. W. PELHAM

WHILE you, at Brynhyffyn,
Are taking your muffin,
And shrimps and plum-duff in
   The sight of the sea,
Remember, remember,
The Ides of September,
And this junior member,
   Who wishes to flee!

You, bold as a Viking,
And clad to your liking,
Go bathing or 'biking,'
   Wherever you please;
He, worried and fretting,
Tight-collared and sweating,
Is well-nigh forgetting
   The colour of trees!

No President wrings you,
No work the post brings you,
The salt water stings you
   Wherever you go;
Lost,—lost in the Present,
And free as a pheasant,
Your 'Minutes' are pleasant,
   But his are not so!

For 'F. and H.'[1] grinds him,
And blue paper blinds him,
And red tape enwinds him
   From shoulder to knee;

---

[1] Fisheries and Harbour Department of the Board of Trade.

While you at Brynhyffyn
Grow sleek as a puffin,
With every new snuff in
You take of the sea !

1901 [1899].

TO THE EARL OF CREWE ON HIS MARRIAGE

WITH A VOLUME OF VERSE

In the duo of Love
  There is little libretto ;
There are few rhymes but 'dove'
In the duo of Love ;
Yet we prize it above
  All our Epic falsetto ;—
In the duo of Love
  There is little libretto.

1899

TO THE LADY DOROTHY NEVILL

[*With a Memoir of* HORACE WALPOLE]

HERE is HORACE his Life.   I have ventured to draw him
As the Berrys, the Conways, the Montagus saw him :
Very kind to his friends, to the rest only so-so ;
A Talker, Fine Gentleman, Wit, Virtuoso ;
With—running through all his sham-Gothic gim-crackery—
A dash of Sévigné, Saint-Simon and Thackeray.

For errors of ignorance, haste, execution,
From You, his descendant, I ask absolution.

1901 [1891].

(380)

TO EDMUND GOSSE

[*With a First Edition of* Atalanta in Calydon]

At your pleasure here I hold
'Atalanta snowy-souled':
Rather smudgy tho',—the gold
Not so brilliant as of old;
First Edition,—that is plain;
Monogram of J. B. Payne . . .
Dogg'rel this, but it was reckoned
Metre under George the Second.
Then a man was thought a Bard
If by striving *very* hard
He could write—say once a quarter,
Something just as long, or shorter.
Straight they crowned his head with bay,
Nobles took him home to 'tay';
Maids of honour for his muse
Quite forgot their 'P's' and 'Q's.'
See his name on all the posts;
People rush to buy in hosts
Tonson's last impression with
Author's portrait, done by Smith;
All his little words are quoted;
All his little airs are noted;
And, if he goes trickling on
From his paltry Helicon,
He is made Court-Footman or,
Possibly, Ambassador!

1893 [1878].

Carmina Votiva

TO THE SAME

[*With* CHURCHILL'S Poems (1763)]

WHEN CHURCHILL wrote, th' Aonian maid
He served was scarce of speech afraid;
    She used no phrase to circumvent
    The homely article she meant,
But plainly called a spade a spade.

Nor was the public much dismayed.
He but his age's law obeyed;—
    They liked to see the bludgeon's dent
           When CHURCHILL wrote.

'Tis not so now.   To-day the trade
Demands the finest Sheffield blade;
    We use a subtler instrument;
    We cut for depth and not extent . . .
But would 'twere ours—the Mark they made—
           When CHURCHILL wrote.

1893 [1877].

TO THE SAME

[*With* GOLDSMITH'S Selected Poems]

GRUB-STREET is Milton Street to-day;
    And that *antiqua Mater*
Whom GOLDSMITH served has passed away;
    But is our lot the greater?

Ah no! as some lean rascal hides
    His misery from his betters,
We wrap our trash in parchment sides,
    And call our task-work 'Letters.'

1893 [1887].

(382)

Carmina Votiva

TO THE SAME

[With a Memoir of HORACE WALPOLE]

HAD I but WALPOLE'S wit, I'd write
    A quatrain here to-day
Should turn the wig of PRIOR white,
    And make e'en HORACE gray;

Or had I STANHOPE'S pen (the same
    That once he lent to YOUNG),
I would as neat a couplet frame
    As e'er was said or sung;

But since I've not, I can't, you know;
    The page must go without it;
This is my latest gift; and so . . .
    And so, that's all about it!

1893 [1891].

TO THE SAME

[With At the Sign of the Lyre]

'BOOK against book.' 'Agreed,' I said:
But 'twas the truck of Diomed!

—And yet, in Fairy-land, I'm told
Dead leaves—as these—will turn to gold.
Take them, Sir Alchemist, and see!
Nothing transmutes like sympathy.

1893 [1885].

Carmina Votiva

TO THE SAME

[*With* VINCENT BOURNE'S Poetical Works]

GOSSIP, may we live as now,
Brothers ever, I and thou ;
Us may never Envy's mesh hold,
Anger never cross our threshold ;
Let our modest Lares be
Friendship and Urbanity.

1893 [1876].

TO THE SAME

[*With Eight Volumes of the Author's Works*]
' Exegi monumentum.'

EIGHT volumes !—all well-polished prose
Or better verse (as some suppose) ;
In style more playful than severe ;
Moral in tone (*pour qui sait lire*) ;
All written by my single pen,
And praised by some distinguished men,
But else not widely read, I fear :—

Crown me, MELPOMENE, my Dear !

1901 [1900].

TO THE SAME

[*With a Copy of* WALTON'S ' Lives']

YOU write your Life of Donne.   'Twill be
A masterpiece of sympathy !
Exact, I know, in fact and date,
And skilled to lead, to stimulate,
To show, as you would have him seen,
That morbid, mystic, mighty Dean.

To Edmund Gosse

But will you catch old Izaak's phrase
That glows with energy of praise?
Old Izaak's ambling unpretence
That flames with untaught eloquence?
Will you? I pause for a reply,
And you must answer, Friend, not I.

1901 [1899].

TO FREDERICK LOCKER

Is it to kindest Friend I send
   This nosegay gathered new?
Or is it more to Critic sure,—
   To Singer clear and true?
I know not which, indeed, nor need;
   All Three I found—in You.

1877.

FOR LOCKER'S 'LONDON LYRICS'
1881

APOLLO made, one April day,
A new thing in the rhyming way;
Its turn was neat, its wit was clear,
It wavered 'twixt a smile and tear,
Then MOMUS gave a touch satiric,
And it became a 'London Lyric.'

1881.

Carmina Votiva

TO BRANDER MATTHEWS

[With a Volume of Verses]

In vain to-day I scrape and blot :
  The nimble words, the phrases neat,
  Decline to mingle or to meet ;
My skill is all foregone—forgot.

He will not canter, walk nor trot,
  My Pegasus. I spur, I beat,
      In vain to-day !

And yet 'twere sure the saddest lot
  That I should fail to leave complete
  One poor . . . the rhyme suggests ' conceit !'
Alas ! 'Tis all too clear I'm not
      In *vein* to-day.

1884.

TO H. C. BUNNER

[With a Volume of Verses]

Witness my hand (and seal thereto) :
  All ye who wrong by word or sign
  This unprotected Muse of mine,
I wish you . . . Something else to do !

May all your bills at once fall due !
  May She, whose grace you seek, decline !
      Witness my hand !

But you, acute, accomplished, true
  And *candid*, who in every line
  Discern a spark (or sparks) divine,
Be blessed ! There 's good in store for You,—
      Witness my hand !

1884.

Carmina Votiva

TO GEORGE H. BOUGHTON, R.A.

[With a Volume of Verses]

SPRING stirs and wakes by holt and hill;
In barren copse and bloomless close
Revives the memory of the rose,
And breaks the yellow daffodil.

Look how the spears of crocus fill
The ancient hollows of the snows,—
Spring stirs and wakes!

Yet what to you are months? At will
For you the season comes or goes;
We watch the flower that fades and blows,
But on your happy canvas still
Spring stirs and wakes!

1885.

TO RICHARD WATSON GILDER

[With a Volume of Verses]

OLD friends are best! And so to you
Again I send, in closer throng,
No unfamiliar shapes of song,
But those that once you liked and knew.

You surely will not do them wrong;
For are you not an old friend, too?—
Old friends are best.

Old books, old wine, old Nankin blue;—
All things, in short, to which belong
The charm, the grace that Time makes strong,—
All these I prize, but (*entre nous*)
Old friends are best!

1884.

Carmina Votiva

TO LAURENCE HUTTON

[With a Volume of Verses]

THERE is no 'mighty purpose' in this book.
 Of that I warn you at the opening page,
Lest haply 'twixt the leaves you careless look
 And finding nothing to reform the age,
 Fall with the rhyme and rhymer in a rage.
Let others prate of problems and of powers;
 I bring but fancies born of idle hours,
 That striving only after Art and Ease,
Have scarcely more of moral than the flowers
 And little else of mission than to please.

1884.

VERSES WRITTEN FOR THE MENU OF THE OMAR KHAYYÁM CLUB

MAY 17, 1901

SALAAM TO OMAR! We that meet to-night
Have bid Black Care be banished, and invite
The Rose, the Cup, the not-too-ancient Jest
To help, and cheer us,—but beyond the Rest,
Peaceful Digestion with its blissful Calm.
Therefore to OMAR once again—SALAAM!

SALAAM TO OMAR! Life in truth is short,
And mortal Man of many Ills the Sport;
Yet still th' Oasis of the Board commends
Its Vantage-Ground for cheerful Talk of Friends,
And brings Oblivion, like an Eastern Balm.
Therefore to OMAR once again—SALAAM!

Verses for the Omar Khayyám Club

SALAAM TO OMAR!   Many Things must go
Down the dim Way that leads to Weal or Woe;
But kindly Hearts and kindly Thoughts will last
Till Time himself—the Arch-Iconoclast—
Drops the last Coin in Charon's withered Palm.
Therefore to OMAR once again—SALAAM!

1901.

HILL AND VALLEY

HE.

'COME, let us climb to the height,
    Peak after peak in the sun,
As the rays brighten, grow rosy and lighten,
    Now that the thunder has done.'

SHE.

'Nay; through the leafage, the light
    Gentlier glimmers below;
See through the valley the rivulets sally,
    Singing aloud as they go.'

HE.

'Grandly, ah! grandly the hill
    Broke the black storm on its crest;
All the cliff under went leaping the thunder,
    Growling away in the west.'

SHE.

'Here it is restful and still;
    Only the drops from the trees,
Where the shades darkle, fall slowly and sparkle,—
    Here there is solace and ease.'

(389)

He.

'Child, but the eagle above,
  Now that the mists are withdrawn,
Never wing-weary, sails up from his eyrie,
  E'en to the eye of the dawn.'

She.

'Ah, but below us the dove,
  Crooning for joy on the nest,
Fills with soft slumber the leaves without number,
  Shadow and quiet are best.'

1901 [1881].

ROSE, IN THE HEDGEROW GROWN

Rose, in the hedgerow grown,
  Where the scent of the fresh sweet hay
Comes up from the fields new-mown,
You know it—you know it—alone,
  So I gather you here to-day.

For here—was it not here, say?—
That she came by the woodland way,
  And my heart with a hope unknown
        Rose?

Ah yes!—with her bright hair blown,
  And her eyes like the skies of May,
And her steps like the rose-leaves strown
  When the winds in the rose-trees play—
It was here—O my love!—my own
        Rose!

1876.

LOVE'S FAREWELL

'No more!' I said to Love.   'No more!
   I scorn your baby-arts to know!
Not now am I as once of yore;
   My brow the Sage's line can show!'
'Farewell!' he laughed.   'Farewell! I go!'
   And clove the air with fluttering track.
'Farewell!' he cried far off;—but lo!
   He sent a Parthian arrow back!

1876.

HUITAINS

FOR ANDREW LANG'S 'THE LIBRARY'

I

BOOKS, books again, and books once more!
These are our theme, which some miscall
Mere madness, setting little store
By copies either short or tall.
But you, O Slaves of Shelf and Stall!
We rather write for you that hold
Patched folios dear, and prize 'the small,
Rare volume, black with tarnish'd gold.'[1]

II

'Of making many books,' 'twas said,
'There is no end'; and who thereon
The ever-running ink doth shed
But proves the words of Solomon.
Therefore we now, for colophon,
From London's city drear and dark,
In the year Eighteen-Eighty-One,
Reprint them at the press of CLARK.

1881.

[1] Ferriar's Bibliomania.

Carmina Votiva

A BALLAD OF ANTIQUARIES

THE days decay as flowers of grass,
  The years as silent waters flow ;
All things that are depart, alas !
  As leaves the winnowing breezes strow ;
  And still while yet, full-orbed and slow,
New suns the old horizon climb,
  Old Time must reap, as others sow :
We are the gleaners after Time !

We garner all the things that pass,
  We harbour all the winds may blow ;
As misers we up-store, amass
  All gifts the hurrying Fates bestow ;
  Old chronicles of feast and show,
Old waifs of by-gone rune and rhyme,
  Old jests that made old banquets glow :—
We are the gleaners after Time !

We hoard old lore of lad and lass,
  Old flowers that in old gardens grow,
Old records writ on tomb and brass,
  Old spoils of arrow-head and bow,
  Old wrecks of old worlds' overthrow,
Old relics of Earth's primal slime,
  All drift that wanders to and fro :—
We are the gleaners after Time !

ENVOY.

FRIENDS, that we know not and we know !
  We pray you, by this Christmas chime,
Help us to save the things that go :
  We are the gleaners after Time.

1880.

(392)

Carmina Votiva

A SECOND BALLAD OF ANTIQUARIES

'FRIENDS that we know not,'—late we said.
  We know you now, true friends, who still,
Where'er Time's tireless scythe has led,
  Have wrought with us through good and ill—
  Have toiled the weary sheaves to fill.
Hail then, O known and tried !—and you,
  Who know us not to-day, but will—
Hail to you all, Old Friends and New !

With no scant store our barns are fed :
  The full sacks bulge by door and sill,
With grain the threshing-floors are spread,
  The piled grist feeds the humming mill ;
  And—but for you—all this were nil,
A harvest of lean ears and few,
  But for your service, friends, and skill ;
Hail to you all, Old Friends and New !

But hark !—Is that the Reaper's tread ?
  Come, let us glean once more until
Here, where the snowdrop lifts its head,
  The days bring round the daffodil ;
  Till winds the last June roses kill,
And Autumn fades ; till, 'neath the yew,
  Once more we cry, with Winter chill,
Hail to you all, Old Friends and New !

ENVOY.

Come ! Unto all a horn we spill,
  Brimmed with a foaming Yule-tide brew,
Hail to you all, by vale and hill !—
  Hail to you all, Old Friends and New !
1881.

REGRETS

(AFTER JOACHIM DU BELLAY)

Happy the man, like wise Ulysses tried,
Or him of yore that gat the Fleece of Gold,
Who comes at last, from travels manifold,
Among his kith and kindred to abide!

When shall I see, from my small hamlet-side,
Once more the blue and curling smoke unrolled?
When the poor boundaries of my house behold—
Poor, but to me as any province wide?

Ah, more than these imperious piles of Rome
Laugh the low portals of my boyhood's home!
More than their marble must its slate-roof be!

More than the Tiber's flood my Loire is still!
More than the Palatine my native hill,
And the soft air of Anjou than the sea!

1901 [1886].

REGRETS

(AFTER JOACHIM DU BELLAY)

Alas! where now doth scorn of fortune hide?
And where the heart that still must conqueror be;
Where the strong hope of immortality,
And that fine flame to common souls denied?

Where is the joyance which, at eventide,
Through the brown night the silver moon could see,
With all the Nine, whenas, in fancy free,
I led the dance, some sacred stream beside?

Dame Fortune now is mistress of my soul,
And this my heart that I would fain control
Is grown the thrall of many a fear and sigh.

For after-time no more have I desire ;
No more within I feel that ancient fire,
And the sweet Muses turn from me, and fly.

1901 [1886].

TO MONSIEUR DE LA MOTHE LE VAYER, UPON THE DEATH OF HIS SON

(AFTER MOLIÈRE)

LET thy tears flow, LE VAYER, let them flow :—
None of scant cause thy sorrowing can accuse,
Since, losing that which thou for aye dost lose,
E'en the most wise might find a ground for woe.

Vainly we strive with precepts to forego
The drops of pity that are Pity's dues ;
And Nature's self, indignant, doth refuse
To count for fortitude that heartless show.

No grief, alas ! can now bring back again
The son too dear, by Death untimely ta'en ;
Yet, not the less, his loss is hard to bear,

Graced as he was by all the world reveres,
Large heart, keen wit, a lofty soul and rare,—
—Surely these claim immitigable tears !

1901 [1886].

Carmina Votiva

THE BALLAD OF BITTER FRUIT

(AFTER THÉODORE DE BANVILLE)

IN the wood with its wide arms overspread,
Where the wan morn strives with the waning night,
The dim shapes strung like a chaplet dread
Shudder, and sway to the left, the right;
The soft rays touch them with fingers white
As they swing in the leaves of the oak-tree browned,
Fruits that the Turk and the Moor would fright—
This is King Lewis his orchard-ground.

All of these poor folk, stark and sped,
Dreaming (who knows!) of what dead despight,
In the freshening breeze by the morning fed
Twirl and spin to the mad wind's might;
Over them wavers the warm sun bright;
Look on them, look on them, skies profound,
Look how they dance in the morning light!—
This is King Lewis his orchard-ground.

Dead, these dead, in a language dead,
Cry to their fellows in evil plight,
Day meanwhile thro' the lift o'erhead
Dazzles and flames at the blue vault's height;
Into the air the dews take flight;
Ravens and crows with a jubilant sound
Over them, over them, hover and light;—
This is King Lewis his orchard-ground.

ENVOY.

PRINCE, we wot of no sorrier sight
Under the whispering leafage found,
Bodies that hang like a hideous blight;—
This is King Lewis his orchard-ground.
1889.

(396)

Carmina Votiva

ON 'NOTES AND QUERIES'

In 'N and Q' we meet to weigh
The Hannibals of yesterday;
   We trace, thro' all its moss o'ergrown,
   The script upon Time's oldest stone,
Nor scorn his latest waif and stray.

Letters and Folk-lore, Art, the Play;
Whate'er, in short, men think or say,
   We make our theme—we make our own,
      In 'N and Q.'

Stranger, whoe'er you be, who may
From China to Peru survey,
   Aghast, the waste of things unknown,
   Take heart of grace, you're not alone;
And all (who will) may find their way
      In 'N and Q.'

1901 [1882].

TO THE PUBLISHER OF 'THE NEW MONTHLY REVIEW'

In the first days of this Review,
When Griffith, ay, and Madam, too,
From the old Dunciad in the Row
Instructed folk how they should go,
'Tis rumoured that they kept confined
And cabined in some room behind
A queer slow-witted, stuttering rogue,
An usher, with an Irish brogue,
Who, working then for Grub-Street pay,
Yet lived to write one perfect play

(397)

That still is played; to tell a tale
Still, as the book-stalls show, on sale;
And write, besides, some verse of note
That still old-fashioned persons quote.

Full well, I wot, Sir, your domain
No such back-parlour could contain;
Sure, too, am I you would not choose
The *Dunciad* for your sign to use;
But still I trust that you may light
Upon some genius who will write
Plain-spoken things, and unperplext,
That we may read this year and next,
Though they should fail to last as long
As GOLDSMITH's play and tale and song!

1901 [1900].

R. L. S.

IN MEMORIAM

THESE to his Memory.   May the Age arriving
    As ours recall
That bravest heart, that gay and gallant striving,
    That laurelled pall!

Blithe and rare spirit!   We who later linger
    By bleaker seas,
Sigh for the touch of the Magician's finger,—
    His golden keys!

1901.

FOR A VOLUME OF VERSE

GOOD Sir, or Madam, pray come in,—
. No doubt you'll find a vacant seat.
Our 'plot,' maybe, is somewhat thin,—
    We hope at least the 'parts' complete.

Of themes sublime we seldom treat,—
  Be warned of that ere we begin.
  Good Sir, or Madam, pray come in,—
No doubt you'll find a vacant seat.

Here is the Bill.   You see we spin
  But trifles.   Still, a slight conceit
May prove the pin to prick a sin,—
  The balm to make a virtue sweet.
Good Sir, or Madam, pray come in,—
  No doubt you'll find a vacant seat.

1901 [1877].

'ALBI, NE DOLEAS'

(HORACE, i. 33)

LOVE mocks us all.   Then cast aside
These tuneful plaints, my Albius tried
  For heartless Glycera, from thee
  Fled to a younger lover.   See,
Low-browed Lycoris burns denied

For Cyrus; he—though goats shall bide
With wolves ere she in him confide—
  Turns, with base suit, to Pholoë:—
    Love mocks us all!

So Venus wills, and joys to guide
'Neath brazen yoke pairs ill-allied
  In form and mind.   So linked she me
  (Whom worthier wooed) to Myrtale,
Fair, but less kind than Hadria's tide:—
    Love mocks us all!

1887.

Carmina Votiva

AD LYRAM

(HORACE, i. 32)

THE Muses call!   Now, Shell, inspire
   If aught, to last this year and more,
    Lightly, we two have wrought before ;—
Come now, a song like his whose fire

First touched thee, from th' Aonian choir
   Catching, thro' camp and tempest's roar,
    The Muses' call,—

Singing the Queen of all desire,
   Bacchus, and Cupid flutt'ring o'er,
    And Lycus : thou, that Phoebus bore,
Dear to Jove's feast—O aid me, Lyre !
    The Muses call !

1887.

LUDIBRIA VENTIS

'*Enough of these Toyes.*'—Bacon.

A BALLAD OF INCAPACITY

'My Lord, I cannot speak.'—MACLEAN THE HIGHWAYMAN
(on his trial).

'SILENCE is golden,' saith the saw,
  And rightly is extolled;
For Speech, too oft, outrides the law
  By waxing overbold:
  Yet he, I think (of mortal mould!),
Most needs the aid of 'cheek,'—
  The man who can *no* tale unfold,—
The man who cannot speak!

He listens with a kind of awe,
  And hears around him rolled
The long, reverberate guffaw
  That greets the quicker-souled;
  He hears the jest, or new or old,
And mutely eats his 'leek,'—
  Is classed as either dull or cold,—
The man who cannot speak!

He may have 'Latin in his mawe,'
  He may keep down controlled
Potentialities of 'jaw'
  Unmatched by any scold;
  He may have thoughts of sterling gold
For each day in the week;
  But he must all these things withhold,—
The man who cannot speak.

(403)

Ludibria Ventis

FRIENDS, 'tis of me the fable's told ;
   Your sufferance I seek ;
In me that shameless sight behold,—
   The man who cannot speak !

1909 [1901].

'A VOICE IN THE SCENTED NIGHT'

(Villanelle at Verona)

A VOICE in the scented night,—
   A step where the rose-trees blow,—
O Love, and O Love's delight !

Cold star at the blue vault's height,
   What is it that shakes you so ?
A voice in the scented night !

She comes in her beauty bright,—
   She comes in her young love's glow,—
O Love, and O Love's delight !

She bends from her casement white,
   And she hears it, hushed and low,
A voice in the scented night.

And he climbs by that stairway slight,—
   Her passionate ROMEO :—
O Love, and O Love's delight !

For it stirs us still in spite
   Of its 'ever so long ago,'
That voice in the scented night,—
   O Love, and O Love's delight !

1902.

Ludibria Ventis

A WELCOME FROM THE JOHNSON CLUB

To WILLIAM JOHN COURTHOPE, March 12, 1903

WHEN POPE came back from Trojan wars once more,
He found a Bard, to meet him on the shore,
And hail his advent with a strain as clear
As e'er was sung by BYRON or by FRERE.

You, SIR, have travelled from no distant clime,
Yet would JOHN GAY might welcome you in rhyme;
And by some Fable, not too coldly penned,
Teach how with judgment one may praise a Friend.

There is no need that I should tell in words
Your prowess from *The Paradise of Birds*;
No need to show how surely you have traced
The Life in Poetry, the Law in Taste;
Or mark with what unwearied strength you wear
The weight that WARTON found too great to bear.
There is no need for this or that.   My plan
Is less to laud the Matter than the Man.

This is my brief.   We recognize in you
The mind judicial, the untroubled view;
The Critic who, without pedantic pose,
Takes his firm foothold on the thing he knows;
Who, free alike from passion and pretence,
Holds the good rule of calm and common sense;
And be the subject or perplexed or plain,
Clear or confusing, is throughout urbane,
Patient, persuasive, logical, precise,
And only hard to vanity and vice.

More I could add, but brevity is best;—
These are our claims to honour you as Guest.

1903.

Ludibria Ventis

SURGE ET AMBULA

'ARISE, and walk'—the One Voice said;
   And lo! the sinews shrunk and dry
   Loosed, and the cripple leaped on high,
Wondering, and bare aloft his bed.

The Age of Miracle is fled.
Who to the halt to-day shall cry—
       ' Arise, and walk! '

Yet though the Power to raise the dead
   Treads earth no more, we still may try
   To smooth the couch where sick men lie,
Whispering—to hopeless heart and head—
       ' Arise, and walk! '

1904

SNAP-SHOT

A SWAN and cygnets, nothing more.
Background of silver, reedy shore,
Dim shapes of rounded trees, the high
Effulgence of a summer sky.

Only a snap-shot. Just a flash,
And it was fixed,—the mimic wash,
The parent bird on-oaring slow,
Her fussy little fleet in tow,
The all-pervading sultry haze,
The white lights on the waterways,—
A scene that never was before,
A scene that will be—Nevermore!

Alas! for us. We look and wait,
And labour but to imitate;
Vainly for new effects we seek . . .
Earth's shortest second is unique!

1904.

Ludibria Ventis

HORATIAN ODE ON THE TERCENTENARY OF 'DON QUIXOTE'

(Published at Madrid, by Francisco de Robles, January 1605.)

'*Para mi sola nació don Quixote, y yo para él.*'—CERVANTES

ADVENTS we greet of great and small ;
 Much we extol that may not live ;
 Yet to the new-born Type we give
  No care at all !

This year,[1]—three centuries past,—by age
 More maimed than by LEPANTO's fight,—
 This year CERVANTES gave to light
  His matchless page,

Whence first outrode th' immortal Pair,—
 The half-crazed Hero and his hind,—
 To make sad laughter for mankind ;
  And whence they fare

Throughout all Fiction still, where chance
 Allies Life's dulness with its dreams,—
 Allies what is, with what but seems,—
  Fact and Romance :—

O Knight of fire and Squire of earth !—
 O changing give-and-take between
 The aim too high, the aim too mean,
  I hail your birth—

Three centuries past—in sunburned SPAIN.
 And hang, on Time's PANTHEON wall,
 My votive tablet to recall
  That lasting gain !

1905.

[1] i.e. January 1905.

Ludibria Ventis

PEPYS' DIARY

(TO ONE WHO ASKED WHY HE WROTE IT)

You ask me what was his intent?
　In truth I'm not a German ;—
'Tis plain though that he neither meant
　A Lecture nor a Sermon.

But there it is, the thing's a Fact.
　I find no other reason
But that some scribbling itch attacked
　Him in and out of season,

To write what no one else should read,—
　With this for second meaning,
To 'cleanse his bosom' (and indeed
　It sometimes wanted cleaning) ;

To speak, as 'twere, his private mind
　Unhindered by repression,
To make his motley life a kind
　Of Midas' ears confession ;

And thus outgrew this work *per se*,—
　This queer, kaleidoscopic,
Delightful, blabbing, vivid, free
　Hotch-pot of daily topic,

So artless in its vanity,
　So fleeting, so eternal,
So packed with 'poor Humanity'—
　We know as Pepys his Journal.

1905.

THE SIMPLE LIFE

'*And 'a babbled of green fields.*'—SHAKESPEARE-CUM-THEOBALD.

WHEN the starlings dot the lawn,
Cheerily we rise at dawn;
Cheerily, with blameless cup,
Greet the wise world waking up;—
Ah, they little know of this,—
They of Megalopolis!

Comes the long, still morning when
Work we ply with book and pen;
Then,—the pure air in our lungs,—
Then ' persuasion tips our tongues ';
Then we write as would, I wis,
Men in Megalopolis!

Next (and not a stroke too soon!)
PHYLLIS spreads the meal of noon,
Simple, frugal, choicely clean,
Gastronomically mean;—
Appetite our entrée is,
Far from Megalopolis!

Salad in our garden grown,
Endive, beetroot,—all our own;
Bread,—we saw it made and how;
Milk and cream,—we know the cow;
Nothing here of 'Force' or 'Vis'
As at Megalopolis!

(409)

Ludibria Ventis

After, surely, there should be,
Somewhere, seats beneath a tree,
Where we—'twixt the curling rings—
Dream of transitory things;
Chiefly of what people miss
Drowsed in Megalopolis!

Then, before the sunlight wanes,
Comes the lounge along the lanes;
Comes the rocking shallop tied
By the reedy river-side;—
Clearer waves the light keel kiss
Than by Megalopolis!

So we speed the golden hours
In this Hermitage of ours
(*Hermits* we are not, believe!
Every Adam has his Eve,
Loved with a serener bliss
Than in Megalopolis):—

So—until the shadows fall:
Then Good Night say each and all
Sleep secure from smoke and din,
Quiet Conscience tucks us in;
Ah, they nothing know of *this*,—
They of Megalopolis!

(*Thus* URBANUS *to his Wife
Babbled of* The Simple Life.
*Then—his glances unawares
Lighting on a List of Shares—
Gulping all his breakfast down,
Bustled, by the Train, to* TOWN.)

1905.

A NEW YEAR'S THOUGHT

YET once again in wintry ways
The grey world rolls its tale of days ;
   And though its breast be chill and frore,
   Still holds the songs of Spring in store,
The Autumn rains, the Summer blaze.

Season to season, phase to phase
Succeed, and pass : what seems a maze
   Is but Life's ordered course gone o'er
       Yet once again.

So, through this drear December haze,
We, fearless, turn our forward gaze,
   As those who know, from days before,
   What has been once will be once more,—
Good Hap or ill, and Blame, and Praise,
       Yet once again !

1906.

RICHARD GARNETT

' Sit tibi terra levis !'

OF him, we may say justly—Here was one
   Who knew of most things more than any other ;
Who loved all learning underneath the sun,
   And looked on every learner as a brother.

Nor was this all.   For those who knew him knew
   Though far and wide his lore's domain extended
It held its quiet Poet's Corner too,
   Where Mirth and Song and Irony were blended.

1906.

Ludibria Ventis

THE PASSIONATE PRINTER TO HIS LOVE

(Whose name is Amanda.)

With Apologies to the Shade of Christopher Marlowe.

COME live with me and be my Dear;
　　And till that happy bond shall lapse,
I'll set your Poutings in *Brevier*,[1]
　　Your Praises in the largest CAPS.

There's *Diamond*—'tis for your Eyes;
　　There's *Ruby*—that will match your Lips;
Pearl, for your Teeth; and *Minion*-size
　　To suit your dainty Finger-tips.

In *Nonpareil* I'll put your Face;
　　In *Rubric* shall your Blushes rise;
There is no *Bourgeois* in your *Case*;
　　Your *Form* can never need '*Revise*.'

Your Cheeks seem '*Ready for the Press*';
　　Your Laugh as *Clarendon* is clear;
There's more distinction in your Dress
　　Than in the oldest *Elzevir*.

So with me live, and with me die;
　　And may no 'FINIS' e'er intrude
To break into mere '*Printers' Pie*'
　　The Type of our Beatitude!

(ERRATUM.—If my suit you flout,
　　And choose some happier Youth to wed,
'Tis but to cross AMANDA out,
　　And read another name instead.)

AMANDUS TYPOGRAPHICUS.

1906.

[1] ' Pronounced Bre-veer ' (Printers' Vocabulary).

Ludibria Ventis

AN EPISTLE TO AN EDITOR

' *Jamais les arbres verts n'ont essayé d'être bleus.*'
—Théophile Gautier.

' A NEW Review !'   You make me tremble
(Though as to that, I can dissemble
Till I hear more).   But is it 'new'?
And will it be a *real* Review ?—
I mean, a Court in which the scales
Weigh equally both him that fails,
And him that hits the mark ?—a place
Where the accus'd can plead his case,
If wrong'd ?   All this I need to know
Before I (arrogant !) say 'Go.'

' We, that are very old ' (the phrase
Is STEELE'S, not mine !), in former days,
Have seen so many 'new Reviews'
Arise, arraign, absolve, abuse ;—
Proclaim their mission to the top
(Where there 's still room !), then slowly drop,
Sink down, fade out, and *sans* preferment,
Depart to their obscure interment ;—
We should be pardon'd if we doubt
That a new venture *can* hold out.

It *will*, you say.   Then don't be 'new';
Be 'old.'   The Old is still the True.
Nature (said GAUTIER) never tries
To alter her accustom'd dyes ;
And all your novelties at best
Are ancient puppets, newly drest.
What you must do, is not to shrink
From speaking out the thing you think ;
And blaming where 'tis right to blame
Despite tradition and a Name.

Yet don't expand a trifling blot,
Or ban the book for what it's not
(That is the poor device of those
Who cavil where they can't oppose!);
Moreover (this is *very* old!),
Be courteous—even when you scold!

Blame I put first, but not at heart.
You must give Praise the foremost part;—
Praise that to those who write is breath
Of Life, if just; if unjust, Death.
Praise then the things that men revere;
Praise what they love, not what they fear;
Praise too the young; praise those who try;
Praise those who fail, but by and by
May do good work. Those who succeed,
You'll praise perforce,—so there's no need
To speak of that. And as to each,
See you keep measure in your speech;—
See that your praise be so exprest
That the best man shall get the best;
Nor fail of the fit word you meant
Because your epithets are spent.
Remember that our language gives
No limitless superlatives;
And SHAKESPEARE, HOMER, *should* have more
Than the last knocker at the door!

'We, that are very old!'—May this
Excuse the hint you find amiss.
My thoughts, I feel, are what to-day
Men call *vieux jeu*. Well!—'let them say.'
The Old, at least, we know: the New
(A changing Shape that all pursue!)
Has been,—may be, a fraud.
                        —But there!
Wind to your sail! *Vogue la galère!*
1906.

Ludibria Ventis

TO THOMAS BAILEY ALDRICH

AT seventy years one well might choose
To pause in service to the Muse;
    Nor counts it much for blame or praise
    To him whose brow is bound with bays
If she be kindly, or refuse.

Least—least of all, need we excuse
The Bard who, backward-looking, views
    But blameless songs and blameless days
        At seventy years!

And yet, Sing on.   While life renews
Its morning skies, its evening hues,
    Still may you walk in rhythmic ways
    Companioned of the lyre whose lays
None—in this tuneless time—would lose
        At seventy years!

1906.

TO MYRTALÉ

(With his verses)

MYRTALÉ, when I am gone
(Who was once Anacreon),
Lay these annals of my heart
In some secret shrine apart;
Into it put all my sighs,
All my lover's litanies,
All my vows and protestations,
All my jealous accusations,
All my hopes and all my fears,
All the tribute of my tears,—

(415)

Let it all be there inurned,
All my passion as it burned;
Label it, when I am gone,
' Ashes of Anacreon.'

1906.

' FAME IS A FOOD THAT DEAD MEN EAT '

(TO EDMUND GOSSE)

FAME is a food that dead men eat,—
I have no stomach for such meat.
In little light and narrow room,
They eat it in the silent tomb,
With no kind voice of comrade near
To bid the feaster be of cheer.

But Friendship is a nobler thing,—
Of Friendship it is good to sing.
For truly, when a man shall end,
He lives in memory of his friend,
Who doth his better part recall
And of his fault make funeral.

1906.

A WAIF

RAGGED and starved, with shifting look, and eyes
    Too old for childhood, and too dull for joy,
How shall you guess, thro' this forlorn disguise,
    The Man you hope for, in this hopeless Boy?

There is no heart so cold but may be warmed;
And—by the grace of God—can be transformed.

1907.

(416)

Ludibria Ventis

LONGFELLOW

(Born at Portland, Maine, U.S.A., February 27th, 1807.)

'AND his old age made beautiful with song.'
   These were thy words of Chaucer who, grown old,
   Like thee, those wand'ring 'Wayside' tales retold,
Which all men hearken to, when hours are long.

But thou hadst added to the rest a throng
   From Western Worlds; and Northern Runes unroll'd;
   And sought in Gestes and Fables manifold
Thy 'Birds of Passage,' fleet of wing and strong.

Bard of the bygone days when we were young!
Be this thy praise, that never flower'd among
   Thy 'Garden of Romance' aught base or mean;
And still, through all the changes of the year,
Thy stream of verse came welling pure and clear,
   A stainless fount,—the truest Hippocrene.

1907.

A PLEASANT INVECTIVE AGAINST PRINTING

'*Flee fro the* Prees, *and dwelle with sothfastnesse.*'
—CHAUCER, *Balade de Bon Conseil.*

THE Press is too much with us: small and great;
We are undone of chatter and *on dit*,
Report, retort, rejoinder, repartee,
Mole-hill and mare's nest, fiction up-to-date,
Babble of booklets, bicker of debate,
Aspect of A., and attitude of B.—
A waste of words that drive us like a sea,
Mere derelict of Ourselves, and helpless freight!

'O for a lodge in some vast wilderness!'
Some region unapproachable of Print,
Where never cablegram could gain access,
And telephones were not, nor any hint
Of tidings new or old, but Man might pipe
His soul to Nature,—careless of the Type!

1907.

THE FRIEND OF HUMANITY AND THE RHYMER

'Emam tua carmina sanus?'—MARTIAL.

F. OF H. I WANT a verse.   It gives you little pains;—
You just sit down, and draw upon your brains.
Come, now, be amiable.

R.   To hear you talk,
You'd make it easier to fly than walk.
You seem to think that rhyming is a thing
You can produce if you but touch a spring;
That fancy, fervour, passion—and what not,
Are just a case of 'penny in the slot.'
You should reflect that no evasive bird
Is half so shy as is your fittest word;
And even similes, however wrought,
Like hares, before you cook them, must be caught;—
Impromptus, too, require elaboration,
And (unlike eggs) grow fresh by incubation;
Then,—as to epigrams . . .

F. OF H.   Nay, nay, I've done.
I did but make petition.   You make fun.

R. Stay.   I am grave.   Forgive me if I ramble:
But then a negative needs some preamble
To break the blow.   I feel with you, in truth,
These complex miseries of Age and Youth;

The Friend of Humanity

I feel with you—and none can feel it more
Than I—this burning Problem of the Poor;
The Want that grinds, the Mystery of Pain,
The Hearts that sink, and never rise again;—
How shall I set this to some careless screed,
Or jigging stave, when Help is what you need,
Help, Help,—more Help?

F. OF H.   I fancied that with ease
    You'd scribble off some verses that might please,
    And so give help to us.

R.   Why then—TAKE THESE!
    1907.

TO A FRIEND

WHO DEPLORED THE BRIEF LIFE OF LITERARY PERSONALITY

IT is most true—and most untrue!
Though all should die of Me and You
And all of later men who press
This weary ball, 'tis like, no less,
That our stray thistle-down of thought
Claimed of some winnowing breeze, and brought
To some safe seeding-place, may lie
Securely there, and fructify;
And—in a world still out of joint—
May serve some bard for starting-point
Of some yet larger utterance whence
New bards shall borrow, aeons hence.

What skills it then, though We be done:
Our thought is living—and lives on!
    1907.

Ludibria Ventis

A PROEM

(To Mr. Arthur Rackham's edition of *Alice in Wonderland*.)

'Tis two-score years since Carroll's art,
    With topsy-turvy magic,
Sent Alice wandering through a part
    Half-comic and half-tragic.

Enchanting Alice! Black-and-white
    Has made your charm perennial;
And nought save 'Chaos and old Night'
    Can part you now from Tenniel;

But still you are a Type, and based
    In Truth, like Lear and Hamlet;
And Types may be re-draped to taste
    In cloth of gold or camlet.

Here comes a fresh Costumier then;
    That Taste may gain a wrinkle
From him who drew with such deft pen
    The rags of Rip van Winkle.

1908 [1907].

THE LAST PROOF

AN EPILOGUE TO ANY BOOK

'Finissons. Mais demain, Muse, à recommencer.'—Boileau.

'Finis at last—the end, the End, the End!
No more of paragraphs to prune or mend;
No more blue pencil, with its ruthless line,
To blot the phrase "particularly fine";
No more of "slips," and "galleys," and "revises,"
Of words "transmogrified," and "wild surmises";

(420)

The Last Proof

No more of *n*'s that masquerade as *u*'s,
No nice perplexities of p's and q's ;
No more mishaps of *ante* and of *post*,
That most mislead when they should help the most ;
No more of " friend " as " fiend," and " warm " as " worm ";
No more negations where we would affirm ;
No more of those mysterious freaks of fate
That make us bless when we should execrate ;
No more of those last blunders that remain
Where we no more can set them right again :
No more apologies for doubtful data ;
No more fresh facts that figure as Errata ;
No more, in short, O Type, of wayward lore
From thy most *un*-Pierian fount—NO MORE ! '
So spoke PAPYRIUS. Yet his hand meanwhile
Went vaguely seeking for the vacant file,
Late stored with long array of notes, but now
Bare-wired and barren as a leafless bough ;—
And even as he spoke, his mind began
Again to scheme, to purpose and to plan.

There is no end to Labour 'neath the sun ;
There is no end of labouring—but One ;
And though we 'twitch [or not] our Mantle blue,'
'To-morrow to fresh Woods, and Pastures new.'

   1907.

AN EPITAPH

(FOR A PARISH MAGAZINE)

' *On n'y lit aucun nom.*'—VICTOR HUGO.

HERE sleeps, at last, in narrow bed,
   A man of whom, whate'er is spoken,
This may with certainty be said
   His promises were never broken.

(421)

Ludibria Ventis

He boasted no high-sounding name,
  Or graced with academic letters;
He paid his way though, all the same,
  And—more than once—forgave his debtors.

He never joined the cry of those
  Who prate about the Public Morals;
But reconciled some private foes,
  And patched up sundry standing quarrels.

It never came within his plan
  To 'demonstrate' on Want or Labour;
He strove to serve his fellow-man,
  And did his best to love his neighbour.

When Doubt disturbed his honest soul,
  He found in this his consolation :—
We see a part, and not the whole,
  With only scant illumination.

And this, at least, he felt was sure :—
  To give the sick man's hurt a plaster,
To soothe the pain no art can cure,—
  Was but the bidding of his Master.

So, all unpraised, he ran his race;
  But we, who watched his life, and knew it,
Thus mark his nameless resting-place,
  Because he died too poor to do it.

1908.

THE HAPPY PRINTER

' Hoc est vivere.'—MARTIAL.

THE Printer's is a happy lot :
    Alone of all professions,
No fateful smudges ever blot
    His earliest ' impressions.'

The outgrowth of his youthful ken
    No cold obstruction fetters ;
He quickly learns the ' types' of men,
    And all the world of ' letters.'

With ' forms' he scorns to compromise ;
    For him no ' rule' has terrors ;
The ' slips' he makes, he can ' revise '—
    They are but ' printers' errors.'

From doubtful questions of the ' Press'
    He wisely holds aloof ;
In all polemics, more or less,
    His argument is ' proof.'

Save in their ' case,' with High and Low,
    Small need has he to grapple !
Without dissent he still can go
    To his accustomed ' Chapel.' [1]

From ills that others scape or shirk,
    He rarely fails to rally ;
For him, his most ' composing' work
    Is labour of the ' galley.'

[1] This—derived, it is said, from Caxton's connexion with Westminster Abbey—is the name given to the meetings held by printers to consider trade affairs, appeals, &c. (Printers' Vocabulary).

Ludibria Ventis

Though ways be foul, and days are dim,
    He makes no lamentation;
The primal 'fount' of woe to him
    Is—want of occupation:

And when, at last, Time finds him gray
    With over-close attention,
He solves the problem of the day,
    And gets an Old Age pension.

1908.

A MILTONIC EXERCISE

(TERCENTENARY, 1608–1908)

' *Stops of various Quills.*'—LYCIDAS.

WHAT need of votive Verse
    To strew thy *Laureat Herse*
With that mix'd *Flora* of th' *Aonian Hill?*
    Or *Mincian* vocall Reed,
    That *Cam* and *Isis* breed,
When thine own Words are burning in us still?

    Bard, Prophet, Archimage!
    In this Cash-cradled Age,
We grate our scrannel Musick, and we dote:
    Where is the Strain unknown,
    Through Bronze or Silver blown,
That thrill'd the Welkin with thy woven Note?

    Yes—'we are selfish Men':
    Yet would we once again
Might see *Sabrina* braid her amber Tire;
    Or watch the *Comus* Crew
    Sweep down the Glade; or view
Strange-streamer'd Craft from *Javan* or *Gadire!*

A Miltonic Exercise

Or could we catch once more,
High up, the Clang and Roar
Of Angel Conflict,—Angel Overthrow;
Or, with a World begun,
Behold the young-ray'd Sun
Flame in the Groves where the *Four Rivers* go!

. . . .

Ay me, I fondly dream!
Only the Storm-bird's Scream
Foretells of Tempest in the Days to come;
Nowhere is heard up-climb
The lofty lyric Rhyme,
And the 'God-gifted Organ-voice' is dumb.

1908.

PROLOGUE

TO 'DE LIBRIS'

LECTOR Benevole!—for so
They used to call you, years ago,—
I can't pretend to make you read
The pages that to this succeed;
Nor would I, if I could, excuse
The wayward promptings of the Muse,
At whose command I wrote them down.

I have no hope to 'please the town.'
I did but think some friendly soul
(Not ill-advised, upon the whole!)
Might like them; and—'to interpose
A little ease,'—between the prose,
Slipped in the scraps of verse, that thus
Things might be less monotonous.

Then, *Lector*, be *Benevolus!*

1908.

Ludibria Ventis

A SONG OF THE GREENAWAY CHILD

As I went a-walking on *Lavender Hill*,
O, I met a Darling in frock and frill ;
And she looked at me shyly, with eyes of blue,
'Are you going a-walking ? Then take me too !'

So we strolled to the field where the cowslips grow,
And we played—and we played for an hour or so ;
Then we climbed to the top of the old park wall,
And the Darling she threaded a cowslip ball.

Then we played again, till I said—'My Dear,
This pain in my side, it has grown severe ;
I ought to have told you I'm past three score,
And I fear that I scarcely can play any more !'

But the Darling she answered,—'O no ! O no !
You must play—you must play.—I shan't let you go !'
—And I woke with a start and a sigh of despair
And I found myself safe in my Grandfather's-chair !

1908.

'K. G.'

(November 6, 1901)

FAREWELL, kind heart ! And if there be
In that unshored immensity
Child-Angels, they will welcome thee.

Clean-souled, clear-eyed, unspoiled, discreet,
Thou gav'st thy gifts to make Life sweet,—
These shall be flowers about thy feet !

1902.

Ludibria Ventis

FOR A VISITORS' BOOK

(TO THE LADY OF THE CASTLE)

' HE who fears the trial,
    Naught can hope to gain ' :—
Shall I make denial
    À la Châtelaine ?

Come then, MUSE, and lend me
    All that poets feign :
Let my verse commend me
    À la Châtelaine !

.   .   .   .   .

TIME, that rarely lingers,—
    TIME, that churl ingrain,—
Kisses courtier fingers
    À la Châtelaine ;

Leads her by soft places
    Free from stone and stain ;
Spares his sterner traces
    À la Châtelaine !

.   .   .   .   .

Ah ! benign, caressing,
    Still, O TIME, remain ;
Send thy chiefest blessing
    À la Châtelaine !

Make her sorest troubles
    Light as summer rain ;
Crosses be but bubbles
    À la Châtelaine !

Neither mar nor mend her ;
    Save her toil and pain ;
TIME, be always tender
    A la Châtelaine !

1908.

Ludibria Ventis

'TWO MAIDS UPROSE IN THE SHIMMERING LIGHT'

'Qui gagne bataille
Aura mes amours.'—
'Qu'il gagne ou qu'il perde
Les aura toujours.'

Two maids uprose in the shimmering light
 Of the clanging battle-morn;
And one was tressed like the bird of night,
 And one like the ripening corn.

Then out spoke she with the raven locks,
 And her dark eyes glowed like wine:—
'If he slay the foe, the knight I know,
 He shall win this heart of mine!'

But softlier she of the yellow hair,
 And her blue eyes 'gan to fill:
'Though he gain or lose, the man I choose,
 He shall be my true love still!'

1908.

ELIM

(Exodus xv. 27)

PALM-TREES and wells they found of yore,
Who—that Egyptian bondage o'er—
 Had sight betimes of feathering green,
 Of lengthened shadows, and between,
The cool, deep-garnered water-store.

Dear,—dear is Rest by sea and shore:
But dearest to the travel-sore,
 Whose camping-place not yet has been
 Palm-trees and wells!

(428)

For such we plead.   Shall we ignore
The long Procession of the Poor,
    Still faring through the night-wind keen,
    With faltering steps, to the Unseen?—
Nay : let us seek for these once more
        · Palm-trees and wells !

1909.

COLLABORATION : AN ECLOGUE

' *Alternis dicetis : amant alterna Camenae.*'—VIRG.

SCENE.—*A Seat on the Thames Embankment.*

BROWN.   BLACK.

(BROWN *has fair hair, displays a velvet coat,*
Pince-nez on nose, and wisp about his throat ;
BLACK *is stiff-bearded, sturdy, brown of boot,*
Wears Harris tweeds, and smokes a brier-root.)

Br. I cannot rhyme, yet feel poetic throes.
Bl. Rhymes I can manage.   But my taste is prose.
Br. A happy thought !   Supposing we combine ?
    I'll find the subject,
Bl.   And I'll cap the line.
Br. Let me premise that, whether blank or not,
    Verse should be rhythmical at any rate.
Bl. I don't object.   But it must 'touch the spot' ;
    And not be 'precious' or 'alembicate.'

Br. Begin then, Muse,—begin the lofty Song !
Bl. In plainer English,—'Roll the ball along !'
Br. 'Life is a Dream'—as Calderon has said—
Bl. And ought to know, for he has long been dead.
Br. A perilous Journey to a Goal unknown—
Bl. Unless you have some income of your own.

Ludibria Ventis

Br. Love is a Need, in Natures incomplete —
Bl. Platonic rubbish !—and a mere conceit.
Br. A gilded Apple, bitter to the Core—
Bl. Also, a metaphor much heard before.
Br. But Love the Need and Life the Dream exist —
Bl. Though—as abstractions—neither would be missed.

Br. And even Sentiment, Affection's Priest—
Bl. Is but an entrée in the daily feast.
Br. An entrée, yes,—and often overlooked—
Bl. Provided that your standing-dish be cooked.
Br. Provided, too, you banish Thought and Care—
Bl. Both needless extras in a bill of fare.

Br. That makes four verses.   Only, your replies
    Have more of crambo than of consequence.
Bl. They have, of course.   No Pegasus that flies
    Can soar when handicapped by Common-sense.

Br. Which makes another.   Underneath the lamp,
    I'll write them down—
Bl.   And I'll provide the stamp.
Br. 'The stamp !' For what ? You think some Magazine ?—
Bl. Why not ?   That is precisely what I mean.

*(So said, so done.   We find them here and guess
They must forthwith have posted that MS.:—
Each Bard believing, as they both retired,
That what he spoke, would be the more admired.)*

1909.

Ludibria Ventis

ENTENTE CORDIALE

Now side by side curvet and prance
The flower of England and of France,
   Tried champions, comrades leal and true,
   Resolved, in all, to dare and do,—
Whom pen and pencil serve for lance.

'Knights of the Joyous Countenance!'—
In wit, skill, gaiety, romance,
   Who shall to-day contend with you,
      Now side by side?

Salut, MESSIRES! May no mischance
To this fair bond bring severance!
   Salut! Salut! Red, White and Blue;—
   Salut! to our grim Lion too,
Who laughs to see the lines advance
      Now side by side!

1909

LATER ADDITIONS AND
TRANSLATIONS

VERSES WRITTEN FOR THE MENU
OF THE OMAR KHAYYÁM CLUB

APRIL 22, 1910

Roses and Wine your OMAR brings,
    Yet o'er the Cup, a Moment-Space,
    Peers into Naught with wistful Face,
As One who views but bygone Things.

Not so with Us. Our larger Scope
    Looks backward through the Past to see
    Not what has been, but what may be—
We drink, not Memory, but Hope.

1910.

LA BONNE COMÉDIE

*'Les "Précieuses Ridicules" allèrent aux nues dès le premier jour.
Un vieillard s'écria du milieu du parterre: "Courage, Molière! voilà de
la bonne comédie!"'* (*Notice sur Molière.*)

TRUE Comedy *circum praecordia ludit*—
It warms the heart's cockles. 'Twas thus that he viewed it,
That simple old Critic, who smote on his knee,
And named it no more than he knew it to be.

'True Comedy!' Yes! there is this thing about it,
If it makes the House merry, you never need doubt it:
It lashes the vicious; it laughs at the fool;
And it brings all the prigs and pretenders to school.

(435)

To the poor it is kind ; to the plain it is gentle ;
It is neither too tragic nor too sentimental ;
Its thrust, like a rapier's, though cutting, is clean,
And it pricks Affectation all over the scene.

Its rules are the rules ARISTOTLE has taught us ;
Its ways have not altered since TERENCE and PLAUTUS ;
Its mission is neither to praise nor to blame ;
Its weapon is Ridicule ; Folly, its game.

'True Comedy !'—such as our POQUELIN made it !
'True Comedy !'—such as our COQUELIN played it !
It clears out the cobwebs ; it freshens the air ;
And it treads in the steps of its Master, MOLIÈRE !

1910.

IN MEMORIAM

(FRIDAY, MAY 20, 1910)

'*Exstinctus amabitur idem.*'
Hor. *Epist.* ii. 1. 14.

HE that was King an hour ago
   Is King no more ; and we that bend
Beside the bier, too surely know
     We lose a Friend.

His was no 'blood-and-iron' blend
   To write in tears a ruthless reign ;
Rather he strove to make an end
     Of strife and pain.

Rather he strove to heal again
   The half-healed wound, to hide the scar,
To purge away the lingering stain
     Of racial war.

(436)

In Memoriam

Thus, though no trophies deck his car
    Of captured guns or banners torn,
Men hailed him as they hail a star
    That comes with morn:

A star of brotherhood, not scorn,
    A morn of loosing and release—
A fruitful time of oil and corn—
    An Age of Peace!

Sleep then, O Dead beloved! and sleep
    As one who, when his course is run,
May yet, in slumber, memory keep
    Of duty done;

Sleep then, our England's King, as one
    Who knows the lofty aim and pure,
Beyond all din of battles won,
    Must still endure.

1910.

THREESCORE AND TEN

*'Age **never** droops into decrepitude while Fancy stands at his side.'*

So LANDOR wrote, and so I quote,
    And wonder if he knew;
There is so much to doubt about—
    So much but partly true!

Can one make points with stiffened joints?
    Or songs that breathe and burn?
Will not the jaded Muse refuse
    An acrobatic turn?

There was a time when dancing rhyme
    Ran readily to cantos;
But now it seems too late a date
    For galliards and corantos.

(437)

One must beware, too, lest one's pace
    Disgrace one's ROXALANE,
For e'en Decrepitude, my Friend,
    Must bend—in a *pavane*.

No! on the whole the fittest rôle
    For Age is the spectator's,
In roomy stall reclined behind
    The 'paters' and the 'maters,'

That fondly watch the pose of those
    Whose thought is still creative—
Whose point of view is fresh and new,
    Not feebly imitative.

Time can no more lost Youth restore
    Or rectify defect;
But it can clear a failing sight
    With light of retrospect.

1911.

AN HORATIAN ODE TO THE KING'S MOST EXCELLENT MAJESTY

(22ND JUNE, 1911)

NOT with high-vaulting phrase, or rush
    Of weak-winged epithets that tire
With their own weight, or formal gush,
    We greet thee, Sire!

To flights less lofty we aspire.
    We pray, in speech unskilled to feign,
That all good things good men desire
    May crown Thy reign;

(438)

That our State ' Dreadnought' once again
　　May leave in broken seas to veer,
And shape her course direct and plain,
　　　　With Thee to steer,

Into blue sky and water clear,
　　Where she on even keel shall ride,
Secure from reef and shoal, or fear
　　　　Of wind and tide.

So may it be, Sire !—so abide !
　　Till, by God's grace, this Empire shine
More great in power than great in pride,
　　　　Through Thee and Thine ;

Nor from her honoured past resign
　　One least bequest ; or vail her claim
To aught that dowers an ancient line—
　　　　An ancient fame !

1911.

WILLIAM MAKEPEACE THACKERAY

('JULY 18, THACKERAY B. 1811')

AH ! what a world the words bring back—
Those bald words in the Almanac !

　Once more they come—from days long fled—
The towering form, the grand white head ;
The upturned look that seems to scent
The paltry and the fraudulent ;
The kind eyes that too soon confess
Their sympathy with wretchedness ;
Nor only these, but all the train
That issued from that teeming brain.

Trooping they enter, one by one,
Distinct and vivid, strangers none;
Nay—if that can be—better known
Than mortal kinsfolk of our own:
'Becky,' 'Amelia,' 'Dobbin,' 'Jos,'
'Pendennis,' 'Warrington,' and 'Cos'—
'Cos' with his 'oi'—Pen's uncle too!
'Florac,' the Colonel, 'Ethel,' 'Kew,'
''Trix' and her mother, and not less
That later ''Trix'—the Baroness.
'Esmond' of course, and 'George,' and 'Harry,'
The rogues and rascals—'Deuceace,' 'Barry,'
Evil or good, none immature,
From 'Yellowplush' to 'Barbazure';
None dimly seen or half-achieved,
Or drawn too vague to be believed;
But each, however small the rôle,
A thing complete, a finished whole.

These are no puppets, smartly drest,
But jerked by strings too manifest;
No dummies wearing surface skin
Without organic frame within;
Nor do they deal in words and looks
Found only in the story-books.
No!—for these beings use their brains,
Have pulse and vigour in their veins;
They move, they act; they take and give
E'en as the master wills; they *live*—
Live to the limit of their scope,
Their anger, pleasure, terror, hope!

Because he touched the flaw in all,
There were who called him 'cynical';
Because his mood to pity leant,
They styled it 'mawkish sentiment';

William Makepeace Thackeray

Because—disdaining to make light
Of wrong by treating it as right—
He probed the wound he saw exist,
They dubbed him 'heartless satirist'!

We have reversed all that to-day :
We know him better—or we may.
We know he strove by ridicule
To shame the hypocrite and fool;
We know—alike in age and youth—
He sought unshrinkingly for truth ;
Made of no smallest virtue sport ;
Loved honesty and good report ;
Went manfully his destined way,
Doing, as far as in him lay,
His daily task without pretence—
With dignity and reticence.

Peace to his memory—and his type !
Too rare, in times grown over-ripe !
Peace to his memory !   Let him rest
Among our bravest and our best ;
Secure, that through the years to come,
His voice shall speak, though he be dumb,
Since men unborn, or glad or vext,
Must need his Sermon and his Text.

He painted Life—the life he knew :
The roundabout of false and true,
The ups-and-downs of good and bad,
The strange vicissitudes and sad,
The things unsolved, the seeming-chance
Complexities of Circumstance,
Yet failed not, humbly, to recall
The Power above, controlling all.

1911.

TO HUGH THOMSON

(WITH A COPY OF SIR JOHN GILBERT'S SHAKESPEARE)

In Fifty-six, when GILBERT drew
These brave conceptions, people knew
   Little that we to-day repeat
   (Quoting the prophet in the street)
Of Value, Tone, and Point of View!

Their tastes were plain; their wants were few;
They liked red suns and skies of blue . . .
   They were so frankly incomplete
        In Fifty-six!

And yet they prized their GILBERT too—
His Knights and Dames, his ruffling crew,
   Where banners fly, and drums are beat,
   And cloth-of-gold and drugget meet . . .
I was a lad then!   Where were you
        In Fifty-six?

1913 [1911].

TO TIME, THE TYRANT

Ave, Imperator, senectus te salutat.

TIME, in whose kingship is Song,
   What shall I bring to thee now,
   Weary of heart and of brow—
Now, that the shadows are long?

Not with the young and the strong
   Numbered am I.   And I bow,
       TIME!

(442)

To Time, the Tyrant

Yet—let me stand in the throng;
  Yet—let me hail and allow
  Youth, that no Combat can cow,
Strength, that is stronger than Wrong,
      TIME !

1911.

A FABLE

(IN THE MANNER OF MR. JOHN GAY)

How much would end in mode abrupt,
If listeners might but interrupt !
Once in a corner of the lawn,
When none was stirring with the dawn,
Save BETTY, who not less, alas !
Still lingered at her looking-glass,
A TORTOISE of didactic habits
Addressed some half-a-dozen Rabbits.

  It was a Tortoise who, 'tis said,
Contrived to break a wise man's head ;
Since then the sect, report avers,
Have set up for Philosophers.

  No harm in this one could be found ;
He weighed so much ; was so much round ;
Not slower than his kin, or quicker
(Although his shell was somewhat thicker),
And wearing just that look of thought
Which speaks profundity,—or nought.

  'My text (he said) is PROMPTITUDE.'
He stretched his throat, and thus pursued ;
'In this discourse I hope to bring
Before you *Promptitude* the Thing ;
Next, if my limits space afford,
I shall take *Promptitude* the Word ;

(443)

Lastly, to make my meaning better,
I shall examine every Letter.

'And first, my Friends, however viewed,
How beautiful is *Promptitude !*
How are we quickened, roused, renewed,
By dwelling upon *Promptitude !*
In short, how much may we discover
By simply saying the word over !

'How much, too, in this vale below,
To this one quality we owe !
'Twas *Promptitude* the battles won
Of CAESAR, and NAPOLEON ;
By *Promptitude* to-day we boast
The blessings of the Penny Post ;
By *Promptitude* (I dare affirm)
The early bird secures the worm. . . .'

The Rabbits are a docile race,
And patient under commonplace ;
But here, one rather puzzle-pated
In Gallic style 'interpellated' :
'If *Promptitude* so much can do,
Why don't *you* try the practice, too ?'

This was, as HAMLET says, 'a hit' ;
Clergy was posed by *Mother-wit*.
The Tortoise the horizon scanned ;
He had no repartee at hand ;
So, finding inspiration fail,
He drew his head in, then his tail.
His audience scampered off in glee :
Risu solvuntur tabulae.

1880 [1877].

ON A PICTURE BY HOPPNER

(MRS. GWYN—GOLDSMITH'S 'JESSAMY BRIDE')

'AND you went once with myrtle crowned!'
    You once were she, for whom
Poor GOLDSMITH'S gentle genius found
    That name of jasmine-bloom!

How strange it seems! You whom he loved,
    You who were breathing, vital,
Not feigned in books, for us have proved
    Scarce but a fragrant title;

A shade too shadowy far to stand
    Beside the girl PRIMROSES—
Beside the dear old VICAR, and
    Our more-than-brother, MOSES!

We cannot guess your voice, who know
    Scamp TONY'S view-halloo;
For us e'en thin Beau TIBBS must show
    More palpable than you!

Yet some scant news we have. You came,
    When that kind soul had fled;
You begged his hair; you kept his name
    Long on your lips, 'tis said;

You lived—and died. Or when, or how,
    Who asks? This age of ours
But marks your grass-grown headstone now
    By GOLDSMITH'S jasmine flowers!

1883.

ON THE BELFRY TOWER

A SKETCH

'Look down the road.   You see that mound
Rise on the right, its grassy round
Broken as by a scar?'

          (We stood,
Where every landscape-lover should,
High on the gray old belfry's lead,
Scored with rude names, and to the tread
Waved like a sea.   Below us spread
Cool grave-stones, watched by one great yew.
To right were ricks; thatched roofs a few;
Next came the rectory, with its lawn
And nestling schoolhouse; next, withdrawn
Beyond a maze of apple boughs,
The long, low-latticed Manor-house.
The wide door showed an antlered hall;
Then, over roof and chimney stack,
You caught the fish-pond at the back,
The roses, and the old red wall.
Behind, the Dorset ridges go
With straggling, wind-clipped trees, and so
The eye came down the slope to follow
The white road winding in the hollow
Beside the mound of which he spoke.)

'There,' said the Rector, 'from the town
The Roundheads rode across the down.
Sir Miles—'twas then Sir Miles's day—
Was posted farther south, and lay
Watching at Weymouth; but his son—
Rupert by name—an only one,

(446)

On the Belfry Tower

The veriest youth, it would appear,
Scrambling about for jackdaws here,
Spied them a league off.   People say,
Scorning the tedious turret-way
(Or else because the butler's care
Had turned the key to keep him there),
He slid down by the rain-pipe.   Then,
Arming the hinds and serving-men
With half-pike and with harquebuss,
Snatched from the wainscot's overplus,
Himself in rusty steel cap clad,
With flapping ear-pieces, the lad
Led them by stealth around the ridge,
So flanked the others at the bridge.
They were just six to half a score,
And yet five crop-ears, if not more,
Sleep in that mound.   But, sad to tell,
The boy, by some stray petronel,
Or friend's or foe's—report is vague—
Was killed; and then, for fear of plague,
Buried within twelve hours or so.

'Such is the story.   Shall we go?
I have his portrait here below:
Grave, olive-cheeked, a Southern face.
His mother, who was dead, had been
Something, I think, about the Queen,
Long ere the day of that disgrace,
Saddest our England yet has seen.
Poor child!   The last of all his race.'

1887.

TO A FRIEND

(ON RECEIVING HIS 'COMPLETE POEMS')

Not yet 'complete,' old Friend, not yet!
What Imp of the Perverse could set
That fateful epithet before
A reader who must wish for more!

'Complete,' in truth, each piece may be
Seen in its several symmetry;
Complete as are the stones that gem
The rondure of the diadem.

But who of men shall so forecast
His latest as to call it last?
Or, if he make an end, be sure
'Tis not profanely premature?

None.   For while yet we breathe and speak,
The Unachieved is still to seek;
Nor may the quest relax while Hope
Still hides in every horoscope!

1909.

THE SONNET OF THE MOUNTAIN

(AFTER MELIN DE SAINT-GELAIS)

When from afar these mountain tops I view,
I do but mete mine own distress thereby:
High is their head, and my desire is high;
Firm is their foot, my faith is certain too.

The Sonnet of the Mountain

E'en as the winds about their summits blue,
From me escapes betimes the wistful sigh;
And as from them the brooks and streamlets hie,
So from mine eyes the tears run down anew.

A thousand flocks upon them feed and stray;
As many loves within me see the day,
And all my heart for pasture ground divide.

No fruit have they, my lot as fruitless is;
And 'twixt us now nought diverse is but this—
In them the snows, in me the fires abide.

1886.

TO MAECENAS

WITH AN INVITATION

(HORACE, I. 20)

But common Sabine on the board
In homely ware you'll find.   Yet stored
And sealed in Grecian jar 'twas first,
Dear Knight, what time your praises burst
From the full circus' serried ranks,
And your own Tiber from his banks,
And the great Mount, rang back reply.

No Caecuban like yours have I;
No press of Cales yet for me
Crushed the fat grape.   These cups of mine
Neither the hills of Formiae
Have tempered, nor Falernian vine.

1913.

RONDEAUS OF THE GREAT WAR AND OTHER POEMS

The glint of a raindrop ;
The song of a bird ;
The laughter of children,—
Just overheard ;
These make up your magic,—
These sing in your song ;
May you sing it for ever,
And ever so long !

[Undated.   First appearance in print.]

A RALLY

We that are English born and bred,
We that are proud of our mighty dead,
Are we at last to end as slaves,
Crawling into dishonoured graves?
Truculent Teutons! Arrogant Huns!
Answer them—answer them, England's sons!

We whose record at least is clean,
Fixed our word as our bond has been,
Are we no longer to hold in scorn
Promises broken and treaties torn?
Double-tongued Teutons! treacherous Huns!
Answer them—answer them, England's sons!

We whose life-blood no land has lacked,
We who never a Louvain sacked,
We who never held Might is Right,
Should we fold hands to-day—or fight?
Merciless Teutons! barbarous Huns!
Answer them—answer them, England's sons!

We whose past is a well-fought page,
Shall we sink now into vassalage?
We with an honour that knows no stain,
Pass to the rule of a Suzerain?
Credulous Teutons! innocent Huns!
Answer them—answer them, England's sons!

[Written in 1914.   First appearance in print.]

CHRISTMAS BELLS, 1914

WHAT do your clear bells ring to me
In this glad hour of jubilee?
Not joy—not joy.   **I** hear instead
So many dead! so many dead!

So many, who but yesterday
Went out, great-hearted, to the fray,
Giving up all that they could give
To fight, forsooth! for 'right to live.'

Life was before them, larger scope,
Room for the morrow's quenchless hope . . .
Now they are stark and cold afar,—
Pawns in this ruthless Game of War!

Glory and power, honour, ease,
What are all those to-day to these?
What their laudation, now they lie
'Piled in the trenches, three feet high!'

This only—that to duty's call
They answered nobly, each and all:
This also—that their blood is seed
For bonds unloosed, for peoples freed.
.   .   .   .

Not less, your peal of bells to me
Rings mourning more than jubilee!
Listen—and with uncovered head—
So many dead! so many dead!

1914.

THAT WOODEN CROSS

THAT wooden cross beside the road
Marks—as the now-blurred legend showed—
  That there a 'soldat anglais' dead
  Has found betimes his foreign bed—
His last impregnable abode.

'Tis no uncommon episode,
You say, of war's barbaric code,
  For which so many men have bled—
    That wooden cross!

Nay, but this blood was well bestowed;
'Twas shed for nations 'neath the load
  Of mailed oppression fury-fed,
  And ruthless rapine, sore bestead.
Surely it needs no funeral ode—
    That wooden cross!

1914.

FOR THE BLINDED SOLDIERS

WE that look on, with God's goodwill,
Have one plain duty to fulfil:
  To drive—by all fair means—afar
  This hideous Juggernaut of War,
And teach the Future not to kill.

But there's a plainer duty still:
We need to meet the instant ill,
  To heal the wound, to hide the scar—
    We that look on!

(455)

What timelier task for brain and quill
Than aiding eyes no light can thrill,
   No sight of all good things that are,
   No morning sky, no evening star—
Shall we not help with all our skill,
     We that look on?

1915.

'WE HOPE TO WIN'

'WE hope to win?' By God's help—'Yes':
Though of the 'when,' no man can guess,
   Since there may yet be long-drawn strain,
   Alternate change of pride and pain,
Till Victory come—at last—to bless.

But there are other wars that press—
Wars bred of surfeit and success—
   Which, if we would our place maintain,
     We hope to win.

There is the war with Selfishness—
The purblind fiend that 'doubts' distress;
   With hearts that fail and lips that feign;
   With Drink, with Lust, with Greed of Gain . . .
These are the wars in which, not less,
     We hope to win.

1915.

'WHEN THERE IS PEACE'

' *WHEN there is Peace our land no more*
Will be the land we knew of yore.'
   Thus do our facile seers foretell
   The truth that none can buy or sell
And e'en the wisest must ignore.

'When there is Peace'

When we have bled at every pore,
Shall we still strive for gear and store?
　　Will it be Heaven?　Will it be Hell?
　　　　When there is Peace.

This let us pray for, this implore:
That all base dreams thrust out at door,
　　We may in loftier aims excel
　　And, like men waking from a spell,
Grow stronger, nobler, than before,
　　　　When there is Peace.

1916.

TO BELGIUM

For Right, not Might, you fought.　The foe,
Checked in his wild World-overthrow,
　　Ravaged, with his remorseless band,
　　Your ancient fanes and peaceful land,
Thinking to crush you at a blow.

You are not crushed, as well we know.
If you are trodden, 'tis to grow;
　　Nor can they fail at last who stand
　　　　For Right, not Might!

God speed you, Belgium!　Time will show
How large a debt to you we owe.
　　To you—through all reverses grand—
　　Men stretch to-day a grateful hand . . .
God speed you still—in weal and woe—
　　　　For Right, not Might.

1917.

CLEAN HANDS

MAKE this thing plain to us, O Lord!
That not the triumph of the sword—
   Not that alone—can end the strife,
   But reformation of the life—
But full submission to Thy Word!

Not all the stream of blood outpoured
Can Peace—the Long-Desired—afford;
   Not tears of Mother, Maid or Wife . . .
     Make this thing plain!

We must root out our sins ignored,
By whatsoever name adored;
   Our secret sins, that, ever rife,
   Shrink from the operating knife;
Then shall we rise, renewed, restored . . .
     Make this thing plain!

1919.

AN ARCTIC EPITAPH

No grave more nobly graced,
No whiter pall than that which wraps the heads
Of those who sleep where the lone land outspreads
   Its ice-bound waste.

These, Mother, were thy sons,
Brood of thy brood, whose seed by sea and land
Still man to-day, and in days gone have manned
   Our English guns.

No mortal foe defied.
What Nature in her silent holds of snow
Hides from all outer ken, they strove to know,
   And striving—died.

1917.

Rondeaus and other Poems

PROLOGUE TO 'A BOOKMAN'S BUDGET'

GOOD-BYE, my Book. To other eyes
      With equal mind, I now address you,
Since in Dame Fortune's lap it lies
      Either to ban you or to bless you.

You have been long a 'care not light':
      If those for whom you were intended
Refuse to read your page aright,
      You must not therefore feel offended.

This is a Game we play, my Book:
      Sometimes one scores, sometimes one misses,
And though the lot for which we look
      Be neither bread-and-cheese nor kisses,

The point is: Was your purpose good?
      Your meaning plain to comprehension?
Have you successfully withstood
      All tedium, tattle, spite, pretension?

Have you contrived no verbal haze
      To hide your poverty of matter?
Have you, unjustly, failed to praise,
      Or have you, feebly, stooped to flatter?

You won't be free from fault, I know.
      None would believe me if I said it.
But still—you did your best, and so,
      That should be counted to your credit.

1917.

ON THE FUTURE OF POETRY

BARDS of the Future ! you that come
With striding march, and roll of drum,
What will your newest challenge be
To our prose-bound community ?

What magic will you find to stir
The limp and languid listener ?
Will it be daring and dramatic ?
Will it be frankly democratic ?

Will Pegasus return again
In guise of modern aeroplane,
Descending from a cloudless blue
To drop on us a bomb or two ?

I know not.   Far be it from me
To darken dark futurity ;
Still less to render more perplexed
The last vagary, or the next.

Leave Pindus Hill to those who list,
Iconoclast or anarchist—
So be it.   'They that break shall pay.'
I stand upon the ancient way.

I hold it for a certain thing,
That, blank or rhyming, song must sing ;
And more, that what is good for verse,
Need not, by dint of rhyme, grow worse.

(460)

On the Future of Poetry

I hold that they who deal in rhyme
Must take the standpoint of the time—
But not to catch the public ear,
As mountebank or pulpiteer;

That the old notes are still the new,
If the musician's touch be true—
Nor can the hand that knows its trade
Achieve the trite and ready-made;

That your first theme is Human Life,
Its hopes and fears, its love and strife—
A theme no custom can efface,
Common, but never commonplace;

For this, beyond all doubt, is plain:
The Truth that pleased will please again,
And move men as in bygone years
When Hector's wife smiled through her tears.

1914 [1913].

ON THE SHELF

(LIBER LOQUITUR)

'Bouquin de rebut acheté au rabais.'—ALFRED DE MUSSET.

I WAS once on the table; I'm now on the shelf.
Let me give a look round, and take stock for myself.

We are not a large party: an ancient *Who's Who*
(Grim sepulchre now of some names that were new!);
Spectator, vol. four, and a *Scot's Magazine*,
With a bulky *Burn's Justice* wedged tightly between;
The excellent Hanway, his *Essay on Tea*,
And *Rhymes for the Roadway*—by 'Nemo.' That's me!

Naught else but a packet of fish-hooks and floats;
A cracked Toby jug and a sample of oats.

No mortal disturbs our seclusion, save when
Some ruddy-armed handmaid comes now and again
To bang us together, and fill up the cup
By putting us back with the bottom-side up;
Or the Farmer that owns us, when smoking at night,
Will ruthlessly tear out a leaf for a light,
Since the ledge that we live on stands over the settle
Where he nods by the fire-log or blinks at the kettle.

But how did I come here? I came—as I think—
With a light-hearted tourist who stopped for a drink,
And tested our home-brewed so long on the lawn
That he either forgot me—or left me in pawn.
The former, I fancy. At end I've a scrawl:
'*Price fourpence, and bought at a market-place stall.*
Not bad too, as verse—with a lingering note
That gives you a curious lump in the throat.'

I was one of three hundred. First twenty went off,
'Complimentary copies,' for critics to scoff,
Who were kind, on the whole. Other eighty were sold
(Less so much in the shilling); then, shop-worn and old,
And so for all saleable purposes dead,
We were promptly 'remaindered' at twopence a head.

O impotent close! But, however you doubt it,
Your twopenny readers are not to be flouted!
For the rich, though they buy, yet they never may need you,
While the poor, if they buy, are quite likely to read you.
And who knows but the laggard who left me behind
May not have been Poet, too, after his kind?

On the Shelf

A mute one, perchance, but still ready to snatch
From my numbers the lilt that he hungered to catch;
Or to find, in the verses there writ, without knowing,
That procreant hint which could set him a-going.
Who shall mete the mysterious commerce of souls?
Was the flambeau of Coleridge not kindled by Bowles?
I myself may have failed.   You may count me 'poor stuff';
But I light a new beacon.   And that is enough.

1914.

THE RIDDLE

'*Others abide our question.*'—MATTHEW ARNOLD.

WHAT like wert thou, O Riddle of our Race!
    Whose intent eye the minds of men could see,
And, by excess of intuition, trace
    In the dull germ its full maturity?

Thou, 'of imagination all compact,'
    Alone among thy fellows, could'st ally
The thought and word, the impulse and the act,
    Cause and effect, unerringly.   But why?

None can make answer!   To our ken a shade,
    Thou—for whom souls lay open—art as dark
As formless phantoms of the night that fade
    With daybreak and the singing of the lark.

We may explore thy Secret still, yet thou,
    Serene, unsearchable, above us all,
Look'st down, as from some lofty mountain-brow,
    And art thyself thine own Memorial.

1916.

Rondeaus and other Poems

A 'CORNHILL' RONDEAU

(FOR THE FIVE-HUNDREDTH NUMBER OF THE
'CORNHILL MAGAZINE')

FOR two-score years the tumbling spray
Has fallen from our bows away;
    What change of skipper and of crew,
    Since first the CORNHILL sailed the blue,
Grain-laden, Master, THACKERAY!

TROLLOPE, GEORGE ELIOT, GASKELL—nay,
Our own dear 'Blackstick' of to-day,—
    What wealth of genius old and new
        For two-score years!

Once more we steer across the bay.
With no vain thought our hearts are gay;
    Our log is clean, our course is true;
    What we have done, we mean to do;
We hope, once more, to lead the way
        For two-score years!

1901.

TO GEORGE H. BOUGHTON, R.A.

(In anticipation of a promised water-colour to illustrate the poem
'Love in Winter.' See page 74.)

THE Spring will come, but ah! will She?—
The girl that BOUGHTON promised me?—
My Bella, who he said should go,
In fitting tint across the snow!
Yet why, forsooth, shall I complain,
Since this my loss is others' gain;—
Since BOUGHTON, even now, perhaps,
Is painting frows in Friesland caps;
Or puts, maybe, the final touch
To some fresh Lovelace in Low Dutch;

To George H. Boughton, R.A.

Or else he makes the world more rich
By still one more New-England witch ;
Or sees upon his canvass grow
Some priestess crowned with mistletoe.
Then, by and by, the crowd will rush
To praise these fruits of BOUGHTON's brush,
And bless the artist who can blend
Unfading beauty with Ostend ;
Or trace immortal truth behind
The furrowed face of humankind.
So why (I say) should I complain
Since this my loss is others' gain !
And yet, and yet, I fain would see
The girl that BOUGHTON promised me !

[Written in 1884.   First appearance in print.]

TO ARTHUR JAMES BALFOUR

NOT to look down, or blanch, or care,
    But fearless still the foe to meet,
And fearless still to do or dare—
    Ah ! there are honours of defeat.

[Written in 1905.   First appearance in print.]

TO ARTHUR WAUGH

(1890-1917)

TIME marks our days with white and black
In his Perennial Almanack ;

But there 's one day I don't forget,
And that 's the day when first we met.

1917.

Rondeaus and other Poems

TO JOHN WADDON MARTYN

(WITH A COPY OF 'SIDE-WALK STUDIES')

As one who on the idle shore
Bends at the Galley bench no more,
I look back to the days when we
Tugged the long sweeps in company.
Yet there were moments even then
When there was thought of Books and Men,
When there was talk of Verse and Prose—
I send you these remembering those.

[Written in 1902. First appearance in print.]

TO RICHARD WATSON GILDER

FRIEND, on whose face I may not look,
  So space and chance divide,
Once more I thank you for a book
  Across the sundering tide ;

And know once more from this, as each,
  In notes or soft or strong,
You speak the universal Speech,
  The Volapuk of Song.

We live, alas ! in prose-rid days :
  Yet though the crowd regard
Not greatly now the verse-man's lays,
  The frenzy of the Bard,

Take heart.   No word sincere, distinct,
  Is lost.   The heartfelt rhyme
May pulse for ever on the linked
  Telegraphy of Time.

[Written in 1899. First appearance in print.]

THE BALLAD OF THE BEGGAR

THE starlings fly in the windy sky,
The rabbits run out a-row,
The pheasants stalk in the stubble dry,
As I tramp in the evenglow,—
As I tramp, tramp, tramp, and grow
More weary at every stride,
And think, as the riders pass and go—
If I had a horse to ride!

The Farmer trots by on his roadster high,
The Squire on his pony low;
Young Miss sweeps out from the Park-Gate nigh,
And canters away with her beau :—
They are proud of themselves, I trow,
But couldn't I too show pride?
And couldn't I too cut a dash and show,
If I had a horse to ride?

The Farmer is four times as fat as I,
The Squire he is blind and slow;
Young Miss has not nearly so bright an eye
As Bess at the 'Barley Mow';—
Ah, wouldn't I cry 'Gee-hup, Gee-ho,'
And wouldn't I bang his side,
And wouldn't I teach him to gallop it though,
If I had a horse to ride!

ENVOY.

It was only a Beggar that grumbled so,
As his blistered feet he eyed;
But the cry is a cry that we all of us know—
If I had a horse to ride!

[Undated.   First appearance in print.]

A BALLAD OF NAMES

SOME love the Laureate's 'tall Elaine';
  There are, who leaving Maud and May,
With Morris, of Yolande are 'fain'
    (And add thereto, perchance, 'le Fay');
  Some shepherding with Phillis stray,
And some with Greek Autonoë;—
  I care not who shall say me nay;
But Rose is still the name for me.

To Bulwer's Blanche some true remain;
  Some Ethel love with Thackeray;
Some turn to Dickens' Nell, again;
    Some choose the Ruth of Wordsworth's lay;
    And some Sir Walter's Di. obey;
Some Christabel, of *S.T.C.*;
    And some with Herrick's Julia play;
But Rose is still the name for me.

'By Celia's arbour' some complain;
  Some with Olivia 'make their hay';
To some not e'en Amelia Jane,
    Or Ann-Matilda strike dismay;
    To some Susanna's charms convey
'The chaste—the inexpressive She';
    Some Hetty, Letty, Tetty sway;—
But Rose is still the name for me.

ENVOY.

Maids, in all names a maiden may
  Allure 'the inexpressive He,'—
This none deny;—I simply say—
    'But Rose is still the name for me.'

[Written in 1878. First appearance in print.]

(468)

ON READING A VOLUME OF POEMS

Too oft, when our new minstrels sing,
How fine so-e'er the Song be wrought,
We catch behind the stricken string
Some touch that tells the music taught
Less by an impulse than a thought :—
Not so with thine, O Poet, where
We breathe again the passionate air,
And feel, at Love's divine commands,
Once more the joy too keen to bear,
And the hot tears upon our hands.

[Undated.   First appearance in print.]

ALTER EGO

Where is the boyish Poet
    Who used with you to write ?
Alas ! his songs are ended :
    I dug his grave last night.

Beneath a flowering myrtle,
    His face against the East,
I buried him at midnight ;
    Without a book or priest.

He had grown older, graver,—
    The iron hand of Time
Had chilled the early laughter
    That rippled in his rhyme.

He had grown graver, sadder,
    Before the darkening years ;
His voice, once clear and joyous,
    Took evermore of tears.

(469)

What should he do but dwindle,
    What should he do but go?
He could not sing the summer,
    He would not sing the snow.

His lyre was carved for pleasure,
    His lot was cast in pain;
Till this gray world grow brighter,
    He may not rise again!

So, 'neath a flowering myrtle
    Without a book or priest,
I buried him at midnight,
    His face against the East.

[Written in 1888. First appearance in print.]

SAT EST VIXISSE

OTHERS there have been of the great Ones dead
Who still met Fortune with uplifted head,
    Still to the blackest morn,
    Returning scorn for scorn;

Others there were from whom no sorest fate
Could wring one cry of misery or hate,
    Faring, with set lips prest,
    Silent, towards their rest;

But thou, as dauntless, as unvanquished, thou,
With equal mind, and with unclouded brow,
    Spared'st not to welcome still
    The morrow, good or ill;

And hastening forward with unslackened pace
Still to the Unknown turned a cheery face,
    Then, at the end of strife,
    Thanked Life for life.

[Written in 1891. First appearance in print.]

'THIS MORN FOR YOU'

FROM THE FRENCH OF MADAME DESBORDES-VALMORE

THIS morn for you I Roses bound,
So many that the ribbon wound
About them snapped, with all that bloom distent.

The ribbon snapped; away they flew;
The wind that bore them seaward blew,—
Adown the wind, to come no more, they went.

The wave, that took them, flushed like wine,
And still these lawny folds of mine
Retain to-night the memory and the scent.

[Undated.   First appearance in print.]

FOR A VOLUME OF ESSAYS

(TO GEORGE SAINTSBURY)

HERE, with little variation,
Comes another 'cold collation.'

Naught, indeed, the taste to tickle—
Coan lees, or roes in pickle;
No comparison between a
Severn lamprey and muraena;
Nothing to derange the peptics
Of the Scholars or the sceptics—
Only useful antiseptics!

Naught for Bacchus, naught for Venus—
Nothing that Nasidienus
Howsoever at a loss for
Novelty, could find a sauce for;
Naught, in truth, to please the palate
Save the dressing of the sallet!

If you care for such-like dishes,
Take it—with my best good wishes!

1920.

BY WAY OF PREFACE

(A REVERIE)

' Hoc opus, hic labor est.'

'A PREFACE?' Yes. It might be well,
If it could make the volume sell.
But 'tis a thing one may misuse.

For think—'twixt 'Qui s'excuse, s'accuse,'
And the temptation to explain
Where explanation must be vain ;
Where everything you try to say
But seems to give yourself away ;
And though you pause on every letter,
Suggests that silence would be better—
The feat is surely one for those
Who deal with jugglery in prose,
And, often, leads to little more
Than simply blocking up the door.

Moreover, there are complications.
If you admit your limitations,
Review your lapses, or refine them,
The Critic can but underline them, ·
And, to your indiscreet confessing,
Respond by blandly acquiescing,
As he, of course, is free to do
(In his place you would do it too !).
Thus, by the give-and-take of war,
You merely hoist with your petar ;
In other words, for all your candour,
Get nothing but a neat back-hander ;

No. On the whole, 'twere surely best
To let a risky matter rest;
And, in default of special pleader,
Refer the ruling ... to the Reader !

1920.

ERRATA: AN ECLOGUE

Author

THIS text is not what it should be.
There are some strange mistakes I see
I must have missed.   For who, right witted,
Would dream of putting 'filled' for 'fitted'?
Or 'light' for 'tight'?   Or 'sleep' for 'steep'?
—Such things would make the angels weep.

Publisher

That is so.   Still they *do* occur
To the most proved artificer.
You must have failed to cross your 't's':
GENIUS is prone to that disease!

Author

True.   (And sometimes, by accident,
The blunder betters what was meant!)
But tell me.   What is my position?
Correction?   In a new edition?
—Those 'new editions' have a knack,
Unluckily, of holding back . . .

Publisher

That is because men take more pains
To feed their bodies than their brains;
Or else because they really care
For little save the lighter fare;
And then—though this is poor relief—
The life of modern books is brief.
—We'll paste in an '*Errata*' slip . . .

Author

Which none will look at but to skip.
No; the misfortune must be gulped,
Until the masterpiece is . . . pulped!

1920.

AN OLD MAGAZINE [1]

' Tout passe, tout casse, tout lasse.'

WHEN first we issued from the Press,
    In days less strenuous and prolific,
The folks who bought us could not guess
    That we should serve for soporific.

The small-paned shop where we were sold,
    Down a blind-alley in the City,
Where friendly Bookmen met of old,
    Is now no more—and more's the pity!

That was the Age of Auction Sales,
    When lives of Books were somewhat longer;
Our sign-board was *The Crab and Scales*,
    And he that 'kept' there, was a Conger—

Our Publisher—a man of might
    (As large as *Johnson* was, and louder),
Who planned new things from morn to night,
    And owned a famous Fever Powder.

We scored at first. We took high ground,
    Preached *Aristotle* from our garret,
Called *Gray* 'remote' and *Locke* 'unsound,'
    And gave strange plates of plant and parrot;

Our *Rebuses* were reckoned neat,
    Our *Logogriphs* were much debated;
Our note, in Ethics, was 'discreet,'
    In Politics, 'twas 'plainly stated.'

We had our views. In Art and Song
    We were—above all—patriotic;
We hated the imported throng
    Of Fiddlers, Singers, Cooks exotic. . . .

[1] A tattered number is supposed to speak.

An Old Magazine

Then matters changed.   Our Foremost Bard
  (Later a copious rhetorician)
Found *crambo*-rhyming far too hard,
  And ' odes Pindarick' not his mission ;

Our Fictionist, whose ' High-Life' page
  Failed to provide the funds he needed,
Threw up his post for ' living wage,'
  And as a ' Pen-cutter' succeeded ;

The cunning Artist, too, that drew
  Our stage *Roxana* and *Statira*,
Flamed out in *folio* with a new
  (Subscription) *Ruins of Palmyra*,

Which he set off to visit.   Next
  Our Essayist, the kind, the gentle,
Whose wayward Humour never vexed,
  Whose Wit was never detrimental,

Fell sick and died.   Then came a day,
  Day to be draped with black, and banished !
When all our sales had ebbed away,
  And what we had of vogue, had vanished—

When, by some stroke of Fate concealed
  (Or stress of butcher and of baker),
Our stock-in-trade entire was wheeled
  To ' Mr. *Pastem*, the Trunk Maker !'
   .   .   .   .   .   .

Such is our mournful history !
  You'll need some tranquillizing slumber.
I offer it.   ' Times change, and we'. . .
  I am a genuine Back-Number !

1920.

NEW AND OLD

(TO A YOUNG LADY)

FOR what is old you nothing care—
   'Antiques,' you say, but leave you cold;
And yet the sun that gilds your hair
   Is more than many aeons old.

The very song I hear you sing
   Is little but a variation
Of some foregone primaeval thing—
   Some early mortal inspiration!

Ah, never say you hate the old,
   It always hides the new within it;
'Twill last until the stars are cold,
   The other only stays a minute!

1920.

TO E. G.

WERE I to pause and hesitate
For something 'picked,' 'alembicate,'
I might, by chance, no further get
Than mere parade of epithet;
So I'll just wish to You and Yours
Strength to achieve while strength endures;
And, when the power to do is done,
Remembered radiance of the sun!

1920.

TO A LYRIC POET

WHEN you bid me discuss
   The status poetic,
'Tis likely that thus
   I may grow homiletic.

Who looks with old eyes
   On the verse-world around him,
Sees much to surprise,
   And more to astound him.

The old lights have ceased ;
   Late suns are subsiding ;
New stars have increased—
   There are others in hiding !

Old themes are out-classed ;
   Old standards are altered
(Let us not stone the Past
   If its mission has faltered !) ;

And then, as it seems,
   Defying Apollo,
There are metrical schemes
   Not easy to follow !

But, where there are bells
   There must also be ringers,
And where the heart swells
   There will always be singers.

And each singer that sings,
   Must chant as he chooses,
And the least likely things
   To be ' scrapped ' are the Muses.

Yes : Song must endure,
    Nothing mortal can stop it ;
Let us build it up sure,
    Let us skilfully prop it !

It lightens men's play,
    It softens their sorrow ;
It will serve for To-day,
    It will stay for To-morrow ;

It will end—with the Race ;
    And one minstrel rejoices
To have lived—by God's grace—
    To join in the voices.

1920.

TO EDMUND GOSSE

IN darkening days, when old desires
Die slowly down, like fading fires,
What cheers us most is still the cry
Of those who look for larger sky,
And find, with every cloud withdrawn,
Fresh promise of an ampler dawn.
Your voice of yore was joined with these,
I wish you therefore Hope and Ease,
Health, and continued power to please.

1922 [1920].

FOR A CLOSING PAGE

' Never a palinode ! '—' Q.'

LIFE, like a page unpenned,
  Spreads out its whiteness ;
Nothing, from end to end,
  Marring its brightness.

Surely a field to claim
  Steadfast endeavour ?
Where one might win a name
  Sounding for ever ?

. . . . . .

Now—to review it all—
  What a prosaic,
Forced, ineffectual,
  Paltry mosaic !

Plans that ne'er found a base ;
  Wingless upyearning ;
Speed that ne'er won the race ;
  Fire without burning ;

Doubt never set at rest
  Stifle or falter it ;
Good that was not the best . . .
  Yet—would you alter it ?

Yet—would you tread again
  All the road over ?
Face the old joy and pain—
  Hemlock and clover ?

. . . . . .

Yes.   For it still was good,
   Good to be living;
Buoyant of heart and blood;
   Fighting, forgiving;

Glad for the earth and sky;
   Glad—for mere gladness;
Grateful, one knew not why,
   Even for sadness;

Finding the ray of hope
   Gleam through distresses;
Building a larger scope
   Out from successes;

Blithe to the close, and still
   Tendering ever,
Both for the Good and Ill,
   Thanks to the GIVER.

.   .   .   .   .   .

So, though the script is slow,
   Blurred though the line is,
Let the poor record go
   Onward to Finis.

1913.

In After Days

In after days when grasses high
O'er-top the stone where I shall lie,
    Though ill or well the world adjust
    My slender claim to honoured dust,
I shall not question or reply.

I shall not see the morning sky;
I shall not hear the night-wind sigh;
    I shall be mute, as all men must
        In after days!

But yet, now living, fain were I
That some one then should testify,
    Saying—'He held his pen in trust
    To Art, not serving shame or lust.'
Will none?— Then let my memory die
        In after days!

1884.

NOTES

NOTES

'*What God withholds no man can know.*'—PAGE 9.

'Nescire velle quæ Magister optimus
Docere non vult, erudita inscitia est.'—SCALIGER.

A GENTLEWOMAN OF THE OLD SCHOOL.—PAGE 11.

The Bachelor Samson Carrasco in *Don Quixote* had his doubt about
Second Parts, and there is a like prejudice against Companion
Pictures. *A Gentlewoman of the Old School* would probably have
remained unwritten if an uninvited pendant to its forerunner (which
originally came out in *St. Paul's* for July 1870) had not made its
appearance in *Chambers's Journal* for July 8, 1871.

THE BALLAD OF 'BEAU BROCADE.'—PAGE 14.

There is no foundation in fact for this ballad. It has, however,
been gravely asked how a story, some of the incidents of which take
place in 1740, can possibly have been suggested by a book published
in 1739. Those who are embarrassed by this delicate difficulty can—
if they choose—mentally substitute Forty-Nine for Thirty-Nine in the
final line.

'*Shared its glories with* Westminster.'—PAGE 14.

Westminster is now 'swallowed up in the general vortex of modern
London' (Wheatley and Cunningham's *London*, 1891, iii. 460).

'*Went out of town to* Marybone.'—PAGE 14.

'Many persons arrived in town from their country-houses in Marybone.' (*Daily Journal*, October 15, 1728.)

'*WHITEFIELD preached to the colliers grim.*'—PAGE 15.

'*Bristol.* The Rev. Mr. *Whitefield* . . . has been wonderfully
laborious and successful, especially among the poor Prisoners in
Newgate and the rude Colliers of *Kingswood*. . . . On Saturday the 18th
instant [March] he preached at *Hannum Mount* to 5 or 6000 Persons,
amongst them many Colliers' (*Gentleman's Magazine*, March 1739,
vol. ix, p. 162).

'*WALPOLE talked of "a man and his price".*'—PAGE 15.

This has been contradicted by the more literal historians. But it is
sufficiently true for poetical purposes.

Notes

'*There was Barber* Dick.'—Page 15.

These two personages are borrowed from Plate II of Hogarth's *Election Series*, 1757 ('Canvassing for Votes').

'*Guard in the basket armed to the teeth.*'—Page 15.

The basket was a cumbrous wicker appendage for luggage (and frequently passengers) at the back of the coach. (See Hogarth's *Country Inn Yard*, 1747.) 'Its [London's] fopperies come down to us . . . in the very basket'—says Mr. Hardcastle in Act I. Scene i, of *She Stoops to Conquer*, 1773. In 1741 a highwayman was shot from the basket by a Captain Mawley (*Gentleman's Magazine*, xi. 498).

'*Highwayman's manners.*'—Page 16.

'On Friday in the Afternoon, between Three and Four o'clock, the Bath Stage-Coach was robbed by a single Highwayman about two Miles this Side of Maidenhead, who took from the passengers between four and five Pounds, *behaved very genteelly*, and made off' (*Covent Garden Journal*, 10th March, 1752).

'*(That 's where the best strong waters are!)*'—Page 16.

Strong waters—e. g. *Barbadoes-water, citron-water*, &c.—were restorative cordials, much affected by the fair sex. In Richardson's *Familiar Letters*, 1741, p. 163, a sailor sends his Peggy from Barbadoes six bottles of citron-water. 'It is what, they say, Ladies drink, when they can get it.'

'*Ensign (of* Bragg's).'—Page 16.

Despite its suspicious appropriateness in this case, 'Bragg's' Regiment of Foot-Guards really existed, and was ordered to Flanders in April 1742 (see *Gentleman's Magazine*, 1742, i. p. 217). In 1759 Wolfe was leading it at Quebec when he was mortally wounded.

'*But for the Ladies had drawn his hanger!*'—Page 16.

A hanger is 'a broad, crooked, short sword' (Bailey). Tom Bowling (*Roderick Random*, ch. iii) wears 'an hanger with a brass handle'; and Commodore Trunnion, going to his marriage, is equipped with 'a huge hanger, with a hilt like that of a backsword' (*Peregrine Pickle*, ch. viii).

'*For* George *was in league.*'—Page 17.

'That these suspicions [of connivance] were not without foundation is proved by the dying speeches of some penitent robbers of that age, who appear to have received from the innkeepers services much resembling those which Farquhar's Boniface [in the *Beaux' Stratagem*] rendered to Gibbet' (Macaulay's *History of England*, ed. 1864, i. p. 181)

Notes

'PORTO-BELLO *at last was ta'en.*'—PAGE 17.

Porto-Bello was taken in November 1739, but Vice-Admiral Vernon's dispatches did not reach England until the following March (see *Gentleman's Magazine*, 1740, i. 124 *et seq.*).

'*With the* B—SH—P *of* L—ND—N's "*Pastoral Letter*".'—PAGE 18.

A Pastoral Letter was issued by the Bishop of London in August, 1739. It was at once answered by Whitefield.

'*In his famous gold-sprigged tambour vest.*'—PAGE 19.

This embroidery was so called from being worked on a drum-shaped frame. 'Your occasional tropes and flowers suit the general coarseness of your style, as *tambour sprigs* would a ground of linsey-woolsey' (Sheridan's *Critic*, 1779, Act I. Scene i).

'*London-Spaw.*'—PAGE 19.

A tavern and pleasure garden at the corner of Rosoman Street and Exmouth Street, Clerkenwell, having a noted chalybeate spring on the premises.

> 'Sweethearts with their sweethearts go
> To Islington or *London-Spaw*;
> Some go but just to drink the water,
> Some for the ale which they like better.'
>
> (*Poor Robin's Almanack*, 1733)

'*A freak of the* "Rose" *or the* "Rummer" *set.*'—PAGE 19.

The 'Rose' was a famous tavern at Covent Garden; the 'Rummer' was at Charing Cross.

'*His* solitaire.'—PAGE 19.

A loose neck-tie of black silk, generally affixed to the bag of the wig (Fairholt).

'(*Called after* BET *of Portugal Street*).'—PAGE 20.

Portugal Street, Lincoln's Inn Fields.

'*In the fresh contours of his* "Milkmaid's" *face.*'—PAGE 20.

See the *Enraged Musician*, an engraving of which was published in November of the following year (1741).

'*Served—for a day.*'—PAGE 20.

Walpole (*Letters*, 1857, ii. 219) says that 'half White's,' with Lord Mountford at their head, went to see James Maclean (the 'gentleman highwayman') in prison. Also that Lady Caroline Petersham and Miss Ashe had been to comfort and weep over him. Maclean was hanged on October 3, 1750, for robbing the Salisbury Coach, near Turnham Green.

Notes

'*To the world of* St. James's Street *and* " White's ".'—PAGE 20.

'White's' was a famous coffee-house in St. James's Street.

'*Aim-well.* Pray, Sir, ha'n't I seen your Face at Will's Coffee-house?
'*Gibbet.* Yes, Sir, and at *White's* too.' (Farquhar's *Beaux' Stratagem*, Act III, Scene ii.)

'*With a pomp befitting his high degree.*'—PAGE 20.

Fielding (*Covent Garden Journal*, 27th April 1752) says : 'This Day five Malefactors were executed at Tyburn. No Heroes within the Memory of Man ever met their Fate with more Boldness and Intrepidity, and consequently with *more felonious Glory.*'

Elsewhere he says (March 27) : 'The real Fact at present is, that instead of making the Gallows an Object of Terror, our Executions contribute to make it an Object of Contempt in the Eye of a Malefactor ; and we sacrifice the Lives of Men, not for [the italics are Fielding's] *the Reformation, but for the Diversion of the Populace.*' Cf. also Macaulay's *History of England*, ed. 1864, i. 182.

'*Bouquet of pinks.*'—PAGE 20.

'Another curious custom observed at this Church [St. Sepulchre's] was that of presenting a nosegay to every criminal on his way to Tyburn' (Wheatley and Cunningham's *London*, 1891, iii. 229, 230). When, as a boy of eight [1774], J. T. Smith watched the notorious John Rann, commonly called 'Sixteen-string Jack,' on his road to Tyburn, he noticed that the robber (who was gallantly clad in bright pea green) was equipped with an immense nosegay which had come to him in this way (*Book for a Rainy Day*, 3rd ed., 1861, pp. 29-30).

'*Flagon of ale at* Holborn Bar.*'—PAGE 20.

Holborn Bar, or Bars, marks the boundary in Holborn of the City Liberties. It was on the official route from Newgate to Tyburn.

'*Friends (in mourning) to follow his Car.*'—PAGE 20.

'He [Richard Turpin, *alias* John Palmer, hanged at York, 7th April 1739] gave 3*l.* 10*s.* to 5 Men who were to follow the Cart as Mourners, with Hatbands and Gloves to them and several others' (*Gentleman's Magazine*, 1739, vol. ix. 213).

'*Topsman.*'—PAGE 21.

i. e. the hangman. In the Tyburn Scene of Hogarth's *Apprentice Series* (Plate XI) he may be seen sitting at the top of the triple tree.

'*An Incident in the Life of François Boucher.*'—PAGE 25.

See *Boucher* by Arsène Houssaye, *Galerie du XVIIIᵉ Siècle* (*Cinquième Série; Sculpteurs, Peintres, Musiciens*). The 'incident' is, however, thus briefly referred to in Charles Blanc's *Histoire des*

Notes

Peintres de toutes les Écoles:—'*Une fois cependant Boucher se laissa prendre à un amour simple et candide. Un jour, en passant dans la Rue Ste-Anne, il aperçut une jeune fruitière dont la beauté l'éblouit. C'était au temps des cerises. Le peintre la regarda et elle se laissa regarder sans songer à ses paniers. Ses lèvres parurent plus belles que ses cerises. Un amour naïf et tendre naquit de cette échange de regards ; Boucher y trouva quelques jours de délices ; Rosine y trouva la mort après une rapide bonheur.*'

'*The scene, a wood.*'—Page 25.

The picture referred to is *Le Panier Mystérieux* by F. Boucher ; engraved by R. Gaillard.

'*"He thinks she thinks he thinks she sleeps", in fact.*'—Page 25.

This, as well as another reference (in *The Misogynist*) to the *Angel in the House*, led the author of that book at first, I am afraid, to doubt whether I was an entirely sympathetic student of his works. But when, in the later years of Coventry Patmore's life, I had the advantage of his personal acquaintance, it was not difficult to convince him that he had no more devoted admirer than myself.

'*And far afield were sun-baked savage creatures.*'—Page 26.

See *Les Caractères de* La Bruyère, *De l'homme,* 128.

'*Whose greatest grace was jupes à la Camargo.*'—Page 26.

'*C'était le beau temps où Camargo trouvait ses jupes trop longues pour danser la gargouillade.*'—Arsène Houssaye.

'*The grass he called "too green."*'—Page 27.

'*Il trouvait la nature trop verte et mal éclairée. Et son ami Lancret, le peintre des salons à la mode, lui répondait : "Je suis de votre sentiment, la nature manque d'harmonie et de séduction."*'—Charles Blanc.

'*Fresh as a fresh young pear-tree blossoming.*'—Page 28.

'She was wel more blisful on to see
Than is the newe perjenete tree.'
—Chaucer, *The Millere's Tale.*

'*Tout vient à point à qui sait attendre.*'—Page 36.

According to a correspondent of *The Times,* 6th February 1903, this proverb, on a carving in the Tower of London, dated 1571, runs— '*Tout vient a poient, quy peult attendre.*' Littré, however, gives it as given here.

'*Nay,*—'*twas a song of* Saint-Aulaire.'—Page 36.

It is but just to the octogenarian Marquis, whom the Duchess of Maine surnamed her '*vieux berger,*' to say that he is guiltless of the

Notes

song here ascribed to him.   For it, and for the similar pieces in these *Proverbs*, I am alone responsible.   In the *Secrets of the Heart*, however, I have, without attempting to revive the persons, borrowed the names of the charming heroines of *À quoi rêvent les Jeunes Filles*.

'*Love was a Shepherd.*'—PAGE 47.

See the lines on p. 364, which have hitherto only appeared in the Notes to *Collected Poems*.

'*Go, little book* . . .'—PAGE 54.

These lines were first printed as a prologue to *Vignettes in Rhyme*, 1873.   In the second and third editions they appear as an Envoi at the end of the volume.   They have not appeared in any edition of '*Collected Poems*' (*Editor's* note).

'*Sing me of Her, whose name may not be told.*'—PAGE 62

> '*Dicat Opuntiæ*
> *Frater Megillæ, quo beatus*
> *Vulnere, qua pereat sagitta.*'—HOR. i. 27.

How this stanza originally stood escapes me ; but—as I well remember—it owes its final turn to the late ANTHONY TROLLOPE,—kindest and most capable of Editors,—who referred me to the foregoing quotation.

'*I am a Shade: a Shadowe too arte thou.*'—PAGE 101.

A motto in this spirit occurs at Stirling.

THE CHILD-MUSICIAN.—PAGE 105.

These verses originated in an 'American story' told me orally by a friend who had found it copied into some English paper.   I 'romanced' it after my own fashion.   After it was published, by the courtesy of one of the most graceful and finished of Trans-Atlantic poets, I was furnished with a more accurate version of the facts.   Those who wish to read the true and authentic story of poor little James Speaight must do so in the pathetic prose setting of Mr. THOMAS BAILEY ALDRICH.

THE CRADLE.—PAGE 106.

The leading idea of these lines is taken from a French Sonnet,—*Le Berceau*, by Eugène Manuel.

'*Some moneyed mourner's " love or pride ".*'—PAGE 108.

> '*Thus much alone we know—Metella died,*
> *The wealthiest Roman's wife : Behold his love or pride !*'
> > —*Childe Harold*, iv. 103.

'*Huddling they came, with shag sides caked of mire.*'—PAGE 120.

See the picture of *Circe* by Mr. BRITON RIVIERE, R.A.

Notes

'A bolder rider than Bellerophon.'—PAGE 123.

'Eques ipso melior Bellerophonte.'—HOR. iii. 12.

'The Thefts of Mercury.'—PAGE 123.

'Te, boves olim nisi reddidisses
Per dolum amotas, puerum minaci
Voce dum terret, viduus pharetra
        Risit Apollo.'—HOR. i. 10.

'Have I not writ thy Laws?'—PAGE 134.

The lines in italic type which follow, are freely paraphrased from the ancient *Code d'Amour* of the twelfth century, as given by André le Chapelain himself.

'To brandish the poles of that old Sedan chair!'—PAGE 148.

A friendly but anonymous critic, whose versatile pen it is, nevertheless, not easy to mistake, recalls, *à-propos* of the above, the following passage from Molière, which shows that Chairmen are much the same all the world over:—

1. Porteur (prenant un des bâtons de sa chaise). *Çà, payez-nous vitement!*

Mascarille. *Quoi?*

1. Porteur. *Je dis que je veux avoir de l'argent tout à l'heure.*

Mascarille. *Il est raisonnable, celui-là,* &c.

            —*Les Précieuses Ridicules*, Sc. vii.

'It has waited by portals where Garrick has played.'—PAGE 148.

According to Mrs. Elizabeth Carter (Smith's *Nollekens*, 1828, i. 211), when Garrick acted, the hackney-chairs often stood 'all round the piazzas [Covent Garden], down Southampton-street, and extended more than half-way along Maiden-lane'.

'A skill PRÉVILLE *could not disown.'*—PAGE 157.

Préville was the French Foote *circa* 1760. His gifts as a comedian were of the highest order; and he had an extraordinary faculty for entering completely into the parts he played. Sterne, in a letter to Garrick from Paris, in January 1762, calls him 'Mercury himself'.

MOLLY TREFUSIS.—PAGE 163.

The epigram here quoted from an 'old magazine' is to be found in Lord Neaves's admirable little volume, *The Greek Anthology* (*Blackwood's Ancient Classics for English Readers*). Those familiar with eighteenth-century literature will recognize in the succeeding verses but another echo of those lively stanzas of John Gay to 'Molly Mog' of the Rose Inn at Wokingham, which, in their own day, found so many imitators.

Notes

An Eastern Apologue.—Page 169.

The initials 'E. H. P.' are those of the eminent (and ill-fated) Orientalist, Professor Palmer. As my lines entirely owed their origin to his translations from Zoheir, I sent them to him. He was indulgent enough to praise them warmly. It is true he found anachronisms; but as he said that these would cause no serious disturbance to orthodox Persians, I concluded I had succeeded in my little *pastiche*, and, with his permission, inscribed it to him. I wish now that it had been a more worthy tribute to one of the most erudite and versatile scholars this age has seen.

A Revolutionary Relic.—Page 172.

'373. St. Pierre (Bernardin de), *Paul et Virginie*, 12mo, old calf. Paris, 1787. This copy is pierced throughout by a bullet-hole, and bears on one of the covers, the words: "*à Lucile St. A. . . . chez M. Batemans, à Edmonds-Bury, en Angleterre*," very faintly written in pencil.' (Extract from Catalogue.)

'*Did she wander like that other?*'—Page 174.

Lucile Desmoulins. See Carlyle's *French Revolution*, Vol. iii, Book vi, Chap. ii.

'*And its tender rain shall lave it.*'—Page 175.

It is by no means uncommon for an editor to interrupt some of these revolutionary letters by a 'Here there are traces of tears'.

A Roman Round-Robin.—Page 182.

This piece of flippancy first appeared in the *Spectator* for 13th November 1875, and was pleasantly rallied in a later number by the late Poet Laureate, Mr. Alfred Austin.

To a Child.—Page 190.

These lines were written for the *Garland of Rachel* (an English imitation of the famous *Guirlande de Julie*), which was issued in 1881 from the private press of Mr. H. Daniel of Oxford.

'*By "Bysshe" his epithet.*'—Page 192.

i. e. *The Art of English Poetry*, by Edward Bysshe, 1702.

The Book-Plate's Petition.—Page 196.

These lines were reprinted in Mr. Andrew Lang's instructive volume *The Library*, 1881, where the curious will find full information as to the enormities of the book mutilators.

A Dialogue, &c.—Page 207.

This dialogue, first printed in *Scribner's Magazine* for May 1888, was afterwards read by Professor HENRY MORLEY at the opening of the Pope Loan Museum at Twickenham (July 31st), to the Catalogue of which exhibition it was prefixed.

'*The "crooked Body with a crooked Mind".'*—PAGE 207.

' Mens curva in corpore curvo.'

Said of Pope by Lord Orrery.

' *Neither as* LOCKE *was, nor as* BLAKE.'—PAGE 212.

The Shire Hall at Taunton, where, on September 4, 1883, these verses were read at the unveiling, by JAMES RUSSELL LOWELL, of Miss MARGARET THOMAS's bust of Fielding, also contains busts of Admiral Blake and John Locke.

'*The Journal of his middle-age.'*—PAGE 214.

It is, perhaps, needless to say that the reference here is to the *Journal of a Voyage to Lisbo* published posthumously in February 1755,—a record which for it intrinsic pathos and dignity may be compared with the prologue and dedication which Fielding's predecessor and model, Cervantes, prefixed to his last romance of *Persiles and Sigismunda*.

A POSTSCRIPT TO ' RETALIATION '.—PAGE 215.

On the 22nd June, 1896, these verses were read for the author by the Master of the Temple (Canon AINGER) at the dinner given in celebration of the five hundredth meeting of the Johnson Society of Pembroke College, Oxford. They then concluded with a couplet appropriate to that occasion. In their present place, it has been thought preferable to leave them—like Goldsmith's epitaph on Reynolds—unfinished.

' *When his pistol miss'd fire, he would use the butt-end.'*—PAGE 215.

' He [Johnson] had recourse to the device which Goldsmith imputed to him in the witty words of one of Cibber's comedies : " There is no arguing with Johnson ; for when his pistol misses fire, he knocks you down with the butt end of it." ' (Hill's *Boswell*, 1887, ii. 100.)

'*You found he had nought of the bear but the skin.'*—PAGE 216.

' Let me impress upon my readers a just and happy saying of my friend Goldsmith, who knew him [Johnson] well : " Johnson, to be sure, has a roughness in his manner ; but no man alive has a more tender heart. *He has nothing of the bear but his skin*." ' (Hill's *Boswell*, 1887, ii. 66.)

Notes

'*That he made little fishes talk vastly like whales.*'—Page 216.

' If you were to make little fishes talk, they would talk like Whales.'
(Goldsmith to Johnson, Hill's *Boswell*, 1887, ii. 231.)

> '*But read him for Style,—and dismiss from your thoughts,*
> *The crowd of compilers who copied his faults.*'—Page 216.

These, or like rhymes, are to be found in *Edwin and Angelina*,
and—for the matter of that—in *Retaliation* itself :—

> ' Say, where has our poet this malady caught?
> Or, wherefore his characters thus without fault?'

But the practice is not confined to Goldsmith: it is also followed
by Pope and Prior.

> '*With that he made a Leg.*'—Page 229.
> '*Jove* made his Leg and kiss'd the Dame,
> Obsequious Hermes did the same.'
> —Prior.

'*So took his Virtù off to* Cock's.'—Page 229.

Cock, the auctioneer of Covent Garden, was the Christie and
Manson of the last century. The leading idea of this fable, it should
be added, is taken from one by Gellert.

'*Of Van's* "*Goose-Pie*".'—Page 230.

> ' At length they in the Rubbish spy
> A Thing resembling a Goose Py.'
> —Swift's verses on *Vanbrugh's House*, 1706.

'*The Oaf preferred the* "Tongs and Bones".'—Page 234.

' I have a reasonable good ear in music : let us have the tongs and
the bones.'

> — *Midsummer Night's Dream*, Act IV, Sc. i.

'*And sighed o'er Chaos wine for Stingo.*'—Page 234.

Squire Homespun probably meant Cahors.

The Water-Cure.—Page 257.

These verses were suggested by the recollection of an anecdote in
Madame de Genlis, which seemed to lend itself to eighteenth-century
treatment. It was therefore somewhat depressing, not long after
they were written, to find that the subject had already been annexed
in the *Tatler* by an actual eighteenth-century writer, Swift's 'little
Harrison,' who, moreover, claimed to have founded his story on a
contemporary incident. Burton, nevertheless, had told it before him,
as early as 1621, in the *Anatomy of Melancholy*.

(494)

Notes

'*In Babylonian numbers hidden.*'—Page 259.

'—nec Babylonios
Tentaris numeros.'

—Hor. i. 11.

A City Flower.—Page 269.

These verses—as far as I can remember—were my first contribution to a magazine, their appearance in *Temple Bar* being welcomed with extreme cordiality by the editor, Edmund Yates.

Of his Mistress.—Page 300.

This translation was made at the request of Professor Saintsbury, who included it in his study of the author of the *Mémoires de Grammont* (*Essays on French Novelists*, Percival, 1891).

To One who bids me Sing.—Page 306.

This piece was written in response to a graceful expostulatory villanelle which appeared in *Temple Bar* for February 1895, and was signed 'Cecil Harley'. [The *Editor* of this volume has since accidentally discovered that the writer was C. H. St. L. Russell, at one time his form master at Clifton College, and still a master there.]

'*All grinning as one in a gust of good-nature.*'—Page 312.

See Hogarth's *Pleased Audience at a Play*, 1733.

'*And spite of the mourning that most of us wear.*'—Page 312.

In March 1773, when *She Stoops to Conquer* was first played, there was a court-mourning for the King of Sardinia (Forster's *Goldsmith*, Book iv, Chap. 15).

'*But he grows every day more and more like the print.*'—Page 312.

'Mr. *Wilkes*, with his usual good humour, has been heard to observe, that he is every day growing more and more like his portrait by *Hogarth* [i. e. the print of May 16, 1763].'

—*Biographical Anecdotes of William Hogarth*, 1782, pp. 305-6.

'*The furious troops in battle joined.*'—Page 317.

The quotation is from Addison's *Campaign*.

'*They are a school to win.*'—Page 321.

In view of the very prolonged popularity which has attended the use of these old French forms in England and America, the following dates may here be preserved. Some of the *Triolets* at p. 461 appeared in the *Graphic* for May 23, 1874; the *Rondeau* at p. 466 and the *Ballade* at p. 486 in *Evening Hours* for May 1876; the *Villanelle* at p. 482 in *Proverbs in Porcelain*, May 1877; the *Chant Royal* at p. 504 in the *Architect* for July 14, 1877; and the *Ballade à double refrain* at p. 500 in *Belgravia* for January 1878.

Notes

'PERSICOS ODI.'—PAGE 325.

This 'Pocket Version' was appended to the preceding poem, when it first appeared in the *second* edition of *Proverbs in Porcelain*, 1878.

Monsieur Isaac de Benserade, in the Hotel de Rambouillet days, translated the entire *Metamorphoses* of Ovid into Rondeaus. In this, and some similar pieces that follow (cf. pp. 326, 335, 336, 337, 339, 348), I have imitated his temerity but not his excess.

'YOU BID ME TRY.'—PAGE 327.

Lope de Vega and Hurtado de Mendoza wrote sonnets on Sonnet-making ; Voiture imitated them as regards the Rondeau. These lines are a paraphrase of Voiture and have hitherto appeared in the Notes to *Collected Poems*.

'MORE POETS YET.'—PAGE 328.

The dedicatory initials of this rondeau stand for 'John Leicester Warren' (afterwards Lord DE TABLEY). He was so kind as to read the proofs of the volume in which it appeared ; and I remember that, years after, at one of our rare meetings, he pleasantly—and with perfect accuracy—recalled the fact that the Homeric epithet 'many-buttoned,' applied to the page in *A Nightingale in Kensington Gardens*, had been suggested by himself. This suggestion by no means exhausts my debt to his fine scholarship and fastidious taste. When, some months before his death in 1895, he sent me his last book, I returned him a few verses of acknowledgement. As they pleased him—and as, more-over, Mr. EDMUND GOSSE has been good enough to give them the currency of his delightful *Critical Kit-Cats*—I may perhaps be pardoned if I reproduce them again. See page 378.

CARMINA VOTIVA.—PAGE 353.

Editor's note.—As explained in the Preface, this section, as the result of rearrangement, now contains, with one or two exceptions, all the poems which originally appeared in the privately printed volume *Carmina Votiva*. The following poems from that volume have not, however, before appeared in any edition of *Collected Poems* :

> Notes of a Honeymoon.
> 'Change.'
> 'Fair.'
> To F. M. D. (In *Carmina Votiva* entitled To a Lady.)
> A 'Departmental Ditty'.
> To the Earl of Crewe on his Marriage.
> To Edmund Gosse. (You write your Life of Donne.)
> To George H. Boughton, R.A.

Notes

' *Our* RUSTUM *here, without red coat*.'—PAGE 357.

Field-Marshal Viscount Wolseley.

' *But that's* FIRDAUSI *in the Chair*.'—PAGE 357.

Mr. EDMUND GOSSE, whose *Firdausi in Exile and other Poems* was published in 1885.

THE PHILOSOPHY OF THE PORCH.—PAGE 367.

The author of *Dorothy, a Country Story*, and the friend of R. D. Blackmore, ARTHUR JOSEPH MUNBY, to whom these verses were inscribed, died at Buttercup Farm, Pyrford, near Ripley, in Surrey, on Saturday, January 29, 1910, aged 81. He lies in the quiet little churchyard of Pyrford Church, of which there is a picture (by Mr. HUGH THOMSON) in Mr. ERIC PARKER's *Highways and Byways in Surrey*, 1908, p. 232. ' *Ah ! mollitter ossa quiescant !* '

JULY.—PAGE 371.

This was, after its first appearance, revised for the late Mr. GLEESON WHITE's *Ballades and Rondeaus*, 1887.

THE SONG OF THE SEA WIND.—PAGE 376.

Mons. MAURICE BOUCHOR's *Le Vent beugle, beugle, beugle*, suggested this ; but it does not reproduce his poem.

' *That once he lent to* YOUNG.'—PAGE 383.

The allusion is to the admirable epigram attributed to Young, and written with a pencil borrowed from Lord Chesterfield :—

'Accept a miracle instead of wit,—
See two dull lines by STANHOPE's pencil writ.'

' *Salaam to Omar !* '—PAGE 388.

' It does not appear that there was any danger in holding and singing Súfi Pantheism, so long as the Poet made his Salaam to Mohammed at the beginning and end of his Song ' (FITZGERALD, Prefaces to *Rubaiyat*, 1872). The last stanza here printed was an afterthought, and was not included in the version on the menu. A third piece, written for the Omar Khayyám dinner of March 1903, and kindly read for the author in his absence by Mr. HENRY NEWBOLT, appears on p. 361. These lines have hitherto appeared in the Notes to *Collected Poems*.

Notes

Rose, in the Hedgerow Grown.—Page 390.

This is a rondeau on the De Musset pattern, and therefore not strict in form.

To Monsieur de la Mothe le Vayer.—Page 395.

From pp. 266-7 of *Sonnets of Europe*, I transcribe Mr. Waddington's note: 'François de la Mothe le Vayer, member of the French Academy, and preceptor of Louis XIV., lost his son in 1664, and Molière, in forwarding him this sonnet, observes,—"*Vous voyez bien, Monsieur, que je m'écarte fort du chemin qu'on suit d'ordinaire en pareille rencontre, que le Sonnet que je vous envoye n'est rien moins qu'une consolation ; mais j'ay cru qu'il falloit en user de la sorte avec vous & que c'est consoler un Philosophe que de luy justifier ses larmes, & de mettre sa douleur en liberté. Si je n'ay pas trouvé d'assez fortes raisons pour affranchir vostre tendresse des sévères leçons de la Philosophie, & pour vous obliger à pleurer sans contrainte, il en faut accuser le peu d'éloquence d'un homme qui ne sçauroit persuader ce qu'il sçait si bien faire.*" '

A Ballad of Incapacity.—Page 403.

Recited by the author at a dinner at the Whitefriars Club in November 1901.

'A Voice in the Scented Night.'—Page 404.

This, and the pieces at p. 416 and p. 428, appeared in the *Century Magazine*, and are here reproduced by permission.

'*When* Pope *came back.*'—Page 405.

Alexander Pope: his Safe Return from Troy. A Congratulatory Poem on his Completing his Translation of Homer's Iliad. (In *ottava rima.*) By Mr. Gay, 1720 (?). Frere's burlesque, *Monks and Giants*—it will be remembered—set the tune to Byron's *Beppo*.

'*The Paradise of Birds.*'—Page 405.

Published in 1870.

'*The Life in Poetry.*'—Page 405.

Life in Poetry, Law in Taste, two series of Lectures delivered in Oxford, 1895-1900, 1901.

'*The Weight that* Warton.'—Page 405.

A History of English Poetry, 1895 (in progress).

Pepys' Diary.—Page 408.

Written for the Pepys' Dinner at Magdalene College, Cambridge, February 23, 1905.

Notes

A Miltonic Exercise.—Page 424.

Written, by request, for the celebration at Christ's College, Cambridge, July 10, 1908.

'K. G.'—Page 426.

In the ninth edition of *Collected Poems* these lines appeared in the notes only.

La Bonne Comédie.—Page 435.

This was written as an epilogue for the *Molière* (1910) of my friend, Prof. Brander Matthews, of Columbia University, New York City, although it appeared in *Scribner's Magazine* a little earlier.

Threescore and Ten.—Page 437.

The epigraph is from the dialogue between Titian and Lewis Cornaro in Landor's *Last Fruit off an Old Tree*, 1853, p. 4.

'With dignity and reticence.'—Page 441.

'Servetur ad imum
Qualis ab incepto processerit, et sibi constet.'
Ars Poetica, lines 126–7.
(Thackeray's motto to *Esmond*.)

'Must need his Sermon and his Text.'—Page 441.

See the verses headed '*Vanitas Vanitatum*' in the *Cornhill Magazine* for July 1860, and particularly—

Pray choose us out another text,
 O man morose and narrow-minded!
Come turn the page—I read the next,
 And then the next, and still I find it.

Methinks the text is never stale,
 And life is every day renewing
Fresh comments on the old, old tale
 Of Folly, Fortune, Glory, Ruin.

'But marks your grass-grown headstone.'—Page 445.

This is a poetical license, for there is a 'quite typical tablet' to the 'Jessamy Bride' in Weybridge Parish Church, where she lies with her mother and sister, 'Little Comedy'. I take this information from a very interesting paper on 'The Hornecks', by H. P. K. Skipton, in the *Connoisseur* for September, 1910.

'Where every landscape lover should.'—Page 446.

This was the theory of Evelyn and Howell, and the old votaries of

Notes

the 'Grand Tour'. 'I would wish my *Traveler*'—says Lassels in his *Voyage of Italy*, 1670, i. 121—'to make it his constant practise (as I did) to mount up the chief *Steeple* of all great townes.'

To a Friend.—Page 448.

These lines are a variation of some sent in 1908 to the late RICHARD WATSON GILDER, who died November 19, 1909.

The Sonnet of the Mountain.—Page 448.

My friend Mr. SAMUEL WADDINGTON, for whose *Sonnets of Europe* (Walter Scott, 1886) this and the translations on pp. 394-5 were written, pointed out in the *Athenaeum* for May 23, 1891, that an earlier version of this particular poem had been made by Sir Thomas Wyatt 'about the year 1530'.

' The glint of a raindrop.'—Page 452. *

It is not clear for whom these lines were written ; moreover they are undated ; but they are included, as they seemed a suitable prologue to the last section of poems.

A Rally.—Page 453.

These lines, which represent the Poet's first War poem, are copied from a MS. sent to *The Times*, but recalled by the Author before they were printed. It is felt that they should now be included in his *Complete Poetical Works*. In an earlier version, apparently destroyed, the last line of each stanza ended with the word 'guns' instead of ' Sons '.

An Arctic Epitaph.—Page 458.

This was written when it was first known that Captain Scott and his companions had perished in the Antarctic.

On the Future of Poetry.—Page 460.

These lines were suggested by a lecture on ' The Future of English Poetry,' delivered by Edmund Gosse, in June 1913.

The Riddle.—Page 463.

Written for *A Book of Homage to Shakespeare*, 1916.

To George H. Boughton, R.A.—Page 464.

The watercolour drawing to which this poem refers was included in the Austin Dobson books sold at Sotheby's in March, 1922 ; and is now in the possession of the *Editor* of this volume. G. H. Boughton

---

* This and the following *Notes* are contributed by the *Editor* of this volume.

Notes

made several drawings to illustrate the poem ' Love in Winter' (see page 74). Besides the watercolour referred to, he made a pen-and-ink sketch in the Poet's own copy of ' At the Sign of the Lyre', which was used as the frontispiece to *Selected Poems* (1905), 1909 and (Oxford University Press) 1923. He also made a pastel drawing, the whereabouts of which is not known; and finally in 1891, he exhibited an oil-painting on the same theme in the Royal Academy. The lines here reproduced were written by the Author in a presentation volume to the Artist, and have never before been reprinted.

To Arthur James Balfour.—Page 465.

These lines were sent to Mr. Balfour (now the Earl of Balfour) on his defeat at Manchester in the 1905 elections.

To Edmund Gosse.—Page 478.

These lines were sent to Edmund Gosse towards the end of December 1920. As they subsequently proved to be the last poem which the Author committed to writing, it was thought fit to publish them early in 1922, and now to include them in this volume.

For a Closing Page.—Page 479.

Although these stanzas were written so long ago as 1913, it was the Author's express instruction that they should be inserted in their present position, immediately before ' In After Days', which completes the volume.

INDEX TO FIRST LINES

(503)

Index to First Lines

Index to First Lines

Index to First Lines

Index to First Lines

Index to First Lines

Index to First Lines

Index to First Lines

INDEX TO TITLES

Index to Titles

Index to Titles

Index to Titles

Index to Titles

BIBLIOGRAPHICAL INDEX

In the list below the poems appearing in this volume are set out chronologically as to their first appearance in print. Where they were first included in a published volume, as opposed to a periodical, the former is indicated in CAPITALS. Where the title of the poem has changed since its first appearance, the original title is shown in *italics* within the brackets.

Bibliographical Index

Bibliographical Index

* This poem was signed WALTER BRYCE, a signature occasionally adopted by the Author, especially in the SATURDAY JOURNAL.

Bibliographical Index

Bibliographical Index

* This appeared in some Magazine, unknown, as 'A Porcelain Villanelle.'

Bibliographical Index

Bibliographical Index

A Ballad of the Queen's Majesty (Saturday Review. 19 June, 1897)
Verses read at the Dinner of the Omar Khayyám Club (Privately
  printed for Edmund Gosse. 100 copies. March, 1897)

For a Copy of 'The Compleat Angler' (Literature. 15 April, 1899)
To the Earl of Crewe, on his Marriage (Literature. 29 April, 1899)
A Madrigal (CHORAL SONGS IN HONOUR OF QUEEN VICTORIA. 1899)

For 'An Appendix to the Catalogue of the Rowfant Library' (AN
  APPENDIX TO THE CATALOGUE OF MR. LOCKER LAMPSON'S PRINTED
  BOOKS, &c. 1900)
Rank and File (Sphere. 3 February, 1900)
To Maecenas (Cliftonian. April, 1900)

R. L. S. In Memoriam (The Student. (Edinburgh University)
  January, 1901)
A Ballad of Incapacity (Sphere. 30 November, 1901)
For a Charity Annual (The May Book (Charing Cross Hospital). 1901)
Verses written for the Menu of the Omar Khayyám Club (CARMINA
  VOTIVA. 1901)
To the Publisher of 'The New Monthly Review' (CARMINA VOTIVA.
  1901)
After a Holiday (CARMINA VOTIVA. 1901)
For a Volume of Verse (CARMINA VOTIVA. 1901)
To the Lady Dorothy Nevill (CARMINA VOTIVA. 1901)
To Edmund Gosse—You write your life of Donne (CARMINA VOTIVA.
  1901)
'Good Luck to your Fishing' (CARMINA VOTIVA. 1901)
The Song of the Sea Wind (CARMINA VOTIVA. 1901)
A 'Departmental Ditty' (CARMINA VOTIVA. 1901)
Hill and Valley (CARMINA VOTIVA. 1901)
'When this old world was young' (CARMINA VOTIVA. 1901)

'K. G.' (Art Journal. April, 1902)
'A Voice in the Scented Night' (Century. October, 1902)

A Welcome, from the Johnson Club (Privately printed by Clement
  Shorter. March, 1903. Sphere. 21 March, 1903)
'Under which King?' (Tatler. 8 April, 1903)

Snap-shot (Harper's. August, 1904)
Surge et Ambula (WAYFARER'S LOVE. 1904)

Horatian Ode on the Tercentenary of 'Don Quixote' (Cornhill.
  January, 1905)
Pepys' Diary (Cambridge Review. 2 May, 1905)
The Simple Life (QUEEN'S CHRISTMAS CAROL. 1905)
Envoi—No moral (PROVERBS IN PORCELAIN. Pocket Edition. 1905)

A New Year's Thought (Pall Mall Magazine. January, 1906)
Richard Garnett (Library. July, 1906)
To Myrtalé (Harper's. September, 1906)
An Epistle to an Editor (Daily Mail. 27 October, 1906)
'Fame is a Food that Dead Men Eat' (Century. November, 1906)

Bibliographical Index

Bibliographical Index

'When there is Peace' (Spectator. 1 January, 1916)
The Riddle (A BOOK OF HOMAGE TO SHAKESPEARE. 1916)

Prologue to 'A Bookman's Budget' (A BOOKMAN'S BUDGET. 1917)
To Arthur Waugh (A BOOKMAN'S BUDGET. 1917)
An Arctic Epitaph (A BOOKMAN'S BUDGET. 1917)
To Belgium (KING ALBERT'S BOOK. 1917)

Clean Hands (A TREASURY OF WAR POETRY. Second Series. America. 1919)

To E. G. (London Mercury. February, 1920)
To a Lyric Poet (London Mercury. May, 1920)
For a volume of Essays (National Review. July, 1920)
An Old Magazine (LATER ESSAYS. 1920)
Errata: An Eclogue (National Review. July, 1920)
By Way of Preface (LATER ESSAYS. 1920)

To Edmund Gosse (London Mercury. February, 1922)

None of the following poems, included in the present volume, have, it is believed, been printed anywhere previously.

A Ballad of Names (1878)
To George H. Boughton, R.A.—*The Spring will come* (1884)
Alter Ego (1888)
Sat est vixisse (1891)
To Richard Watson Gilder—*Friend, on whose face I may not look* (1899)
To John Waddon Martyn (1902)
To Arthur James Balfour (1905)
A Rally (1914)
New and Old (1920)
The Ballad of the Beggar (Undated)
'This Morn for you' (Undated)
On Reading a Volume of Poems (Undated)
Prologue—*The Glint of a raindrop* (Undated)

As indicated in the Preface, some of Austin Dobson's Poems have been omitted from this Complete Edition. The greater number of these consist of the poems which he himself never reprinted from the magazines in which they made their first and only appearance. The others have actually appeared in book-form at one time or another, but Austin Dobson deliberately omitted them from the editions of the *Collected Poems* which appeared under his own supervision, and this must exclude them from any authorized edition of his *Complete Poems*. A list of these poems, with an indication of the volumes in which they appeared, may, however, be of interest to students, and is here subjoined.

A Song of Angiola on Earth.
A Song of Angiola Dead.
The Bookworm.
The Peacock on the Wall.
  (*Vignettes in Rhyme*. First Edition. 1873)

Bibliographical Index

A Short Vacation (*Vignettes in Rhyme.* Third Edition. 1875)

Poor Miss Tox.
Emblemata Amoris.
Apple Blossoms.
    (*Proverbs in Porcelain.* First Edition. 1877)

A Sabine Farm (*At the Sign of the Lyre.* First Edition. 1885)

To Edmund Clarence Stedman.
The Street Singer.
    (*At the Sign of the Lyre.* American Edition. 1885)

Ah, judge her gently (*Four Frenchwomen*—Madame de Corday.
    1890)

A Ballad of Bygone Bookshops. (*Eighteenth Century Vignettes.*
    (The Two Paynes.) Second Series. 1894)

For a Floral Wreath.
Epigrams.
    (*Carmina Votiva.* 1901)

To Thestylis.
A number of Epigrams.
    (*A Bookman's Budget.* 1917)

Epigrams of the War.
Re-Reading.
    (*Later Essays.* 1920)

*Austin Dobson's bookplate designed for him
by the late Alfred Parsons, R.A.*